Further praise for *The Burden of Heritage*

"Dancing in a village square populated by active ancestors, ghostly hauntings, living memories, poetic interruptions and client narratives, Dr. Aileen Alleyne composes a gripping epic about loss, longing, and the partially submerged worlds of black trauma. Her fluid fingers, careful and masterful, weave practical therapeutic insights, political critique, a cultural situatedness in racialized suffering, and an eye on futurity and justice into a cartography of restoration – a map of hope in dire times."
– Dr. Bayo Akomolafe, author, *These Wilds Beyond our Fences: Letters to My Daughter on Humanity's Search for Home*

"Aileen Alleyne has written one of the most ground-breaking books on the vital subject of intergenerational trauma. This truly heartening and gripping contribution to modern psychology offers many bold and essential insights into the nature of global suffering and hatred. We all have much to learn from the author's wisdom, regardless of the colour of our skin."
– Professor Brett Kahr, Senior Fellow, Tavistock Institute of Medical Psychology, London, and Visiting Professor of Psychoanalysis and Mental Health, Regent's University London.

"Dr. Aileen Alleyne has created a powerful written narrative of the African Holocaust psychological experience that supports, enhances and is a scholarly gift to individuals engaged in doing the healing work of intergenerational and transgenerational trauma. *The Burden of Heritage* begins with the author's own story of being six years old and psychologically experiencing what she later understands to be a collapse of her ego. This experience, that occurred when confronted with white Others and familial relations, contributes to the psychic groundwork for Dr. Alleyne's consciousness as regards her own developing identity, and that of other members of her cultural group. This eventually leads her to become a psychoanalyst. The writing in *The Burden of Heritage* creates a unique and excellent foundation for clinicians, especially those of the African diaspora, to see into their own psychological wounding as well as those of their patients and clients. The book provides the reader with knowledge for self-examination as well as ways to see and move deeper into understanding the racial trauma caused by British government historical racism, exploitation, and economic greed. The root of this racial trauma shows its negative impact not only

to those suffering in the 1600s as Britain spread her 'empire', but also the contemporary psychological suffering experienced by descendants of formerly enslaved Africanist people. Dr. Alleyne's book should be required reading for every clinician seeking to better understand Black psychology and African diaspora intergenerational trauma. *The Burden of Heritage is* a creative work that lovingly explores, teaches, and psychologically deepens who we are, and who we can become in terms of healing individual and cultural group racial trauma."
– **Fanny Brewster, Ph.D., MFA, author of *The Racial Complex: A Jungian Perspective on Culture and Race***

"*The Burden of Heritage* is a powerful reminder of the deep and prolonged impact of racial oppression on black communities, and of the importance for all of us – black and white, people of colour – to acknowledge this and find ways to deal with it. Full of new concepts, written with clarity and passion, this book will be invaluable for all those dedicated to racial justice."
– **Professor Stephen Frosh, Birkbeck, University of London.**

"This book helps to fill an important gap in the psychoanalytic psychotherapeutic theorizing of racial trauma. Focusing on the dual forms of relational transmission of such trauma—the transgenerational and the intergenerational, this book presents an experience-near, personal account of working with racial trauma in psychotherapy. Psychotherapy professionals of all stripes will find it abundantly clear: attending to the sequela of racism must be considered an essential, indeed foundational, aspect of psychotherapeutic work."
– **Anton Hart, Ph.D., FABP, FIPA, Faculty, Training and Supervising Analyst, The William Alanson White Institute Private Practice, New York**

THE
BURDEN
OF
HERITAGE

I dedicate this book to my dear family and loving parents who constantly watch over me. To all agents of psychological change, growth and transformation, I gift this multidimensional text as a practical approach to help in the important process of reframing negative and biased scripts to make all of humanity matter.

Creole Hauntings

Black grandmas spoke of hauntings from 400 years ago
Hovering internally like dark shadows when distress is activated
The experience passed down the generations
Trigger questions when emotions can't be appeased.
So we hear the young black mother shouting at her child
Why yuh so [h]'aunted bwoy?
Wha mek yuh so restless?
Who trouble yuh soul and tek away yuh joy?
Sit still and don't annoy me;
Try hard to be mama's good bwoy.
Nana say yuh behavin like yuh got Saint Vitus' Dance
Shiftin about like yuh gat ants in yuh pants
Maybe the *duppy* disturb yuh,
Or obeah man up to mischief
Whatever it is, we 'ave to find a solution
To this mental pollution
'caue this situation must improve
Or me and you kcant continue in dis groove.

Nowadays such hauntings brand black children with ADHD
And stamp the *chip on the shoulder* label upon the rest of we
But whether such restlessness is Creole or universal,
The clock ticks NOW for a solution to this daily grind.

THE
Aileen Alleyne

BURDEN

Hauntings of
Generational Trauma
on Black Lives

OF

HERITAGE

KARNAC
firing the mind

First published in 2022 by Karnac Books, an imprint of Confer Ltd.

Reprinted in 2026 by Karnac Books Limited
62 Bucknell Road, Bicester, Oxfordshire, OX26 2DS, UK

British Library Cataloguing in Publication Data
A catalogue record for this book is available from the British Library.
ISBN: 978-1-913494-24-7 (paperback)
ISBN: 978-1-913494-25-4 (ebook)

Typeset in Berling by Bespoke Publishing Ltd.
Printed in the UK. Karnac Books Limited is committed to using paper from a sustainable source.

Contents

About the author

Dr Aileen Alleyne is a UKCP-registered psychodynamic psychotherapist, clinical supervisor and organisational consultant in the UK. She lecturers at several training institutions and is a consultant on issues of race and cultural diversity to private organisations and statutory bodies, such as the NHS, Social Services, Education and the Police Services. Her clinical research examining black workers' experiences in three institutional settings makes a significant contribution to the discourse on race. Highlighting the concept of *'the internal oppressor'*, it offers ways of deepening understanding of black psychological reactions to the negative impact of racism. Aileen is the author of several book chapters and journal papers exploring themes on Black–White dynamics, shame and identity wounding, and working with issues of difference and diversity in the workplace.

Aileen presents her first published book, *The Burden of Heritage: Hauntings of Generational Trauma on Black Lives* (Karnac Books, 2022), which she hopes is the first of several to come.

Acknowledgements

I wish to acknowledge my deepest gratitude to all the wonderful women and men whose caring feedback, reliable support and constructive critique have helped me through this journey to make this book happen. In particular, Anita Gaspar, for her consummate professional editing and studious engagement with the tough theme of trauma. I wish to thank the super-efficient and supportive publishing team at Confer for creating a respectful collaborative process throughout. With very special thanks and appreciations to Curlette Beckman, Dr Gill Tuckwell, Dr Elaine Arnold, Dr Isha McKenzie-Mavinga, Eugene Ellis, Dr Lucia Swanepoel, the late Lennox Thomas, Cherry Koster and Wendy Alleyne, Joan Muss, Jane Ryan, Christine Roberts, Regina Zander, Patricia Stafford, Bob Chase, David Jones, and the book endorsers. To those who continually inspire my thinking – my clients, supervisees, students, peers, colleagues – and Michael, thank you all for enriching my learning.

This book reflects my observations, reflections and sense-making of my personal, historical, societal and clinical experiences over time. Although all clients' names, characteristics and descriptions in clinical examples have been changed to protect the privacy of individuals, no characters have been invented and no events fabricated.

The Kiskadee bird symbol will appear at the end of each chapter to signal a break or intermission from reading the text. This favourite native to my birth home, Guyana, is known as a bird with attitude because of its bright yellow breast, proud black and white head and incessant, cheerful, often raucous kiskadee calls. I would like to give special thanks to the artist Catherine Clark at Catherine Clark Studio and the Birdwatchers General Store website: www.birdwatchersgeneralstore.com for permission to use the kiskadee bird illustration in this book.

Preface

The subject of black intergenerational trauma has long occupied my mind. I may not have known it by this term then but, as a child, I remained forever curious as to why older members of my family and black people of a certain age and generation spoke always about 'the white man' with reverence, a certain deference and an observable servility. Why? I thought. What is it about these people that had such an effect on my people? Why did this other seem so big, so powerful, in their minds and in their thinking? Even in my innocent and naïve young years, I questioned this fawning behaviour, this apparent disavowal. I was a prolific reader as a child, and I knew from some of the story books I read that courtiers, and so-called lesser beings, fawned over kings and queens, stooping, bending, submitting and genuflecting in their presence. But I never quite understood why my proud black parents and that older generation gave over their identity pride in this way. It was curious a thing from my child's viewpoint, and it seemed stupefyingly wrong.

In trying to make things congruent in my young mind, I used to ask myself did our people do something wrong or commit a crime that made them humble themselves in the midst of white people? Were they showing gratitude for something that required them to behave in such a beholden way? Were we second class to this first-class, first-world people? These questions left me confused as a child and when, for the very first time, I found myself, aged 6, in very close contact with a white couple, I was almost mute. I remember the experience well. My parents and baby sister had left our home in Guyana in the Caribbean and gone travelling for a whole year to Europe and the UK as part of my father's sabbatical. He worked as a senior agriculturalist for the Guyanese Government in the Ministry of Lands, Mines and Forests. That year, my brother and I, who did not accompany our parents, were very well looked after by our aunt and uncle. I remember also that it was during this year my childhood dreams of becoming an astronaut were reshaped by what I now recognize as a deeply shaming put-down by my paternal grandmother. She dissuaded me from astronomy, as, in her words, black people could not be astronauts, as their nostrils were too large and they would use up far too much oxygen. Nursing, she said, was more suitable and respectable. This puerile and racially reductionist comment made such an impact that my first qualification as an adult was indeed in nursing.

My first contact with white people was on the day of my parent's arrival back in Guyana after my father's sabbatical. He had prearranged with this white couple with a duck-egg blue and cream Volkswagen camper van to pick us up from our aunt and uncle's home to be finally reunited with them. Being in such close proximity with these two white alien beings, and grappling with what I had previously heard and witnessed as a child from my black folks about white people seemed to cause a strange kind of internal collapse. I remember being mute throughout the journey. My behaviour was labelled as shy, but I now know that the child does not only need love and safety for its healthy development, but two other ingredients, namely congruence and continuity. Congruence, in this context, is about things making sense to the child, and continuity, the steadiness and safety of the parent's presence, particularly at a very young age. Congruence lessens confusion and insecurity and, with safety provided by the continuous presence of the parents, the child is less likely to eventually turn its insecurities onto and into itself. Left unchecked, this scenario provides the perfect breeding ground for identity shame: *I am not as good as the other person, I am second best, I am inferior, I am not entitled.*

Sitting in the back seat of the camper van and being so close to these two white people was a powerfully confusing experience. As I quietly observed them, I felt they were ordinary and nothing particularly special. Yet, the woman's blonde hair, blue eyes and both of their very pale, Scandinavian skins and strange accents made them very different to me, the little black girl.

Looking back all those years, the paradox for my child's mind was seeing and experiencing ordinary and extraordinary at the same time. Madan Sarup (1996) says that 'we are not born with an identity; we begin the process of identity-construction with identification'. My internalized parental identifications, which were shaped by my black elders' reverential relationship towards and with the white Other, had collided at the age of 6 with my innocent, normal, curious and more natural child-like experience of noting racial difference. However, with my identifications strongly imprinted, there was internal confusion within my young self – one of feeling a lesser being in the presence of the two white people I had met – and herein lie the dynamics that lead to identity shame-based experiences.

'Identity shame leads to identity disavowal', my own description of the infantilisation the black self experiences in the presence of whiteness, is also expressed by Fanon (1986, p. 154):

> When the negro makes contact with the white world, a certain sensitizing actions takes place. If his psychic structure is weak, one observes a collapse of the ego. The black man stops behaving as an actional person. The goal of his behaviour will be The Other (in the guise of the white man), for The Other alone can give him worth.

Something devastatingly awful happens intrapsychically to cause this collapse, this infantilization, this belittling of the black person's entitled human status. Sixty plus years on, the confused little Guyanese girl has found clarity through her anthropological curiosity, dedication and persistence in making sense of her world. These qualities saw me through my adolescent, teenage and young adult life. It perhaps was no surprise that I would leave my country of origin at barely 19 to travel on my own to the UK. My grandmother's words culminated in my becoming a psychiatric and general trained nurse, and subsequently moving away to train as a psychotherapist.

As a more knowing adult, and someone who enjoys her work in private practice, I can now articulate my adult voice to coin my own phrase about the intergenerational burden: what ceases to be a coincidence must be a phenomenon. This phrase, that many of my clients fondly tease me of using frequently, is one that speaks to the ubiquitous and unique nature of black historical trauma – which no black person seems able to escape, and which leads to the challenging work of healing from identity shame and identity disavowal. This affliction, and Fanon's concept of the collapse of the ego, both speak profoundly to the burden still carried (in varying degrees), and the ever-present 'ruptures' caused by the familiar presence of racial hauntings.

This book is a crucial and timely addition to the library of diverse psychological texts covering the far-reaching impact of trauma. Trauma, as the main tenet of black ancestral or historical baggage, is a subject that has long preoccupied my interest as a psychotherapist. I have been a keen observer and facilitator of our ability as human beings to heal and transcend psychological pain, and the subject of black intergenerational trauma presents a particular challenge in mediating our lives at the intersection of our history, the present and the future. In the context of psychotherapy and psychoanalysis, a major part of this challenge of healing from intergenerational wounds is facilitating work that teaches the art of both remembering and forgetting.

From the perspective of a psychotherapist, and through my Caribbean and British lenses, I have much to say and share about black historical and psychological trauma. I have already investigated this topic at great length for my master's and doctorate degrees. This book further highlights the impact of this unheeded dimension of trauma, where the historical, social, political and spiritual coalesce, with significant psychological and emotional impact. In the immersive process, clarity emerged in both the nature and the understanding of the burden of black heritage and racial hauntings. From my work as a psychotherapist, I am particularly aware of the effects of this trauma on clients' core sense of self, their private and public identities, and their individual capacity for growth and individuation.

What I will try to articulate in this book is the profound and continuing trauma impact on Caribbean and African people by Britain, 'the mother country', a dominant patriarchal force that held rule over her 'subjects' from the sixteenth century, settling in St Kitts in 1624, Barbados, Montserrat and Antigua in 1627, and Nevis in 1628. The mother country, as it was fondly referred to by Caribbean elders, was one of the chief colonizers among other equally notorious European and American colonial powers. They all played their part in engineering the slave trade from as far back as the fifteenth century, with each nation growing their empires from slave-based industries. The justification for the slave trade and slavery itself to be able to flourish for an astonishing 400 years, was, without doubt, the fact of greed – that it was lucrative and easy to invade and exploit so-called third world peoples with impunity. Additionally, within the collective white psyches of the oppressors, shame and guilt found no place, as they were dealing with subhumans: black lives did not matter. The harsh and inhumane treatment of black humans could only be justified by the idea that they were part of an inferior 'race' – and therefore lesser beings. This assuaging of collective guilt placed 'white' people at the top, 'black' people at the bottom and different 'mixed' groups somewhere in between. Invented by white people, this stratification was a way of trying to excuse the brutality of slavery.

Britain's sizeable share of and substantial benefits from colonizing much of the Caribbean, Africa and India puts her front and centre of black and brown people's ongoing difficult relationship with their colonial past. Despite this fact, there remains a knee-jerk tendency in British society to point out the role of African middlemen who were complicit in the human trafficking industry. This reminder seems to act as a rationale, albeit a poor one, for the dehumanizing atrocity of slavery. Such deflection and lack of full ownership of this history quietly contribute to keeping open the deep psychological historical wound. The resultant generational impact on black lives makes black and white people strange bedfellows, who are both dependent on and separate from each other. Each has had their lives shaped and impacted by the other.

Bowlby's Attachment Theory (1969; 1973) tells us that the key attachment figures in any family or group system wield the power to influence attachment patterns of relating, being and growing. In the context of the abused child, it would be the abusive parent, the opportunistic abusive paedophile and the narcissistic and coercive abusive family member. In the context of the colonized and colonizer, Britain's relationship with the many islands of the Caribbean, the vast continents of Africa and India, highlights a parallel history of abuse and infantilisation that has shaped attachment patterns and relationships between these nations and peoples. Behavioural attitudes, relatedness to each other and capacities for growth are key areas where the impact can be studied. In summary, it could be concluded that Britain and her empire have engineered one of the most effective forms of abusive attachment, one that has bred a history of transgenerational dependency, indebtedness, impoverishment and psychological emasculation among her subjects. The concomitant effects of these impactful relationship dynamics are scrutinized within this book.

Since Ghana gained freedom from British rule in 1957, many black (and brown) colonized countries have become independent nations in their own right. Most recently, Barbados became a republic in November 2021, ending the island's nearly 400-year relationship with the British monarchy. However, in the eyes and experiences of the colonized, Britain as 'the mother country' and colonizer has failed in her duty to atone for the atrocities of human trading and the inhumane treatment of these subjects. In this loud silence and collective forgetting, which hide the cruelty of the past, the indelible wounds remain untreated and unhealed. An increasingly nationalistic climate, which justifies the British Empire's dominant slave-trading power as bringing economic development and benefits to so-called 'third world' peoples, means that the transgenerational wound cannot be healed. When Britain's former prime minister, David Cameron (in 2013 on a visit to India), remarked that the Empire should be 'celebrated', transgenerational wounds were reopened and left the painful presence of racial hauntings. Historical wounds will not be given the chance to heal when a YouGov survey finds that 44 per cent of British people were proud of Britain's history of colonialism and thought it was a good thing, whereas only 21 per cent regretted that it happened, and 23 per cent held neither view. This empirical evidence shows that people are not aware of Britain's crimes against black humanity, while many choose to remain silent. Many still hold the view that imperialism was benign and that its overriding purpose was not land-grabbing, greed and exploitation, but 'to humanize the natives'. This airbrushing and total disregard of the past make the work of transgenerational healing even more painful for the wronged. There is a need for a day dedicated to the recognition of those black lives that suffered and were lost, lest we forget. In my view, a national day of commemoration would be fitting, and this would also be a gesture of atonement for Britain's significant and atrocious 400-year past.

At the time of writing, we have all been witness to history and its vicissitudes surfacing in more challenging and even dangerous ways. At a global level, the barbaric actions of a megalomanic despotic leader are reminiscent of how powerful nations wield their might in the pursuit of empire building and ethnic superiority. At a level closer to home, the shocking incident of a 15-year-old black girl on her period, being strip-searched by Metropolitan police officers at a London school, is highly evocative of intimate body searches of black bodies during slavery times. These present-day happenings activate powerful hauntings and reopen deep wounds for black people globally. Our clinical work is shaped overtly or covertly by these reverberations, as clients battle to create safer and quieter mental spaces amid a divided and increasingly hateful world. In this silent tyranny, other recent events such as the spark that gave life to the Black Lives Matter movement, re-trigger hauntings and reopen historical wounds. We are made more aware of our histories and, for black people, a deeper, more painful connection with the legacies of generational trauma is inescapable.

In this journey I am both the observer and the observed; in other words, I have not escaped the impact of what I write about. There is potential for vicarious traumatisation, where my own historical and generational wounds are reopened. I therefore see the writing of this book as an act of sublimation: it is my way of redirecting those energies that stem from a place of wounding towards creativity and healing.

Introduction

This book is essentially a text for therapy practitioners and general readers, about an unheeded dimension of trauma that is, paradoxically, omnipresent. It is everywhere in our midst but, like a virus, is unseen yet impactful. My aim is to reveal its presence and shine a light on its complex workings, offering an in-depth understanding of a historical phenomenon that produces deep psychological wounding to a collective of people.

Race and ethnicity terminology

Racial terminology is daunting, confusing, sensitive and ever-changing. For these reasons, I wish to offer at the outset a definition of some regularly used terms to indicate clearly how I will be using them throughout the book. A full glossary of additional terms is also offered at the end of the book.

I have used the term **'black'** to include people with known African heritage, who can be discriminated against because of the colour of their skin. Black is also used as a political term, rooted in racial oppression that pervaded directly from the trans-Atlantic slave trade, giving birth to the civil rights movement and all subsequent organized political and social justice campaigns for change. Alongside the description of black, I use the inclusive term **'people of colour'**, (also in current use as BIPOC – an acronym meaning, black, indigenous, and people of colour), to embrace a wide range of people who are not white or of full European heritage, that is racial groups whose geographical origins are from south Asia, or the Indian subcontinent, including China, Japan, Malaysia, Mauritius, Pakistan, to name a few. It is important to note that, in some current discourses, the term 'people of colour' is seen as sitting in opposition to or set against white as not being a colour. **Mixed-race** or **mixed-heritage people** of any mix of ethnic origin or background are included in the people of colour category, and the term is also used for diverse minority ethnic groups aggregating in social solidarity, (including those who see themselves as 'white-passing'). Again, some find the term 'mixed', in mixed-race, problematic, as it carries a connotation of impurity or a state of incompleteness. These movements in current discourses, although confusing, are healthy, as they highlight the nature of culture being fluid, dynamic and complex. **'Minority ethnic'** is an umbrella term that is used interchangeably in the book to embrace all of the aforementioned groups, including those from hidden white minorities, such as travellers, Gypsies, Irish and Jewish groups, the last who are often mistakenly seen in narrow terms of being a cultural or religious minority only. The term '**race**' will cover nationality, national origin and ethnicity or ethnic origin, and I also use the term 'race' to highlight and explain social constructs that pathologize skin colour and racial attributes that are not biological fact. '**Ethnic origin**' or '**ethnicity**' is used to define shared history/ancestry, language or distinct shared culture. '**Culture**' incorporates broader aspects of ethnicity, religion/belief, values, behaviours, practices, preferences, styles. I also include my new term '**aggregate collective**' to mean a same race group comprising its own distinct differences. '**White** and **white people**' are used in the book as a racialized classification for Caucasian people, for example of European origin, and as a skin colour specifier for people with white skin.

Because the aetiology of generational trauma does not fall easily into the more well-known categories and classifications of trauma, the overlooked dimension of psychological damage to black lives will be fully explained, contextualized and illuminated. The subject will not be distilled down to addressing intergenerational trauma only by what can be observed to be happening with therapists and clients in the consulting room – the reader will also be given a holistic understanding of a phenomenon that embraces all that is going on for the client at three important meeting places: the past, the present and the future. This is where the burden of heritage and racial hauntings meet and will be fully explored.

Standing at the coalface of this intersection with black clients will mean that we will also be hit vicariously by the invisible historical particles and inevitable obstacles of the past – a past that is both the black client and the practitioner's history. There is no way of dodging this. Black intergenerational trauma is essentially about the psychological impact of unprocessed and reactivated pain, suffering and damage caused by man's inhumanity to man. The perpetuation of this historical malady down the generations has meant that the impact of generational trauma has fundamentally left the colonizer and colonized and the oppressor and oppressed, locked in the position of needing the other, yet ambivalent and watchful of them at the same time.

It feels important at this juncture to include a brief summary of my doctoral research (Alleyne, 2006), which is the forerunner and biggest influence for my developed thinking in writing this book. I refer to the findings in subsequent chapters in the book. The doctorate further developed the race theme focus from my master's degree, and the book is the consummate project that brings together my developed ideas, understanding and practice knowledge in the thorny subject of race trauma.

Summary of doctoral research: psychotherapeutic understanding of black identity in workplace contexts

Thirty years of psychotherapy practice have provided a rich context from which to observe and question workplace conflict as it continues to cause untold psychological damage to black and Asian minority ethnic workers. The repeated clinical observations from this clientele led me to wonder whether it was just mere coincidence that I was noticing significantly more negative and damaging effects suffered by this group when compared with their white counterparts. As a result, I began to question whether there was a real and important phenomenon presenting itself, and whether it was worth further investigation.

It is important to add that, in my psychotherapy practice, white clients also presented with workplace stress caused by acts of bullying, scapegoating and other undermining work dynamics, and they too were negatively affected by their experiences. However, my observations were picking up something distinctly more consistent in the experiences of non-white staff. I coined this continuous occurrence 'workplace oppression', which seemed to affect black and Asian workers of every status, age group, gender, and sexuality, with correspondingly more marked damaging impact not seen in the dominant white workforce. The contributing factors observed for the ethnic minority staff appeared to be:

(a) specific factors of racial bias and racism contributing to the onset of workplace conflict,
(b) the collusive nature of management systems closing ranks and not dealing with the conflict,
(c) the stuck and entrenched positions both sides that ended up in workplace impasses,
(d) heavier penalties meted out to black and Asian workers for situations that would be otherwise ignored and overlooked if it were white staff involved, and
(e) the quite significant effects of these workplace experiences on the emotional, physical health and self-esteem of these workers.

The cumulative effects of workplace oppression for black and Asian workers were the intense feelings of being ground down, made powerless and totally deskilled. The persistent overwhelming patterns and remarkable familiar trajectories observed in my clients' professional and mental collapse prompted rigorous investigation. My doctoral research utilized a phenomenological approach, combining hermenutics and a heuristic enquiry (as opposed to a quantitative survey), to investigate the experiences of 30 workers, mostly black, and Asian workers within three workplace settings – the NHS (National Health Service), education and social services.

Summary of key findings:

- All respondents felt that they were qualified and capable (and in some instances more so than their white counterparts) to carry out their jobs responsibly and effectively.
- All respondents described traumatic events at work in terms of a grinding down and confidence-sapping experience, leading to feelings of powerlessness, low self-esteem and being stuck in victimhood.
- Twenty-eight of the thirty respondents attributed their race and racial bias (conscious and unconscious) as major contributing factors to their workplace difficulties.
- Of the thirty respondents, nine were successful in taking their case to Employment Tribunals and were vindicated. The remaining twenty-one respondents chose to battle on in the workplace with an increasingly high cost to their mental health and well-being.
- Twelve of the thirty respondents were officially diagnosed by their GPs as suffering from clinical depression and post-traumatic stress disorder (PTSD). The latter diagnosis was given to those whose stress symptoms had persisted even after their legal complaint cases were successfully closed.

Subsequent research findings also highlighted important and specific issues for black and Asian workers. They pointed to areas where these minority ethnic staff needed to take notice of what they themselves might have unintentionally contributed to their traumatic experiences. A brief summary of these follows.

Wider analysis of the research findings strongly indicated that, alongside workers, present difficulties, were also negative experiences of black people's historical heritage being activated. Hauntings from a painful past became bound up with the present struggles. I formulated that, as a result of this powerful activation, an internal oppressive force was being created that also had the effect of causing damage. This internal adversary often proved to be more difficult to manage therapeutically than the perceived external oppressor. I coined the phenomenon 'the internal oppressor' (Alleyne, 2004c, 2005b), which acted like an internal enemy and burden on the self. This was borne out of the rich findings which emerged from respondents' stories. The findings highlighted the impact and nature of their trauma experiences seen in the reactive personal scripts, shared attitudinal disposition, the recurring trauma responses and impact of the selfhood. The frequency of these evolving themes in psychotherapy practice highlighted clinical themes of identity shame, deep narcissistic wounding, historical enmeshment issues and real difficulties in negotiating the individuation process – all themes that will be addressed in the forthcoming chapters.

The book is intended for practitioners, thinkers and educators from the fields of psychotherapy, psychoanalysis, counselling, psychology, sociology, education and the community and pastoral sectors. It will offer a useful map for all to orientate themselves and navigate their way in work with black clients found to be presenting with generational trauma issues. Having a rounded understanding of where historical transmissions collide with present-day circumstances will provide an awareness of the real challenges to the client's healing, individuation and personal empowerment. The book will also address the important psychological transmissions of intergenerational trauma; this includes the author's coinage of the term 'racial hauntings', as a new perspective on Professor Stephen Frosh's significant writings (2012, 2013), thereby advancing the concept of hauntings. His work speaks powerfully to one of the most traumatic silencings of recent generations – the Holocaust. The book will offer theoretical and practical tools to support clients in these areas. Journeying with clients in this challenging area of trauma work will also demand that the practitioner develop a thick professional skin – one that paradoxically allows for empathy and authentic engagement, while being able to withstand the inevitable impingements from the client's world experiences. Consequently, the well-researched facts from Newell and MacNeal (2010), Norcross (2000, 2007), Pearlman (1995) show that those who work with trauma conditions will need to be observed. Practitioners may invariably be triggered by their own trauma experiences, making it vital that they receive regular support through supervision, where care for the caretaker is prioritized.

Meeting the subject of black intergenerational trauma will demand that, as therapists, we learn the art of self-regulation when our own feelings and trauma triggers are aroused. Trauma work demands a particular stillness from the practitioner to truly listen, hear and reflect inwardly before responding. This therapeutic posture cannot be achieved if the practitioner's vicarious traumatization reactions interrupt the containment and transitional space for the client's own healing.

Vicarious traumatization: a caution

This text is essentially about trauma, deep historical trauma that profoundly shapes and affects the core sense of self. As with any exposure to emotional pain that closely resembles our own experiences or affects us in other ways, we may find ourselves retriggered in our own pain or shame. I would therefore like to offer a word of caution: do not rush through the text but, rather, pace yourself, leaving space to reflect, debrief and regroup. Engaging with this text will hopefully come about through my passion, use of story-telling, anecdotes, historical facts and analytic thinking about the phenomenon. Whatever personal material that may surface through empathic engagement, over-identification or even being a bystander who experiences guilt and shame, the journey through the book should be monitored closely and space given for reflection and contemplation.

Many readers will appreciate that vicarious traumatization should be understood in the context of a transformation in the self that results from empathic engagement with traumatized clients and events. Psychodynamic and psychoanalytic therapy practitioners will know this as countertransference, which is a form of identification with the other that can open up our own emotional material. In addressing possible vicarious traumatization, I include a debrief symbol to mitigate any potential mental overload or other negative emotional impact while reading this text . The appearance of the Guyanese Kisskadee bird symbol at the end of each chapter will signal a suggested breathing space for an interlude.

What is vicarious trauma?

In short, this is second-hand suffering. This type of trauma can occur when someone speaks to someone who has experienced a trauma or witnessed a trauma first-hand. The person listening can suffer secondary trauma and feel second-hand symptoms experienced by the person explaining the trauma. It is an indirect way of picking up the distress and agony from the person's suffering from an intense ordeal and being impacted by the vivid experiences.

Signs of vicarious traumatization and tips for self-care

- Noticing that you are in a high state of tension and preoccupation with the trauma experiences and stories described in the book.

  Tip: Allow for a break away or recess from the material.

- Remembering and talking excessively about a once forgotten or repressed experience, or a past traumatizing event.

  Tip: Allow for a break away from the material and practise reality orientation: that was then; this is now. I have choices and the power to change things in my own situation.

- Becoming aware that you are feeling overwhelmed and are experiencing a deep sense of hopelessness about the divisive way society is and the way it treats your race. You feel that you are harbouring growing anger or rage that does not subside towards people in, for example, authority and power.

  Tip: Allow for a break from the book and engage your feelings with at least two other people. Sharing is better than being alone with your experiences. Attend to your mental hygiene by engaging in soothing, calming and relaxation activities.

- Feeling stuck with persistent and recurring feelings of dread and a crippling fear for the progress of the next black generation or mankind generally.

Tip: Remember that you are not weak or damaged but may be experiencing the normal ripple effects of compassion fatigue. You are advised to read the text in bite-sized chunks and to discuss your experiences with interested and like-minded people. If you are in therapy training, suggest the text as reading references to your college tutors, university or training institution, to engage practitioners in race conversations and diversity education.

On a more general note, all readers of trauma material may find it helpful to learn mindfulness techniques that focus us to live and be in the moment – not stuck and preoccupied with the past or experiences that cause us pain.

Finally, should vicarious emotional triggers continue to preoccupy the mind to such an extent that they affect regular, normal life routines, it will be advisable to seek out a professional counsellor or therapist for some time-limited support to regain one's emotional equilibrium and focus for life and ontological security.

Context

The main thrust of the book will hover at the intersection where European imperial slave-trade history, most notably Britain's past, meets the present-day trauma experience of black lives, and will describe the healing process involved. The book will focus on the ongoing psychological and emotional trauma impact for black identity development and will address therapeutic processes for psychological healing and the individuation process. As this book has been written mainly for practitioners, by a practitioner and analytic thinker, a major aspect of it is to offer ways to understand the hidden manifestations of historical trauma, which is continually re-enacted in black people's lives – and in the consulting room. The book will also offer tools and ways to work psychodynamically and integratively with the psychological impact of this trauma on clients' lives.

Chapter 1 – Transgenerational and intergenerational trauma delineates the difference between trans- and intergenerational trauma. It defines and explains trauma from the perspectives of history and the impact of the generational baggage on the black diaspora. It discusses how the history of British colonial rule and influence has played – and continues to play a major part in the shaping of black lives through the generations.

Chapter 2 – Trauma legacies focuses on the struggle for mental freedom by first journeying through the 'Cycle of Events' (Alleyne, 1992), which examines what has been passed on to six generations of black Caribbean people. This chapter also describes how the ongoing effects of historical baggage have shaped the racial identity, personal and collective agency of black Caribbean people, and highlights ongoing difficulties for both individual and collective individuation.

Chapter 3 – Understanding trauma addresses trauma and identifies the specific nature of generational trauma. The chapter makes a case for this complex condition in the black context to be recognized as a legitimate psychological condition affecting the quality of mental health of black lives. It illustrates how the manifestations of this condition must be separated, assessed and treated differently from other trauma and psychiatric presentations that are measured by the standard Eurocentric diagnostic guidelines and principles. A robust rationale is put forward for the black lived experience to be recognized under classification of a 'Complex Type III Trauma' utilizing my doctoral research respondents' scripts and observations from psychotherapy practice. The emerging respondents' scripts from my doctoral research (2006), as well as those expressed in clinical practice by black clients will be presented here,

Chapter 4 – The nature of hauntings introduces the new concept of racial hauntings, which is a reworking of the Freudian analytic concept of hauntings. Racial hauntings are discussed as an unheeded dimension of trauma occurring in the light of conscious racialized experiences in the white world. This phenomenon creates psychic ruptures from its capacity to leave a damaging presence and trauma residue that disrupts black ontological security. The visitations of racial hauntings is psychoanalytically positioned as a relational third – the black subject, the white other, and a third unwanted and lingering presence.

Chapter 5 – Shame and its vicissitudes is a chapter that looks at the many faces of shame over time and its application in wider places and spaces. Three strands are addressed with a race thread running throughout. First, the manner of causation of shame is discussed with the help of some personal experiences of childhood to illustrate its profound impact on racial identity formation. The second strand weaves in the context of white identity shame. It highlights how past lineage transgressions, embedded as guilt of exposure in national character, would rather be buried somewhere in the huge planks of the human cargo ships that crossed the oceans. The third strand of this chapter includes the element of societal (universal) shame and its impact in shaping the current zeitgeist.

Chapter 6 – Shame and its role in black identity wounding argues the point that shame overarches much of the therapeutic work of trauma and identity wounding. The chapter discusses how generational trauma carries a particular shame that leaves toxic and epigenetic wounds. It highlights the concept of *the internal oppressor* (Alleyne, 2004c, 2005b), elucidating its workings via case vignettes and clinical casework to highlight unheeded dimensions of the shame trauma and its interruptions to the black individuation process.

Chapter 7 – The chokehold of historical enmeshment explores the ever-present and intertwined nature of the historical past and black people's present-day functioning. It describes the relationship between the burden carried from the past and racial hauntings that dwell in the present. It addresses pitfalls and over-investments with the past that contribute to the psychological chokehold of enmeshment. Areas of untreated trauma are identified that adversely determine a person's ontology and full capacity for individuation. The chapter suggests that enmeshment, as a psychoanalytic concept, can provide deeper understanding of why such co-dependency must be recognized and worked through for the exercising of personal and collective agency.

Chapter 8 – Intersectionality and racialized trauma provides an understanding the interplay between these two concepts. Using carefully chosen examples, the chapter illuminates how multiple oppressions are experienced in the midst of existing racialized and historical trauma. The chapter is a reminder to practitioners to embrace the hybrid nature of black identity and to be mindful of tendencies (conscious and unconscious) toward racial objectification, homogenization and the pathologizing of blackness. The chapter themes remind the reader that oppressive and discriminatory experiences can impact multiple areas of black identity and trigger racial hauntings and dormant wounds of generational trauma.

Chapter 9 – Working therapeutically with generational trauma is an informative and instructive text for analysts, psychotherapists, counsellors, group therapists and general therapy practitioners from all modalities. The chapter offers insights and therapy tools for working with the lived experience of generational trauma in the black context. The chapter provides clear 'banister rails' for practitioners to steady themselves when meeting such painful and damaging experiences in the consulting room. They are reminded of intercultural gaps, pitfalls and racial biases, born out of Eurocentric thinking and black-on-black collusion that may re-wound the wounded and reshame the shamed.

Chapter 10 – Healing from the burden of our heritage explores the concepts of freedom, transcendence, transformation and resilience – the work of psychological (and spiritual) healing from generational trauma. New thinking is presented for the analysis and understanding of 'vertical' and 'horizontal' trauma activation and healing. The chapter delineates what is to be healed and the process of separating from the chokehold of historical enmeshment. The principles of healing offered will be of use to both practitioners and general readers.

APPENDIX 2 – Recognizing My Own Ancestral Burden is an important part of this book, as it is my attempt to discover ME; the make-up of my ethnic origin, to uncover the ancestral origins of my white English-language surname, Alleyne – where did it originate and who are the people behind my genetic makeup? I wanted to uncover this by following all links leading back to the very first genetically related Alleyne in my father's bloodline. The genealogical research is not complete, and may never be possible to complete, but I share my discoveries to date and how they have added meaning to my sense of self and identity.

CHAPTER 1

Transgenerational and intergenerational trauma

In this country white means British. Everybody else has to hyphenate

Difference between transgenerational and intergenerational trauma

Transgenerational and intergenerational trauma are two types of trauma that will be addressed, and the terms are used frequently, throughout the book. They are inextricably linked and impact each other. As they are often confused, it is important to understand the difference between the two.

In short, *trans*generational trauma refers to the negative and damaging impact of an oppressive history on a people, society, group or collective. It is about history and how what happened in one generation can affect future generations, even a few hundred years later. In this context, black historical trauma is 400 years old (1619 to the present day).

*Inter*generational trauma is concerned with the transmission of trauma, arising from that history, within families. It is about what is psychologically – and epigenetically – inherited, internalized and passed on in ways that influence family life, dynamics, behaviours and so on, within and between black families and in black people's experiences in the wider world. In this context, a generation is approximately 25–30 years (an average interval of time between the birth of parents and the birth of their offspring), which sociologists refer to as a 'familial generation'.

The book's focus on the interplay between trans- and inter-generational trauma will highlight psychological ruptures still unhealed, which continue to blight the humanity of a black civilization.

Transgenerational trauma

'If you don't know where you've come from, you don't know where you're going'

Maya Angelou The Arizona Republic interview, 2011

The term 'transgenerational trauma' was first documented in the 1960s to describe the trauma symptoms experienced by descendants of Holocaust survivors. The term 'transgenerational' is used in a similar way throughout this book to describe the workings of a comparable historical trauma, in the black context of slavery. The prefix trans, meaning *through, to the other side and beyond*, denotes here the movement or conveyance of the original trauma and its psychological effects on a colonized people into the future, impacting future generations of the black diaspora.

Transgenerational trauma can be the result of the tyranny of colonization, slavery, genocide, war and the forced relocation of a people, its indelible impact forever shaping the history and identity of a people. In addition to those affected by the Holocaust, there are other well-documented cases of racial, cultural and religious groups who have been impacted by transgenerational trauma, for example the Irish because of the Troubles, and many other indigenous populations where legacies of conflict have left their mark on the mental health and social cohesion of nations and communities. The ancestral baggage that inevitably cascades down the generations weighs heavily on the group and its peoples, and the consequences to their emotional, mental and psychic health are inescapable. The burdens of heritage as a result of black intergenerational trauma are no different.

The black experience of transgenerational trauma has occurred over centuries, rendering an aggregate collective or group of people subjugated and enslaved for four centuries. The devastating impact of this insidious trauma and its negative transmissions are still being re-enacted in many aspects of black life. Why, after four centuries, is the impact still alive?

In his dystopian novel, *Nineteen Eighty-Four*, George Orwell wrote, 'Who controls the past controls the future: who controls the present, controls the past' (Orwell, 1949, p. 44). Orwell's novel describes a dystopian future, in which all citizens are manipulated by a single political party.

Orwell was writing at a time when information was being controlled by a minority of people and his novel contains references to Nazi Germany.

It would be a stretch to suggest that black people live under such subjugation, but the essence of Orwell's quote shapes the central tenet of slavery and transgenerational trauma, as it reminds us of who is still in control of the facts and truths about black history. The history of slavery is mostly argued from the point of view that it happened a long time ago and that we must learn to forget, leave it where it is and move on. Its present-day beneficiaries feel that they need not concern themselves with their ancestors' crimes, and should be allowed to exist with no reminders of its presence, for being reminded risks both shame and guilt. My contention is that this very disavowal is a great hurt, one that contributes to the ongoing nature and damage of transgenerational trauma, as having one's trauma recognized is the first step towards reconciliation and healing. The very fact that the discussion of the injustices of slavery remains tightly controlled and pushed away from consciousness animates the pain of the past.

In Afua Hirsch's article 'Britain was built on the backs of slaves. A memorial is the least they deserve' (*The Guardian*, 2019), she addresses Britain's disavowal of its imperialist past. She cites the powerful example of government failure to support a tireless working party's effort (supported by the UNESCO Slave Route Project) to create Britain's first permanent national memorial to honour millions of unnamed enslaved Africans and their descendants.[1] It was hoped that the memorial, 'Remembering Enslaved Africans and Their Descendants', which was to be erected in the rose gardens in Hyde Park, would give public recognition and acknowledgement to the millions of unnamed Africans who were victims of the transatlantic slave trade, thereby fulfilling the desires of present and future generations to see their ancestors commemorated. The belief was that African slavery is everyone's history and crosses the ethnic divide, as there are beneficiaries of the legacy. The sophisticated £4 million campaign, called Memorial 2007, had high-profile backing, which included Kate Davson, a descendant of abolitionist William Wilberforce, and Doreen Lawrence, the mother of Steven Lawrence. Memorial 2007 repeatedly tried to secure support from every prime minister from Tony Blair to Boris Johnson, but lack of government financial backing and full engagement means that the project has never been granted approval. Hirsch writes:

> This campaign is not requesting a favour for a marginal section of society. The history of how we came to be this nation is a history for us all. If we can't dignify it with a simple memorial, one whose location, design, importance and even planning permission have already been established, then we really have lost the plot. (Hirsch, 2019)

The announcement in 2015 of £50 million in support for a Holocaust memorial raised the group's hopes that there was a renewed interest in remembering painful historic events. That interest did not, however, extend to the country's treatment of black people who have descended from Britain's imperial slave history. This shameless disavowal can be added to a list which includes one of the biggest scandals of institutionalized racism, namely the failure to properly commemorate potentially 350,000 predominantly black and Asian service personnel who died fighting for the British Empire in both world wars. Another example is the attempts to deport members of the Windrush generation just a few years ago; together, these events demonstrate the appalling treatment black people have endured, on top of – and thereby compounding – the original wound.

Timelines

In order to give justice to this black historical context, I have included two brief slavery and abolition timelines, crucial chronological sequences relating to the Caribbean and African experiences. They map the historical background and circumstances from which the collective trauma of the diasporic groups have emerged. The timelines also highlight the role and position of the colonizers in their dealings with the colonized. Angelou's quote provides a poignant reminder that, for ancestral healing to be experienced on all sides of the historical divide, an awareness of one's past is a necessity for both the oppressed and the oppressor. The oppressor/colonizer cannot legitimize its greatness if it is unable to step back, do an honest accounting of its past and recognize the need to atone for its inhumanity. On the other side, the oppressed has to do its work by recognizing the impact of generational trauma and healing from its damaging transmissions and impact on individuation.

The following timelines highlight European competition and Britain's key involvement in the transatlantic slave trade, where black humans were a mere unit of currency and land grabbing was the order of the day.

Slavery and abolition: brief historical timeline (Caribbean)

1562–9   John Hawkins becomes the first Englishman definitely known to have traded in Africans, making three voyages to Sierra Leone and transporting a total of 1200 inhabitants to Hispaniola and St Domingue (Dominican Republic and Haiti). He sells them to the Spanish in exchange for pearls, hides, sugar and ginger.

1618   King James I creates The Company of Adventurers of London Trading in parts of Africa.

1672   The Royal African Company is formed in order to regulate the English slave trade, with a legal monopoly over the 2500 miles of African coast from the Sahara to the Cape of Good Hope. The company is financed by royal, aristocratic and commercial capital.

1698   The Royal African Company monopoly ends, opening the trade to private traders from Bristol and Liverpool.

1713   Under the Treaty of Utrecht following the War of the Spanish Succession, Britain is awarded the 'Asiento' or sole right to import an unlimited number of enslaved people to the Spanish Caribbean colonies for 30 years.

1730   First Maroon War in the British colony of Jamaica. Groups of escaped slaves in the mountains repel British forces and a treaty in 1739 confirms their free status.

1760   Slave revolts in Jamaica last for several months and claim many lives.

1765	Granville Sharp begins legal challenges to the British slave trade with the case of Jonathan Strong.
1772	John Woolman, an American Quaker and early anti-slavery campaigner, comes to England to gather support from English Quakers.
1783	133 Africans are thrown overboard alive from the slave ship *Zong* so that the owners can claim compensation money from their insurance company.
1783	British Quakers form a committee against slavery and the slave trade.
1787	*Thoughts and Sentiments on the Evil and Wicked Traffic of the Slavery and Commerce of the Human Species* by Ottobah Cuguano is published. The Society for Effecting the Abolition of the African Slave Trade is founded in London.
1790	Wilberforce's first Abolition Bill is rejected by Parliament.
1804	St Domingue declared the Republic of Haiti the first independent black state outside of Africa.
1807	The Act to Abolish the Transatlantic Slave Trade is passed in Parliament.
1833	Slavery Abolition Act is passed in Parliament, taking effect in 1834. This act gives all slaves in the Caribbean their freedom, although some other British territories have to wait longer. However, ex-slaves in the Caribbean are forced to undertake a period of 'apprenticeship' (working for former masters for a low wage) which means that slavery is not fully abolished in practice until 1838.

This timeline is adapted from: https://historicengland.org.uk/research/inclusive-heritage/the-slave-trade-and-abolition/time-line

Slavery and abolition: brief historical timeline (African)

1488	Portuguese discover Cape of Good Hope.
1494	Treaty of Tordesilhas; Portuguese King agrees to trade with West African leaders.
1498	Vasco de Gama undertakes first journey to Spice Islands.
1562	Hawkins' first voyage.
1564	Hawkins' second voyage.
1567	Hawkins' third voyage.
1580	Portugal unites with Spain.
1581	Drake rounds Cape of Good Hope.
1602	Dutch East India Company formed.
1618	Royal Charter to The Company of Adventurers of London (Guinea Company).
1621	Dutch West India Company established.
1631	The Company of Merchants Trading to Guinea chartered.
1632	First English factories built in West Africa.
1652	Dutch establish Cape of Good Hope.
1657	The Company of Merchants Trading to Guinea ceases to trade.
1660	Royal African Company established.
1663	Fort James constructed in Gambia.
1668	The Gambia Adventurers is created.
1672	The New Royal African Company created.
1688	Glorious Revolution overthrows King James II.

1694–1700 Komenda Wars.

1698   Royal African Company loses monopoly of trade
              with West Africa.

1713   Asiento allows English to transport slaves to
              Spanish South America.

1758   British capture St Louis in Senegal in Seven Years War.

1772   Somerset case outlaws slavery in Britain itself.

1779   British lose St Louis in Senegal.

1787   Sierra Leone created for freed slaves.

1788   African Association created.

1806   Britain seizes Cape Town from Dutch.

1807   Britain abolishes Slave Trade.

1808   'Slave Squadron' formed to enforce abolition of Slave
              Trade; Britain formally takes control of Sierra Leone.

1824   Asante defeat British expedition.

1830   Royal Geographical Society formed.

1833   Britain abolishes slavery throughout British Empire.

1861   Lagos acquired as a British port.

1872   Diamonds discovered in South Africa.

1874   Wolseley campaign against Asante.

1879   Zulus defeat British at Isandlwana; United African
              Company led by George Goldie.

1881   British defeat Zulus at Ulundi; First Boer War; British
              bombardment of Alexandria.

1884   Berlin Conference.

1885   Gordon killed at Khartoum; gold discovered on

	Witwatersrand; British East Africa Company led by William Mackinnon.
1886	Royal Niger Company.
1888	German East Africa Company led by Karl Peters.
1889	British South Africa Company created by Cecil Rhodes.
1893–1894	First Matabele War.
1895	Jameson Raid.
1896	Italians defeated at Adowa.
1896–1897	Second Matabele War.
1896–1899	Sudan Expedition.
1898	Fashoda Incident.
1899–1902	Second Boer War.
1900	Royal Niger subsumed by British to form Southern Nigeria.
1902	Treaty of Vereeniging.
1914	Northern and Southern Nigeria merge into single colony.
1923	Southern Rhodesian self-government and end of BSAC rule.

This Timeline of The Slave Trade and Abolition was reproduced from https://historicengland.org.uk/research/inclusive-heritage/the-slave-trade-and-abolition/time-line and amalgamates the related Caribbean and African historical events of slavery in a chronological order.

British involvement in the slave trade

History tells us that Britain's involvement in the transatlantic slave trade was officially started by Sir John Hawkins with his first voyage in 1562. In 1573, he received the support and investment of Elizabeth I. Britain outsmarted its European rivals and became the premier trader in the people trafficking and enslavement industry until 1807. Together with Portugal, the two countries accounted for 70 per cent of all Africans transported to the Americas. It has been estimated that 40 per cent of African slaves were transported in British vessels (Lovejoy, 1982). Although the numbers are likely to be much greater, Lovejoy suggests that around six million people were transported from their homelands between 1701 and 1800, and a further two million were exported between 1811 and 1867. This history sits alongside the organized systematic extermination of six million European Jews during the Holocaust.

British plantation and mine owners bought the Africans, and thousands died in the perilous journeys they were forced to make, with many more thousands dying in captivity and hard labour. Slaves were treated inhumanely by their colonial owners, who were at liberty to work their slaves to death, knowing that it was more economical to buy another slave than to keep one alive. The slaves have neither human nor legal rights, marriage was forbidden and existing families were broken up. Parents and their children were often sold to different owners, with the men moved abruptly to work like horses on other plantations. Rape, torture and the beating of slaves to death were accepted practices among slave owners.

Britain's involvement in the slave trade was the most dominant between 1640 and 1807, transporting enslaved African men, women and children to British colonies in the Caribbean, North and South America, and to other countries. The scale and breadth of slavery to Britain's economy were colossal. The slave trade encouraged the development of financial, commercial, legal and insurance institutions to support and protect the activities of the trade. In the process, Britain's economy grew exponentially from the lucrative businesses of the cotton and tobacco industries, and imported products such as sugar. Merchants became bankers, the landed gentry became wealthier from businesses financed by profits from slave trading, and ports like Liverpool, Glasgow and some of the smaller British ports all became significant gateways.

Edward Colston, a notorious Atlantic slave trader, English merchant, philanthropist and Conservative Member of Parliament, was widely commemorated in Bristol for making the city rich from the lootings of the slave trade. The toppling of his statue in June 2020, which had been a constant landmark reminder for many in the city of Bristol, symbolizes, as I see it, a powerful act of attempting to deal with the reverberations of racial hauntings. Colston's erect statue, a celebration of the man and his philanthropy, only serves to cancel out the evils of slavery and transfers the burden and racial hauntings to be carried by the progeny of the historically wounded.

Figure 1.1 gives an overview of the scale and duration of the abhorrent practice.

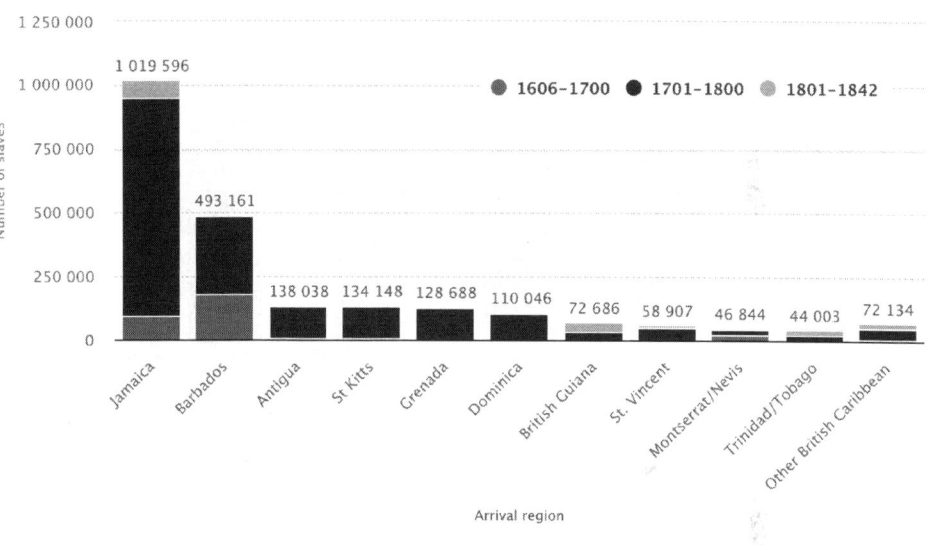

Figure 1.1 *Estimated number of slaves who arrived from Africa in various regions of the British Caribbean in each century from 1606 to 1842*
Source: Slave Voyages © Statista 2020

The historical timelines of 400 years of enslavement of the black African and black Caribbean peoples show the genesis of a historical trauma that follows a similar organized and systematic system. Each 100-year period of the 400 years of enslavement has had the effect of embedding the trauma. Each subsequent generation has inherited the trauma transmissions of the original dehumanizing wound experience, both psychologically and epigenetically (see Chapter 3 for more information on epigenetics).

The wounding after-effects of the slave trade for the colonized and enslaved reverberate deeply. Slavery not only led to the devastation of villages, towns and peoples in Africa through European-fostered wars, but also contributed to the destruction of much indigenous manufacturing and wealth in Africa itself. The movement of Africans for economic survival, and the displacement of many Africans during the period of the slave trade – within Africa and around the world, as well as the emigration of Caribbeans of African descent to other parts of the world – have all contributed to diasporic fragmentation and the ongoing division of black African, black American and black Caribbean peoples. Despite these hard facts of history and evidence of lived lives, the spread of racist ideology to justify the enslavement and treatment of black people, and the continual laundering of the truth, means that the burden and racial hauntings remain in black peoples' midst.

Intergenerational trauma

From this historical transgenerational experience, intergenerational trauma transmissions have occurred between and across generations. These transmissions pass on in the trauma of, for example: holding on to family secrets and perpetuating lies and deception; in hiding the shame of mental health problems; and in not declaring the presence of children born outside of marriage and other relationships. So-called baby mothers and baby fathers are commonly held as secret. These Jamaican terms, used most commonly by the wider black community in Britain, describe the parents of infants who are not married to, or are in exclusive relationships with, each other. The terms also speak to notions of marriage to imply a group with a significant proportion of single mothers and absent fathers.

Intergenerational trauma is noticeable in certain generational illness patterns where, for example: black men who are non-smokers present as 50 per cent more likely to suffer with lung cancer than white men; diabetes showing a 60 per cent more common occurrence in black Americans than in white Americans, killing four times more 35- to 54-year-old black Americans than white Americans; and high blood pressure being commonly known as the silent killer in all black western communities (DeNoon, 2005). These and other psychological manifestations are all continued on in the pedigree (genes/genealogy) and kinship (interactions and social relations) of generations. Manifestations of ongoing intergenerational trauma may be found when a person comments on particular attributes and traits of a family member, for example by commenting on, 'the proud way she carries herself through adversity is the mark of independence all single-parent women of my mother's generation are blessed with'. In this example, the narrative speaks overtly to the strength of black women who soldier on in the absence of support from their menfolk. The above quote speaks of a pattern, repeated down the generations, of black women keeping things together and holding families intact. The example highlights the phenomenon of absent men and the pain women carry most often on their own that becomes normalized.

Intergenerational trauma can continue on in the pedigree of families and spotted in a black person or client's narrative, where reference is made to the curse of one's genes. The burden of such a curse may be expressed thus: 'several men in my father's lineage seemed to suffer in silence ... they ended it quietly when they couldn't carry on.' In this example, the untreated trauma is a clear generational pattern where men suffer shame about their mental suffering in silence and, rather than run the risk of asking for help, which is seen as weakness, take matters into their own hands and end their lives. Intergenerational trauma may also be identified in a person's reference to certain physical family traits that repeat in several generations and cause puzzlement, pain and shame. An example of this trauma can be heard in a remark such as, 'even though we knew the light-skinned ones were throwbacks to slavery, nothing prepared us for an albino baby.' Although the birth of an albino baby is a phenomenon not always related to interracial parentage, and mostly regarded as a rare inherited genetic disorder where there is a complete absence of pigment, the couple's emotional shock is evident in their immediate link to a painful historical past. This is a clear example of how the trigger of a painful historical past becomes activated. Alongside the couple's questioning of their circumstances: a light-skinned baby, although a surprise, is, on another level, disturbing, but rationalized as an expected intergenerational occurrence in black families, from the known fact that children were born to white slave owners. The genetic throwback from this history can be manifest in light-skinned children being born to black families. But, in the case of this couple having an albino baby, the experience may seem exaggerated and inexplicable, leading to questions about their morality, being cursed and even being a punishment.

More generally for black people, intergenerational trauma has strong links to a history that has left the descendants of slaves with many burdens that we continue to bear. My own held script informs me that, when we trace our ancestry, there's abundant evidence to show that we have been marginalized at every point in time and place on meeting the white world. The indelible mark from this historical psychic wound is no different from those carried by other historically oppressed groups. Black history carries the collective memory of these past traumatic events, and current social, cultural and political contexts remind us of how the dominant culture often silences and diminishes the value of the different other.

The formal recognition of transgenerational trauma

The recognition of transgenerational trauma first emerged in research exploring how historical and cultural traumas affect children of survivors over generations. According to Tori DeAngelis's (2019) article in the American Psychological Association, one of the first articles to note the presence of intergenerational trauma appeared in 1966, when Canadian psychiatrist Vivian M. Rakoff and colleagues (Rakoff et al., 1966) documented high rates of psychological distress among children of Holocaust survivors. Since then, researchers have been assessing anxiety, depression and post-traumatic stress disorder (PTSD) in trauma survivors and their offspring. Holocaust survivors and their children were the most widely studied over the longest period of time and most of the studies have found atypically high rates of these disorders.

In the early 1980s, Yael Danieli (1981), in her article addressing the adaptational styles in families of survivors of the Nazi Holocaust, identified at least four adaptive styles to transgenerational trauma that she and others observed among Holocaust survivors. Examples include 'victim', people who have difficulty moving on from the original trauma and are emotionally volatile and overprotective, and 'numb', those who are emotionally detached, intolerant of weakness in others and who maintain a 'conspiracy of silence' within the family. Other styles include 'fighter' and 'those who made it'.

The non-recognition of black people's historical trauma from the white colonizing world and the rest of the world's non-acknowledgement of its impact on a human race, both contribute deeply to an arrested state of being and thus development for the black diaspora. This is neither the adaptive state of victimhood nor numbness mentioned above that can be shoehorned into a category of pathology; rather this should be recognized as a perpetual state of feeling held back and being held back. The continuation of this historical wound into present-day struggles is the hallmark of intergenerational trauma. I believe that to fully understand and appreciate the burden of this heritage is to see the nature of black historical trauma as a type III, complex PTSD. We will return to this need for formal recognition for this category of trauma in Chapter 2: Trauma legacies.

CHAPTER 2

Trauma legacies

Cycle of Events

Cycle of Events (Alleyne, 1992, 2009) is a pictorial and psychodynamic framework of black people's relationship with white people which highlights the nature of traumatic historical transmissions and their ongoing intergenerational impact. I first devised the framework in 1992, and have adapted it as my ideas have developed. It is, sadly, as relevant today as it was back then, illustrating what is passed on from generation to generation and laying out the psychological effects and manifest impact on black–white relationships.

The following pages show the full Cycle of Events and a breakdown of the different stages.

The first and second stages of the Cycle of Events show how a legacy of pain was passed down the generations by black ancestors and their progeny. Brutally enslaved for 400 years by the organized system of slavery, black people found themselves so-called free slaves who then ended up as colonized peoples in nations ruled and governed by the same ancestral lines of white colonizers. This extraordinary legacy of always being controlled and regulated by the white Other has left, in its wake, an indelible impact and mark of identity wounding on the victims of this abhorrent system. The unequal and oppressive relationships that have continued since then have, inevitably, led to unhealthy co-dependencies, preoccupations, unequal relationships, and racial and cultural enmeshments.

What is this legacy of pain for black people and what has been passed on? As I see it, the initial trauma for black people was the systematic dehumanization of African people. We must be reminded that black people's existence did not start with slavery. We now know from fossil discoveries and DNA analysis, that the African continent and, more

27

specifically, the eastern and southern regions are home to the cradle of humankind. There is no doubt that civilizations of black people date back several million years.

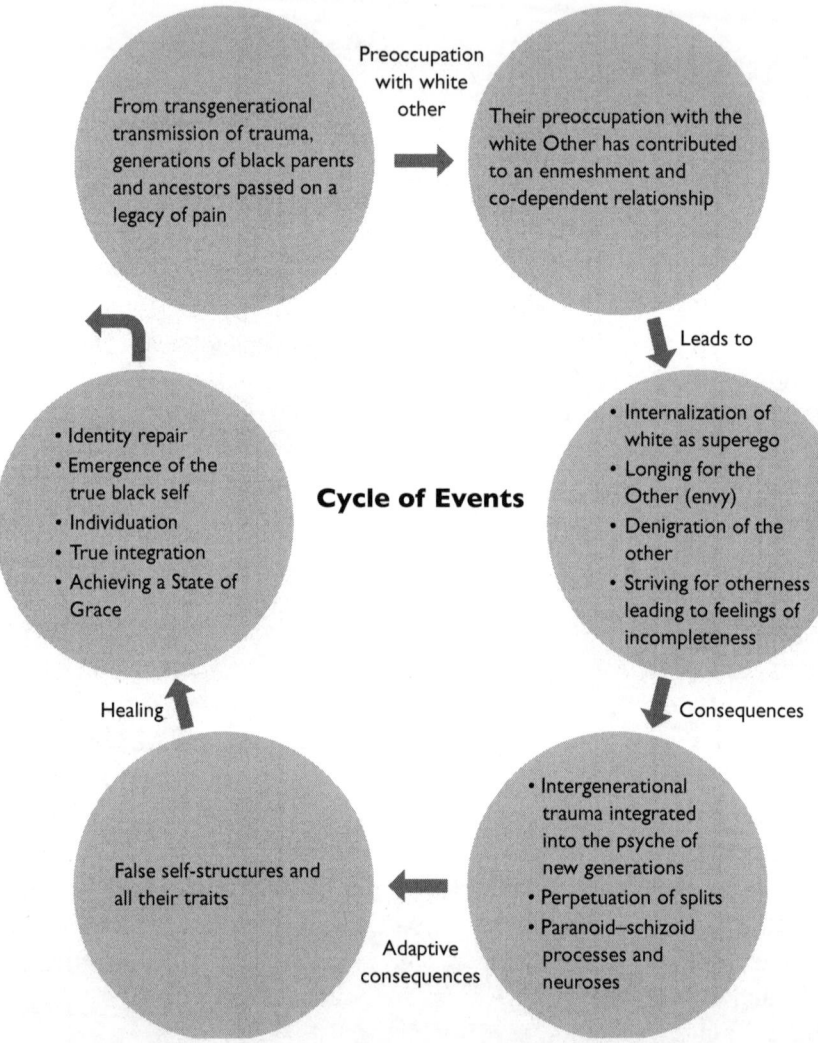

Figure 2.1 Cycle of Events: first stage (Alleyne, 2009)

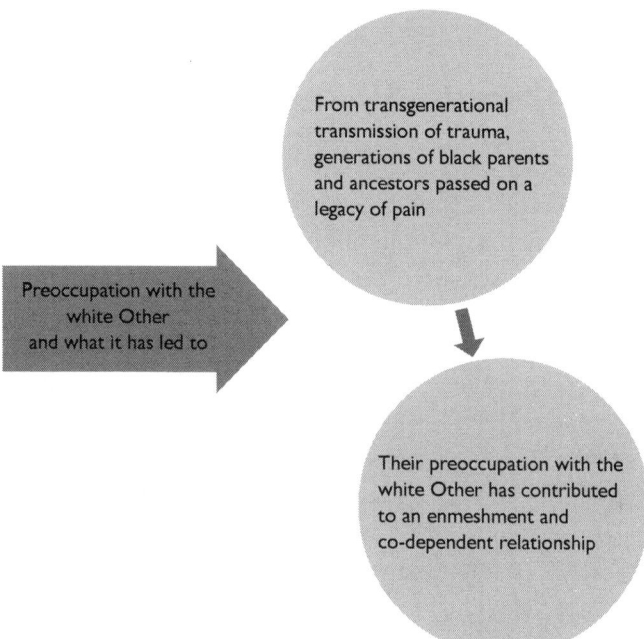

Figure 2.2 *Cycle of Events: second stage*

A potted history of black civilizations

Black civilization in the continent of Africa did not begin from a position of slavery. Many civilizations existed way before the advent of slavery, consisting of complex societies comprising established towns and cities with different forms of government, social stratification, developed systems of communication and interaction. These civilizations functioned in an orderly manner, with structures for living and maintaining order. They developed their own cultural ideologies of progress, created their own architecture and worked the lands for a natural ecological existence. Their economies developed as they engaged in cross-country trading that fostered interdependence and commercial expansion, and they had their own taxation systems.

Starting with the Egyptian civilization, this society had significant histories, proud identities, organizations, technology, the arts, knowledge of science, influential power, all before the arrival of the European. The

Egyptian civilization was already 2000 years old by the time the city of Rome was built.

In West Africa, there was the Kingdom of Ghana, a highly advanced and prosperous civilization, with a vast empire that spread across an area the size of western Europe.

Then there were the Kingdoms of Benin and Ife, with their highly skilled craftsmen, that sprang up between the eleventh and twelfth centuries. From the thirteenth to fifteenth centuries, came the Kingdom of Mali, engaged in the organized trade of gold and agricultural produce.

Among the numerous advanced civilizations and African kingdoms that existed before slavery, some developed into large and powerful empires, the most notable being the Songhai Empire in sub-Saharan Africa, until the British conquest in 1903. Between 1450 and 1550, the Songhai Kingdom grew and expanded from its organized government which had developed a currency to import fabrics from Europe. Timbuktu was an important place within this kingdom known worldwide for its universities, libraries and a meeting place for poets, scholars and artists from other parts of Africa and the Middle East.

An understanding of this history is important at this point in order to avoid possible pathologizing of a whole civilization as having existed only from the point in history that they were conquered and had their identity shaped by European slavery. It is important to note that forms of captivity and servitude did exist in Africa before European slavery – and we know the practice of slavery, in the form of one group of humans subjugating another, has been widespread throughout human history, regardless of skin colour or socio-political context. However, the arrival of European slavery was large scale and created divisions among Africans. The business of slavery itself bred greed and opportunism among African middlemen who were caught up and used by Europeans in the process of boosting white power and dominance in the world. The abomination of European and American slavery, with its sustained involvement in land grabbing and the human trade of Africans over an extensive period, forever remains an indelible stain on the face of humanity.

Returning to the first and second stages of the Cycle of Events, it can be seen how the genesis of the trauma has its beginnings in the wide-scale human tragedy of slavery. Although this was carried out on an industrial scale by mainly enlightened people with high civil values for their own, when it came to the African these values had neither place nor relevance. Until the nineteenth century, African slavery was considered an acceptable economic system in Britain and many other countries in Europe. It was condoned by politicians and businessmen, and even scientists and churches justified the legitimacy of this practice, which can now be recognized and accepted as morally reprehensible.

It is the discomfort that comes from such incongruously different attitudes towards this section of civilization that makes the trauma so painful for black people. You only need to type 'Windrush' into a search engine to see how colonialism is very much not something that has been consigned to the past.

I recall a black client asking in bewilderment as she spoke about her very painful experiences of blatant racism in the workplace, 'Why is it we always seem to be at the bottom of everything? Why does our skin colour evoke such harsh and ugly reactions in others?' The legacy of pain and anger about our past is never far from consciousness. For some, this creates a relationship with this past that is avoidant and detached, for to remember is to keep alive what is unbearable. For others, the pain of this history is constantly triggered and kept alive, thus creating an over-attachment with, and an acting out of, the past. This enmeshment causes historical wounds to be continually reopened and compounds experiences of racial oppression in the present. It is this reopening and retriggering of these traumatic historical imprints that make black identity wounding an ongoing process of trans- and intergenerational trauma. As discussed in Chapter 1, until the historical wound is properly acknowledged through public reparative measures, both individual and collective healing for the black diaspora will be slow to take place. In the absence of these acts of atonement, those carrying the burden of heritage will continue to live with chronic trauma.

The oppression of black people by white colonizers, with the British as chief player in the Caribbean and African colonial experience, spawned numerous negative effects. These adverse effects have motivated many scholars to research the psychological impact of the colonized. Frantz Fanon, a literary scholar and psychiatrist, devoted his life to helping the oppressed, and became the foremost authority on oppression related to colonization. In *Les damnés de la terre*, he begins the chapter 'Colonial War and Mental Disorders' by explaining, 'For many years to come we shall be bandaging the countless and sometimes indelible wounds inflicted in our people by the colonist's onslaught' (Fanon, 1961, p. 181). This quote brings to light the enduring nature of transgenerational trauma within the colonized, and the psychological healing that remains ongoing from every aspect of its destabilizing process.

In Britain, the legacy of transgenerational pain manifests in ways that see us still being plagued by the trauma transmissions. The high numbers of black people being diagnosed with mental disorders who end up sometimes wrongly in mental institutions is a consequence of this malady. Psychotherapists and counsellors in the UK continue to witness the phenomenon of maladaptive behaviours and struggles for actualization that stem primarily from low self-esteem, poor self-worth and struggles with doubt and self-belief. These struggles stem, in part, from what is now known as imposter syndrome, a phenomenon that causes self-doubt in individuals and feelings of being a fraud, even though there is abundant evidence of their abilities or success, and in actualizing desires and entitlements. Psychologists first described the syndrome in 1978 (Clance and Imes, 1978) and, in this context, it arises through the ongoing message (through, for example, institutionalized racism and daily microaggressions) directed at black people and other minority ethnic groups. The negative message becomes internalized and results in a feeling that they do not belong and are 'imposters'.[1] The negative impact is destructive to mental health and psychological well-being.

For many black people, the impact of racism goes unnoticed in many areas of daily life and adds to the burden of carrying the transmissions of untreated transgenerational trauma alone. As black identity is seldom properly and fully seen in its hybrid capacity,[2] a preoccupation with the white Other results in an unhealthy enmeshed and co-dependent relationship, in its search for recognition and affirmation. The white gaze then becomes the superego, whose function alone can give recognition and validation. This preoccupation with the white Other results in a psychological barrier to autonomy and selfhood.

Cycle of Events: third and fourth stages

The third and fourth stages of the Cycle of Events highlight the intra-psychic process at play that contributes to internal struggles and psychic conflict which have a propensity for the unease I describe as racial hauntings, dis-ease and mental disturbances.

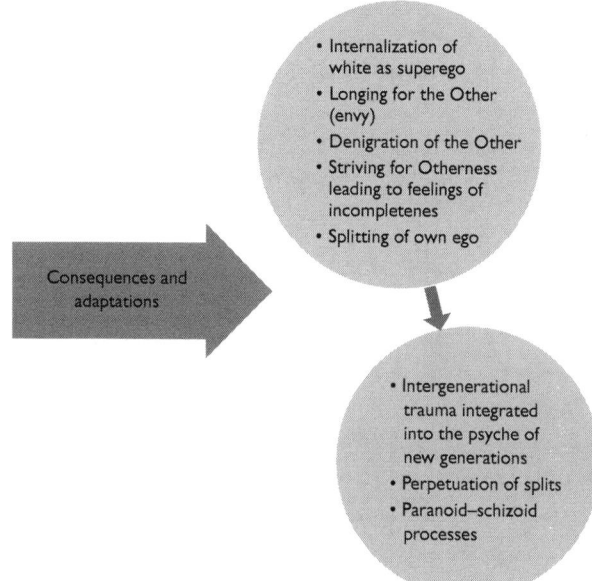

- Internalization of white as superego
- Longing for the Other (envy)
- Denigration of the Other
- Striving for Otherness leading to feelings of incompletenes
- Splitting of own ego

Consequences and adaptations

- Intergenerational trauma integrated into the psyche of new generations
- Perpetuation of splits
- Paranoid–schizoid processes

Figure 2.3 Cycle of Events: third and fourth stages

The internalization of whiteness as superego, formed through previous generations' preoccupation with the oppressor, now serves to create huge conflicts of emotion for subsequent generations. I think that this is the case for black people because we still struggle to locate black identity from multiple other locations, as well as that of the white Other. In addition, the conflict plays out as a longing for the freedom and privileged position of the white Other, while holding a denigration of this dominant Other. In analytic terms, the superego is described as the part of the ego in which self-observation, self-criticism and other reflective activities develop. It is also that part of the ego in which parental introjects are located.

The struggle that arises from internalizing whiteness as superego can be observed in some of the cultural and family scripts that are still kept alive in black people's everyday interactions; A few examples are:

- 'You've got to work twice as hard to prove your worth to white people.'
- 'We can't afford to wash our dirty linen in public – that's like giving white people ammunition – we must stick together.'
- 'You need to play them at their own game or else …'

In these fairly common and familiar scripts, we hear and detect the positions from which self-observation and self-reflection are made. They are clearly made in relation to the white Other, and this key object becomes the representation of our battles and whose standards we feel pressured to gauge ourselves against. The white Other now becomes the object in whose presence we must be ever vigilant and from whom we must protect ourselves, while holding envy for the privileges of white freedom. Being in the subordinate position also means that the white Other will never cease to be the critical judge of black people's very nature and being. Longing for the privileges of the white Other could lead to a striving for Otherness, and sometimes this manifests as a disowning of one's own blackness which, from an analytic point of view, may fester shame and self-hate. All of these internal struggles can lead, in turn, to feelings of incompleteness and to the splitting of the ego.

This love/hate symbiotic relationship has left a people over the generations striving for Otherness, thereby also leading to feelings of incompleteness. In the most severe cases, when these conflicts are not managed, the ongoing internal struggle can lead to splitting of the ego, which is manifest in mental health struggles with identity in society. This can present as experiences of unease and distress acted out in the form of intense agitation, anger, obsessive reliance on drugs and other substance misuse, and through violence and aggression, towards self and others. From experience with black clients, this can present as energy acted inwards and manifesting as low self-esteem, low self-worth, generalized anxiety, depression and mood-related mental health problems.

Distress may also be triggered in social interactions and by news items that highlight discrimination, racial injustice and the impact of racism. Distress of this nature can be experienced on counselling and psychotherapy trainings, in experiential groups, where black students may experience their voices not heard or pathologized as aggressive, too complaining about race issues, particularly if they raise subjects such as inequality where the majority do not feel comfortable. A black student raising the topic of the historical trauma of a people is likely to be dismissed by comments such as: 'Slavery happened a long time ago'; 'We can't keep looking backwards, we must look forward'; 'I don't want to be made to feel guilty for something I didn't do'. All of these responses may, on the surface, seem harmless, but the lack of attention and detachment from these key areas for a black student could demean the dreadful issue of black suffering in a way that, for example, the Holocaust is not demeaned. The Holocaust – everyone knows – is not just an issue for Jews; it is something that defines everyone's humanity. There are very few people in western society who do not know something about this, probably the most heinous crime ever committed in world history. However, this is also true of African slavery, but black people experience the world choosing to relate to this human tragedy very differently.

From an analytic attachment-based perspective, I see no difference between this difficult black/white relational dynamic and that of, say, an adult client in therapy, whose inner child forever yearns for the experience of the parent's full and heartfelt acknowledgement of the suffering caused by their damaging parenting. I see so many parallels in this relationship dynamic and that between the colonized and colonizer, where the black person expends so much energy in asking and being granted the basic human need to simply be heard and be believed. Although it must be underlined that the colonized are not children and the colonizers are not parents, the advantages and privileges gained from this power differential continues to be played out today, keeping alive the unequal status quo.

There is much evidence within individual, family and community value systems to suggest that the strong ambivalent patterns that have developed are continually passed down the generations. Cultural folklore, cultural scripts and cultural behaviours can all verify the fact that this transmission process is alive. Although these patterns may vary within the different generations, the effects of ancestral baggage continue to perpetuate particular forms of paranoid–schizoid (not in the clinical sense, but in the maladaptive psychological sense) behaviours and neuroses.

A few examples demonstrate this: in racially mixed groups, where there is a predominance of white people, black people have been shown to exhibit more elements of hypervigilance, anticipation of conflict occurring and disavowal of personal entitlements. Black people may, for example, contribute less to group discussions because they feel that their voices will not be heard or their contributions viewed as unimportant. Black people will often choose to sit at the back of an audience rather than up front. These behavioral patterns may be hard to acknowledge when stated so frankly but they are true of many situations, for example in the workplace, and are usually attributed to a general lack of trust – what William Grier and Price Cobbs (1968) refer to as 'healthy paranoia.'

Grier and Cobbs were keen to make a distinction between clinical paranoid disorders and the healthy state of paranoia, which is considered to be adaptive behaviour developed from being mistrustful of white people. This distinction has been supported by others in the field, such as Jones and Seagull (1977), who remind practitioners of the need to be flexible with western criteria and values when determining what constitutes normality and abnormality in specific cultural groups.

All of the aforementioned relationship dynamics can lead to false self-structures and all their traits, which form the fifth stage in the Cycle of Events.

The enmeshed attachment patterns in this complex black/white dyadic relationship create the potential for splits and mental dislocation. In this unhealthy enmeshment pattern, recognizing key themes of identity shame and working with the internal oppressor (Alleyne, 2004c) will be helpful to counsellors and psychotherapists working with black clients who present with identity issues arising from low self-esteem and self-worth in a predominantly white society.

African slavery as a critical reference point from which to understand intergenerational trauma and black identity wounding is not an indulgence, but a way of giving special recognition to something very important. It should form part of our minds and memories – not to haunt us, or disable us, but to be known and lived and accepted as one of the greatest facts that has formed all of us. However, when we feel the rest of the world is not with us, it makes it much harder for black people to achieve this. What an anguish it is, first to carry a cultural burden and, then, to carry the further burden of not being granted recognition.

I believe it is this pain – this deep psychic pain – that most, if not every, black person carries knowingly and unknowingly inside them. The world's forgetfulness, its neglect of something so huge increases the anguish and, in turn, keeps something of old generational wounds alive within the wronged. Being forgotten creates a sense of not being properly noticed and valued – and leads to a kind of damaging inward-turning, a stubborn in-dwelling on old wounds so as not to have them forgotten. It is the internalizing of these deep-seated wounds that entangles black people in an uncreative engagement with an acting in and acting out of their past.

The development of a false self-structure, a concept coined by Donald Winnicott (1960), is a defence that describes falseness in the self – a kind of mask of behaviour that creates maladaptive traits, which can eventually lead to a range of difficulties impeding personal growth – and collective progress, when used in the context of the cycle.

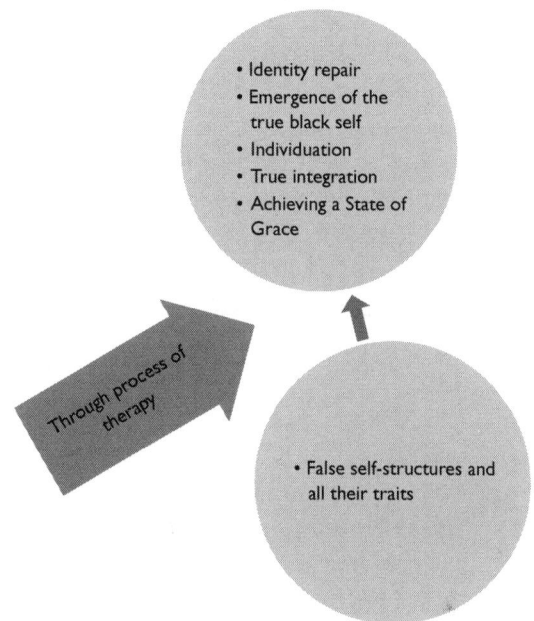

Figure 2.4 *Cycle of Events: fifth and sixth stages*

Fanon (1986), when talking about race and racism, sites problems in being 'actional', a term he uses to describe difficulties in exercising full self-agency, personal entitlements and all our God-given human rights.

These difficulties are currently a major concern in Britain's black communities. Increased black-on-black violence, the proliferation of knife crime, black children underachieving in schools, the damaging impact of absent fathers in the home and higher numbers still of single parents struggling in an unsupported way in our society are just a few of the related problems that arise out of this cultural malady.

Within the false self-structure, maladaptive traits can manifest as an excessive holding on to expectations of being judged negatively. Within this belief system, the self may learn to experience itself only when it acts in opposition to these negative expectations, that is always reacting to the white Other. My clinical work with people who are stuck in this position shows how their own authentic gestures can become hidden, and their own true character and real abilities severely undermined.

Winnicott's false self theory (1960) also suggests that the false self structure can be revealed through compliance, lack of spontaneity and/or originality. An example that might be met in the consulting room is the six-foot strapping black male who constantly worries that his obvious black masculinity might make him an object to be feared. He might describe how he compensates for this worry by clowning around, presenting himself as happy-go lucky, always laughing, dumbing down and deferring to others at work and in social situations. The astute therapist will be noticing that this seemingly benign persona may belie the fact that this individual is trapped in a people-pleasing persona that does not allow him to ever reveal his authentic self. Societal pressure and his own oppressive internalizations push him into psychic spaces where he must comply with the false self-structure. This structure only permits him to be what others want him to be – the harmless eunuch and emasculated court jester. The false self-structure continually robs him of his own spontaneity, his originality, and contributes to his black identity wounding.

How can we, as individuals and therapeutic practitioners, help with this important repair work? At an individual level, an understanding of this Cycle of Events can help to confront the ongoing silent trauma of racism. By having a deep understanding of its subtle and not so subtle workings, we can help release unacknowledged pain – and reframe the resulting, more often than not – unconscious, responses in order to transcend the original trauma.

Emergence of the true black self or true black potential comes via the process of repairing and healing from our historical maladies, which can hopefully lead to full individuation, which in turn leads to the place of becoming our full potential. The work of individuating can help to halt the perpetuation of splits previously described, which can lead to true integration – this is the position most therapies strive for as their ultimate goal. The reclaiming of the self for black people means to hopefully arrive at a state of grace – a term I've chosen to describe the process of tuning out expressions of black rage and pain and delighting in our distinct hybrid vigour.

The impact of carrying alone a trauma of this monumental and significant nature makes it difficult to let go of the past. The trauma interferes consciously and unconsciously with black people's self-structure, and ultimately contributes to difficulties in present-day functioning. This is the legacy of pain held by our parents, grandparents and ancestors, perpetually passed down and across the generations. Over generations, the legacy of this painful ancestral baggage has contributed to an unconscious preoccupation with the white Other, which has, I believe, led to complex attachment and relationship patterns that now exist between black people and white people.

Two notable American writers, Na'im Akbar (1979, 1996) and Joy DeGruy Leary (2005), conceptualize the internal holding on to this ancestral baggage and its negative impact, in terms of a 'post-traumatic [slave] syndrome'. Their theory suggests that 'centuries of the painful history of slavery followed by systemic racism and oppression have resulted in multigenerational adaptive behaviours, some of which have been positive and reflective of resilience, and others detrimental and destructive' (DeGruy Leary, 2005).

Although the Cycle of Events highlights, in a stark fashion, the circular trauma of the historical burden, and all its limiting and unhealthy impacts on black identity structure, these elements are by no means the whole of the black make-up. There are many other facets to black identity that must be noted and celebrated, including strengths that come from experiences of adversity.

Peoples of the black diaspora are recognized the world over for their innate ability to be resourceful and resilient, even in the direst of circumstances. We have only to think of war-torn Africa as an example, to witness how its peoples battle through repeated natural and manmade disasters – many have mastered the amazing art of being resilient. Although battle-weary by life's circumstances, black people are still able to work well, play well, love well and expect well. Many have moved from the position of mere surviving to thriving; countless others are aware of the fact that hurt people who hurt others must seek opportunities to move away from the position of victim to that of victor. These are not trendy soundbites, but celebrated aspects of black life that can sometimes be easily forgotten.

Summary

In the *Cycle of Events* (Alleyne, 2009) I argued that, through the generations, it was possible for us as black people to perpetuate certain false self traits by carrying around the burden, internalized negative patterns of cognition about ourselves in relation to the white Other. I suggested that this complex internal process could lead to internal disturbances, enmeshment dynamics and false self traits. The relevance of the false self concept thus becomes an important construct in understanding black people's struggle for individuation and healthy negotiations in the white world. I also argued that, as it was not possible to erase our history from our identity, its facts and consequences should serve as crucial lessons from which we learn to be more progressive in our relationships and lives generally. This is what I term a reflexive identity, not for survival, but one that is in continuous change for enjoying a quality of life.

The psychological effects of black/white historical attachments, coupled with the impact of racial hauntings activated by virulent aspects of modern-day racism, appear to have affected this moving-on process and the actualization of the full black potential. Within this arrested state, negative self traits develop within a dependent false persona, suppressing the identity and individuation process for black people. The thrust of my Master's thesis (Alleyne, 1992) was based on the belief that a 'psychological metamorphosis' – a reframing of impeding historical life scripts – was a necessary process for black folk to negotiate when dealing with these shame-based neuroses and 'false' self-structures (i.e. manufactured coping personas). Again, I return to the need for a reflexive identity that is always in flux to help with the moving-on process.

In psychotherapy, views on the true and false self (Winnicott 1958), and truth and authenticity, are highly contentious concepts and, as such, I am mindful that some psychoanalytic readers may immediately declare they have problems with them. However, I embrace the Winnicottian stance that distinguishes the true and false self thus; he states that the latter is a defensive structure, a 'false' adaptation to an environment that has not met the needs of the 'true' self during the formative months of infancy. Historical experiences for both black and white may have left the former with issues of shame and inferiority complexes and the latter with feelings of power over others and superiority complexes.

CHAPTER 3

Understanding trauma

We are changed when we are seen ... positively.

Types of trauma

The American Psychiatric Association and the World Health Organization provide distinct trauma diagnoses in the fifth edition of the *Diagnostic and Statistical Manual* (DSM-V), and the forthcoming 11th edition of the *International Classification of Diseases* (ICD-11), respectively. DSM-V conceptualizes PTSD as a single, broad diagnosis, whereas ICD-11 proposes two 'sibling-disorders' of PTSD and complex post-traumatic stress disorder (CPTSD). Although various forms of complex trauma are listed, none sufficiently embraces the real prolonged effects of mental slavery on many indigenous peoples of the world.

Controversies relating to the lack of inclusiveness of the DSM to address changing conceptualizations of trauma have considerable implications for counselling and psychotherapy practice. Currently, the DSM only alludes briefly to other trauma that may be a focus of clinical attention. It is this paucity of information that drew me to the research by psychiatrist Lenore Terr (1991), whose work focused on the adult survivors of childhood trauma. It led me to think more widely about diagnostic implications of multi-systemic and multi-ethnic psychological trauma of which black generational trauma is an overlooked area. Terr (1991) distinguished between type I (single-incident trauma, as in a sudden and unexpected traffic accident) and type II (repeated or prolonged interpersonal trauma usually involving a fundamental betrayal of trust in primary relationships). Authors Eldra P. Solomon and Kathleen M. Heide (1999), built on Terr's study, by proposing a third category, a type III trauma, which was a more complex trauma that individuals experienced as a result of multiple, pervasive, violent events over a long period of time. Incest survivors' trauma experience will meet this type III criterion.

Advancing a theory towards a more effective conceptualization of type III trauma, I wish to make a strong case for the unheeded dimensions of black trans- and intergenerational trauma to be regarded clinically as a new type III, complex post-traumatic stress disorder. At present, the psychological manifestations of this cultural trauma syndrome remain largely unaddressed by the mental health professions in the UK.

The impact of black historical trauma on its progeny appears not to have been given the same status for empirical examination and analysis, despite it being an equally horrific crime arising from man's inhumanity to man. In the latest DSM–V categorization of trauma- and stress-related disorders, there is cursory acknowledgement of 'other conditions that may be a focus of clinical attention'. This 'other' section makes reference to:

> Target of (Perceived) Adverse Discrimination, or Persecution: Inclusion in this category is appropriate when the individual perceives or experiences instances of discrimination or persecution that appear to be due to their membership (or perceived membership) in certain groups such as race, religion, gender, ethnicity, sexual orientation, political affiliation, disability, social status, weight, or appearance.
>
> Unspecified Problem Related to Social Environment (American Psychiatric Association, 2013)

In the work of authors Eldra P. Solomon and Kathleen M. Heide (1999), built on Terr's study, their diagnostic criteria include a number of effects: emotional numbing; major developmental deficits; a poorly developed and often fragmented sense of self; and a core belief that he or she is fatally flawed. They include the fact that such sufferers carry a sense of hopelessness and shame, experience trust issues that interfere with normal relationships and have no concept of a sense of future. They conclude that the treatment of individuals who have sustained type III trauma is much more complex and demanding relative to survivors of type I or type II trauma.

I was able to see further crossovers, which acknowledged the dimensions of historical trauma and their psychological effects. These dimensions warrant fuller and formal recognition in a distinct trauma category recognizing the ongoing trauma-impact of a new type III, complex post-traumatic stress disorder.

My awareness of trauma has been greatly increased by the work of Professor Gill Straker. The texts and experiential work covered in her seminar, as part of a doctoral programme I attended in 2004, offered a transtheoretical approach to trauma (Moosa, Straker and Eagle 2004; Straker, 1999, 2001, 2004). In her stimulating lecture offering perspectives from biological theories, theories on information processing, cognitive theories, psychodynamic theories, Lacanian theories and treatment implication, I understood that, initially, the word trauma in western society was used as an explanatory concept and a metaphor for any psychic pain or psychological distress (Hacking, 1995). Later, cumulative evidence from longitudinal and prospective studies (Wilson and Raphael, 1993) confirmed that trauma (i.e. the cause, whether type I or type II) is predictive of psychopathology, given the wide-ranging manifest and hidden factors and processes that create fault lines in psychic functioning.

Why a new type III complex trauma category?

Although there is a growing body of evidence that multigenerational trauma (also called historical loss, transgenerational trauma) and its consequences are prevalent among historically oppressed and colonized peoples (Levine, 2001; Pupavac, 2002; Stone, 2003; Whitbeck, Chen, Hoyt and Adams, 2004), the psychological and generational impact of 400 years of imposed trauma on the lives of black peoples has been overlooked. The lived experiences of those struggling today and who require psychological and mental health treatment suggest that there is a clear need for a recognized separate category of a type III CPTSD. The ongoing psychological impact of psychic wounds from post-slavery trauma, which are constantly reopened by present-day forms of racism, racial injustice and racial inequality would fall into such a category. All of these experiences do great harm to the ontological security of a people, and the fact that this is an unheeded dimension in mental health presentations is, in itself, an additional wounding that adds to the trauma. The omission and non-recognition of this type III trauma suggests that the world has not yet seen, recognized and accepted that slavery, one of the most heinous historical acts of our time, is – and continues to be – a real and damaging experience for black people and the black diaspora. This suggests that black people's pain is not worthy of being noticed and that, therefore, black lives do not matter. Yet, this complex phenomenon affects black people the world over on a daily basis.

A type III CPTSD category seems more fitting than those that currently exist, to fully encompass the complex nature of historical, collective and intergenerational trauma. I also see it as honouring the experiences of groups of people who share an identity, affiliation or social circumstances, and whose complex collective trauma cascades over time and down the generations. The trauma is characterized by psychological or emotional difficulties that can lead to adaptive coping patterns passed on intergenerationally, with varying effects on identity and sense of self.

Events that may lead to inclusion in this category include personal or generational experience of:

- institutional and individual racism
- modern-day slavery
- forcible removal from a family or community
- genocide
- war (religious and political)
- invasion of people by a foreign invader
- recurrent epidemics
- starvation.

Current system of diagnosis of trauma in the UK and abroad

To further understand the need for a type III CPTSD category, it is necessary to understand the context and structure for mental health diagnoses in the UK and internationally.

The DSM-V does not currently acknowledge complex PTSD, let alone type III trauma, as a separate condition. PTSD is an anxiety disorder that, as previously mentioned, can develop after a person experiences a single traumatic event such as a car collision. A doctor may diagnose complex

PTSD, under the category of type II complex trauma, if a person has experienced prolonged or repeated trauma over a period of months or years. Some examples of type II complex trauma include:

- sibling abuse
- childhood emotional abuse
- domestic violence
- emotional neglect and attachment trauma
- abandonment
- verbal abuse
- coercion
- long-term misdiagnosis of a health problem
- bullying at home, at school or in a work setting
- sexual abuse
- emotional abuse
- physical neglect
- overly strict upbringing, for example religious.

The ICD *does* identify complex PTSD as a separate condition. Complex PTSD is a relatively recent concept and, because of its variable nature, healthcare professionals may instead diagnose conditions. They may use a diagnosis of borderline personality disorder (BPD), when more manifest symptoms of distress or unease are observed in black people (particularly black men) who may be more likely to rush in with a psychotic disorder diagnosis (both in the UK and in the US). The most common misdiagnoses are those of schizophrenia and/or a detention order. This has been my first-hand professional experience, working 11 years in the British mental health system as a registered mental health practitioner at a senior level. Race often seems to play a part in the assessment of black people and men in particular, being out of control, a threat to society and particularly dangerous. From my own experiences as a National Health Service (NHS) psychiatric head nurse, the frequent and guaranteed responses to these biases were – and are still – swiftly managed by administering older anti-psychotic medications to manage suspected threats and danger. These first-generation 1950s' anti-psychotics, as opposed to the newer 1970s' medicines, are still prescribed in higher dosages to black people today, rendering them zombie like and eventually feeling like non-persons.

An analysis of the figures relating to how the Mental Health Act has been applied nationally shows how black minority ethnic groups are over-represented in the detained population. Black people are shown to experience the highest rate of detention (288.7 per 100 000 population) in hospitals, more than four times that of the broad 'white' group, which has the lowest rate (71.8 per 100 000 population). Using the more detailed breakdown of BME (black and minority ethnic) categories shows the inequalities to be even more marked: the 'Black British' subgroup 'Any other Black background' is detained at 10 times the rate of the 'White British' group (745.9 detentions compared with 69.0 detentions per 100 000 population). These figures are generally consistent with past findings (Care Quality Commission, 2019).[1]

The biased tendency to overemphasize the relevance of psychotic symptoms (such as paranoia, being loud and agitated while in a distressed state) lead to harsher treatments, rather than symptoms of depression or deep emotional distress being diagnosed which may require and, indeed, respond well to counselling and antidepressants. Sadly, race still remains a major determining factor, one that readily leads to chemical and physical containment for blacks as opposed to the range of therapeutic interventions and psychological therapies made more readily available to whites. The black person's position, as historically dictated by white-run systems, is observed all over again.

Self-agency

It is important to note at this juncture, however, that black people's lives, do not have to be entirely predetermined by the abhorrence and psychological impact of enslavement. My reasoning behind this statement is heavily influenced by Sartre's (1943) words, 'freedom is what you do with what's been done to you', which profoundly and succinctly identifies the power of self-agency and phenomenal will that is required for healing from all forms of trauma.

Self-agency has been defined (Libet, 1985; Wegner, 2003) as having three criteria: (1) priority, (2) exclusivity and (3) consistency. Priority means that an action must be planned before it is initiated, with the interval between the action and the effect known as intentional binding. Exclusivity means that the effect is due to the person's action and not because of other potential causes for the effect. Consistency means that, once planned, action must occur as planned. Although no models that predict agency have been proved, the conclusion of applying this criterion to the healing process may suggest that the most effective way of breaking and transcending the cycles of the resulting trans- and intergenerational trauma is to repair through individuation. In this context, individuation would mean the process of burning off the trauma (orbit) trails that still seem to have the capacity to fuel our thinking, behaviours, interactions, relatedness, sense of identity, values and belief systems. Granted, such an impactful history will have left indelible traces of trauma, but this does not mean it should be held as the absolute cause of how things are and will always be for black people. That would be a reductive, lazy oversimplification of the nature of trauma and, at worst, could lead to a perpetuation of historical wounds.

Most studies of transgenerational trauma have focused on Holocaust survivors, but the theory is rarely applied to the progeny of slavery by the psychological, sociological, psychiatric and medical communities. It is my view that *both* groups have suffered in heinous and horrific ways, and it is right that both are recognized justifiably in their respective experience of historical trauma, including the unique post-trauma psychological aspects arising intergenerationally. Some psychiatrists do not believe in transgenerational trauma as a significant factor underpinning black mental health disturbance in the UK. It seems that the work of bringing this disregarded phenomenon to light falls to psychological practitioners such as counsellors and psychotherapists, who are in the more privileged position of hearing the trauma narratives and are able to make sense of their impact in a holistic mind, soul, body and spirit assessment capacity.

Trauma in situ

The ongoing reality of trans- and intergenerational transmissions of trauma has resulted in black cultural 'scripts', verbatim examples of which can be seen in Table 1, which are taken from research I undertook for my doctorate (2009). The scripts, although a genuine reflection of the trauma impact, beg the serious question of whether such codes of conduct for living one's life are entitlements or impediments. For therapists meeting such scripts in the consulting room, the therapeutic challenge is working with the trauma impact, as well as helping the client recognize how and where their entitled belief systems can inadvertently become handicaps, which hold back progress, drive and determination. Paradoxically, and symbolically, such scripts make the historical shackle a modern-day self-imposed manacle, which hampers, restrains and checks the individuation process of black people.

Table 3.1 highlights common scripts that speak to managing the impact of widespread occurrences in the lives of black people. Scripts function as codes of conduct and safety shields for living and being. The chosen scripts also suggest the presence of a lived trauma experienced by those carrying such scripts. The scripts are borne out of a burden carried. They come to shape the reality of black life in ways where the recurrence of the trauma experience is no longer a coincidence, but a phenomenon of black life.

Table 3.1 Scripts highlighting the impact of racialized trauma (Alleyne, 2009)

Scripts highlighting black archetypal experiences	Scripts highlighting a defensive (protective) mindset and value system
'People will always see your colour first and personality second'	'I am not interested in theory – I go by my instincts'
'We have to work twice as hard to be noticed'	'What's the point in trying – you'll only get no for an answer'
'No matter how much you succeed, people will always try to beat you down'	'Promotion is not for me – it forces you to conform to the system – I don't want to lose who I am as a black person'
'We can't afford to wash our dirty linen in public – that's like giving whitepeople ammunition – we must stick together'	'I don't do deference where white people are concerned'
	'I can never trust white people – I have a healthy disrespect where they are concerned'
	'You can't afford to show vulnerability – people will walk all over you'

	'When things get too much, I just walk away'
	'You take me as you see me – what you see is what you get – like it or lump it'
	'This is who I am – I say what's on my mind – ain't changing for no one'
	'I don't trust anyone but myself'

Anatomy of racialized trauma

The relationship between internal and external factors – a developmental view – is an aspect of my doctoral research (2006). The developmental process illustrates the relationship between the generational trauma link to the relationship between internal and external factors operating in black lives. From the abundant doctoral research data, scripts within respondent date (similar to those in Table 3.1) illuminated a deeper understanding of black/white relational dynamics within the British context. The process identified through the different stages outlined represents the anatomy of racialized trauma where the past meets internal and external factors.

Figure 3.1 provides a visual image of the developmental process where racial impingements from the outside world impact the internal world. The interplay between generational factors and present-day factors affect black lives in a myriad of emotional and psychological ways. An overview identifies that in (1) a key issue relating to an attachment to the colonial and historical past is observed to be played out in black people's present-day functioning. This finding was clearly evidenced in the scripts as seen in Table 3.1. This was seen in the often-problematic nature of black client's relationship dynamic with white people – a group from whom they often experienced discrimination in their work settings. Evidence of fostering transgenerational trauma (2) was extrapolated from both the expressed texts and pain arising from respondents' narratives (Table 3.1) and in the clinical setting of therapy. The evidence of such pain in somatic reactions and health complaints acted as further confirmation. This evidence was discerned as believable because of my insider knowledge, through surviving as a wounded healer in similar such situations. Development of compensatory personal constructs (3) was perhaps the most vivid psychological theme that was

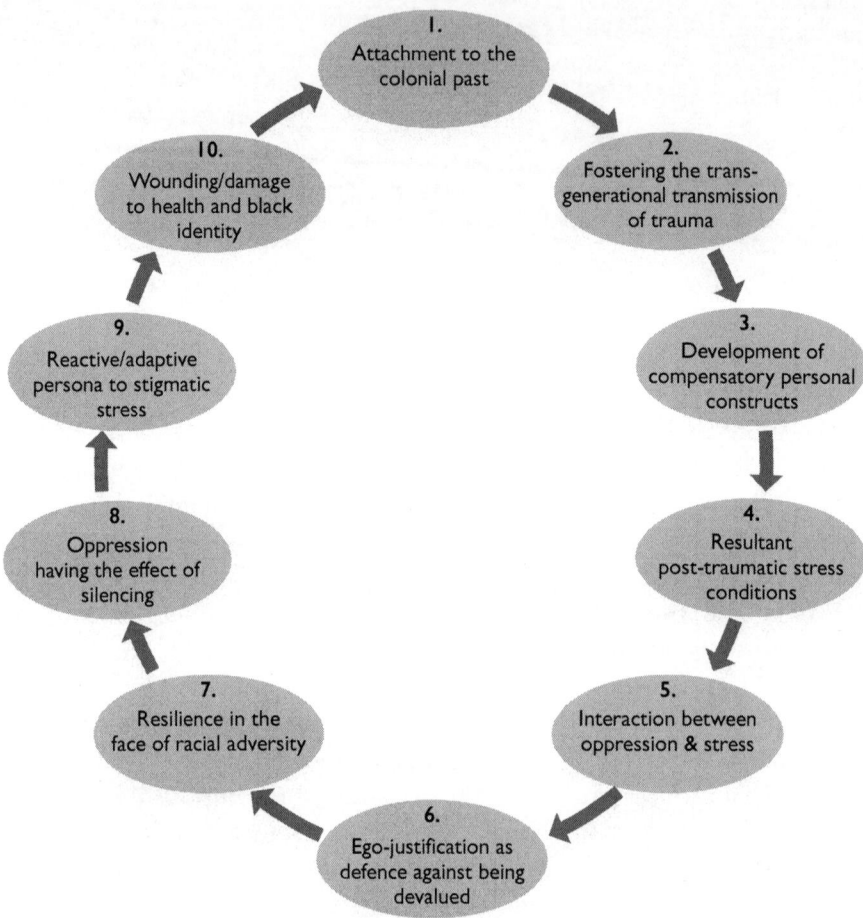

Figure 3.1 Anatomy of racialized trauma

drawn mainly from the verbatim examples. Resultant post-traumatic stress (4) was gauged from the way clients constantly harped back to the past, either through inferences or through actual reference to slavery, white privilege, white power and dominance. This revisiting suggested the presence of unfinished business and the experiences of rewounding in difficult black/white encounters. Overview of the material showed that the severity of societal stress was not originating only from common everyday stress factors but by a definite connection and interaction between stigma-related stress and feeling oppressed (5). Reactions of ego justification (6), resilience and stoicism (7), being silenced, often by the triggering of racial hauntings (8), and made powerless were all evidenced by the felt experiences expressed in clients' stories. I also noted other textural factors such as a dejected manner, emotional pain and, from some clients, an exaggerated determination to be resilient in very difficult and depressing situations. The resultant reactive/adaptive personas to stigma-related stress (9) and consequent wounding/damage to self (10) were clear to see during engagement with clients who were experiencing clear signs of trauma at the coalface. Reactive and adaptive personas were observed in the way some were left permanently angry by their experiences, and indications of damage to the self and black identity were visible in the beaten down, embittered and depressed auras worn by some individuals, while they were striving to maintain resilience in the face of adversity.

Figure 3.2 is my own pictorial representation of the relationship between internal and external trauma factors, and is included to show a creative way of highlighting, through imagery, the inextricable link between social context and the inner world of clients. Inter-cultural, trans-cultural or cross-cultural therapy – whichever is preferred in addressing diversity in counselling and psychotherapy practice – must embrace the impingements from the external world and their impact on the client's internal experience. The minority client's story is the sum total of their background plus their life experiences. Similarly, for the white therapist, their biases will be discovered in their own story – that is, their background plus their life experience. The reader may find it helpful to create their own representation in picture form, as in Figure 3.2, and see it also as a creative tool that could be used to help clients explore their internal and external worlds.

The collage, which can also be used as a facilitative tool in more creative therapeutic contexts, depicts symbolic images in the top half of the collage, to represent external factors that contribute to the wounding experience of racialized trauma. The symbolic images in the bottom half of the collage represent the negative psychological impact and responses to racialized trauma, often compounded by the activation of generational trauma.

Meeting the above realities of black clients' lives in the therapeutic encounter is often a distressing experience and can be vicariously impactful for the aware and culturally competent practitioner. Sadly, inadequate training of race issues on counselling and psychotherapy

External stressors
imagery (left)
Internal stressors
imagery (right)

Figure 3.2 Interplay between internal and external stressors

training means that the challenges for black lives are overlooked by most practitioners who are not attuned to presentations of complex, multidimensional aspects of identity and generational trauma. It is heartening, however, to note that, in the last five years, psychological and mental health professionals in the UK have slowly begun to recognize that there might be a correlation between present-day psychological distresses as seen in the black population, and the connection to unresolved historical and intergenerational trauma. There is, however, no clear clinical integrated framework for professionals to properly address complex manifestations of distress and dis-ease as valid mental and psychological health concerns. Practitioners have no certified yardsticks to measure the effects on black psychological health and to work with the complex presentations in any professionally coherent way. This was not the same in the case of descendants of Holocaust survivors: following the study of PTSD experienced by these survivors, the formal recognition of historical trauma was brought into the mainstream, with much attention, empirical research and meaningful critique (Yehuda and Lehrner, 1998).

Historical trauma

In their paper, 'Historical trauma as public narrative: A conceptual review of how history impacts present-day health' (2014), Mohatt et al. argue that historical trauma functions as a public narrative for particular groups or communities. This shifts the discourse from the influence of past variables on health, to identifying how present-day experiences are connected to public narratives of historical trauma. Their paper looks at sources of present-day stress – as well as resilience – for particular groups, exploring the connection between historical trauma and present-day experiences, related narratives and health.

Mohatt's approach is a healthy perspective on healing from the present-day impact of racialized trauma. For practitioners, this approach suggest that, although it is important to give particular recognition to the activation of generational trauma impact within the context of present-day racism, the clinical imperative is also crucial to highlight what empowerment can look like from the perspective of what people can do with what has been done to them. This is crucial to the individuation process and mitigates becoming stuck in the cycle of pain.

Mohatt et al. make the point that historical trauma originated from the attempt to describe the experience of children of Holocaust survivors (Kellermann, 2001a).They explain how the term has more recently been applied to colonized indigenous groups throughout the world, as well cultural groups and communities 'that share a history of oppression, victimization, or mass group trauma exposure'. Scholars from various disciplines have described the generational aspect of historical trauma as transgenerational, intergenerational, multi-generational or cross-generational (Bar-On et al., 1998; Kellermann, 2001), and have introduced concepts, such as soul wound (Duran, 2006; Duran and Duran, 1995), for the collective experience of Native Peoples of the Americas, especially within the indigenous Native American and/or American Indian population, and post-traumatic slavery syndrome (DeGruy Leary, 2005), to highlight generational trauma within the black experience.

Historical trauma can be understood as consisting of three primary elements: (1) a 'trauma' or wounding, (2) the trauma being shared by a group of people (rather than individually experienced) and (3) the trauma spanning multiple generations, such that descendants of the affected group may experience trauma-related symptoms without having been present at the original traumatizing event or even being aware of its personal impact or damage to self.

History is, in part, collective memory and, like memory, past traumatic events are constructed within social and cultural contexts that often determine what is remembered and how it is interpreted. This is definitely the case for the oppressed and the oppressor. In terms of slavery within the black/white context, the oppressed remembers the pain of the past – enslavement, racial oppression, brutality, disempowerment, humiliation and feelings of inferiority – and relives the mutated reverberations in current times. For black people it is incontestable that hauntings of the past are never far away from the present. On the other side of the context, a lack of consensus, often borne out by an intellectual acceptance that slavery was a bad thing, but also something that now should be forgotten, rankles deeply. Who decides when to forget and how long to remember? Who holds the memory and who does the remembering are areas still to be addressed for individual and collective generational trauma repair and closure. However, this process will always be hindered in the midst of felt and active resistance to take up an unqualified position of contrition for past, and present, abhorrent human practices.

Mohatt et al. refer to Foucault (2003), who, they say, pointed out how 'dominant cultures often silence or diminish the value of other cultural groups' narratives' and in doing so, 'disqualify other people's knowledge and limit what may be discussed publicly' (Mohatt et al., 2014). Therefore, the struggle for narrative recognition is an important element in a group's healing from historical trauma.

Black trans- and intergenerational trauma over six generations

Table 3.2 depicts my observations of the trajectory of trauma within a six-generation time span for black Caribbean peoples. The six-generation traumagram highlights the impact and fragmentation of black life as a result of historical events associated with the rule of the British Empire, its slave trade industry over the period from 1562 to 1838 and the further subjugation of black people even after the abolition of slavery. The six-stage traumagram (Alleyne, 2020) is similar to that of Blanco (in Levine and Kline, 2007), who mapped out the effects of violence on subsequent generations of indigenous Australians, and Atkinson's version of the impact of intergenerational trauma on the Australian Aboriginal peoples (2002).

I have chosen to focus predominantly on the Caribbean Black British and African experience, as they are the closest to my heart, from the points of view of place of birth (Guyana), place of acculturation (Britain) and place of genetic heritage (Africa). To situate the Caribbean historical experience, it is important to note that, as early as 1562, John Hawkins, the first Englishman, was known to have traded African people. Between 1562 and 1569 he transported a total of 1200 slaves to Hispaniola and St Domingue in the Caribbean. Following him, and throughout the transatlantic slave trade, approximately 2.3 million enslaved Africans were shipped to the British Caribbean between the seventeenth century and early nineteenth century. Half of this number were dispensed to Jamaica, which was Britain's most profitable possession at that time, followed by Barbados, the second most common destination for African slaves. The Abolition Act was passed in 1833.

Table 3.2 Trauma passed down six generations following
abolition of slavery 1833

First generation Slavery creates hauntings evoked by the emotional scars carried by black African men, women and children who were enslaved and treated inhumanely. Enforced racial segregation laws and their impact on black lives create reminders of the ever-present racial apartheid and black people's marginalized place in the society. Racial discrimination and economic hardships keep the shadow of slavery present, reminding black people of their subordinate position in relation to others and their value only in terms of the white man's property. Black people's racial differences continue to be treated as an oddity in white society, making them inferior and lesser beings.

Second generation The ongoing devastating effects of human objectification take hold and impact individual and collective identity pride. Cohesion within the family is threatened. Black people continue to be seen as mere units of currency destined to be stuck in a life of servitude. Black women objectified as mules; their bodies not considered their own. Trauma transmission continues, lingers and whiteness is internalized as supreme power and domination. Dehumanization and infantilization remain the order of the day. Societally, black obedience is rewarded, resistance is thwarted; black empowerment is viewed as a threat to white security.

Third generation Post-slavery generational burdens are inherited and cascade down the generations. Trauma transmissions leave a major legacy of mental and psychological destruction as black people are still not treated fully as human. Internalized trauma profoundly affects relationships with self and others. Internalized oppression and disempowerment manifest as domestic violence, and forms of relational transgressions such as acting out, infidelity, secrets, betrayal, deception, commitment and trust issues. Family structures suffer and break down, leading to a pervasiveness of absent fathers, mother-led one-parent families, extended (often secret) family units comprising multiple baby mothers and fathers. Generational trauma becomes trauma re-enactments of historical enslavement.

Fourth generation Established white civil authority and widespread economic suffering spark race tensions and race riots. Racial pride exalting blackness as strong and beautiful, marks the age of the black Renaissance. New political movements demand civil rights, social equality and justice for black people. Alongside the public fight for liberation and social change, the internal impact of intergenerational trauma continues. Discord, divisions and splits occur within black-group relations. Parallel dynamics play out in family life. Untreated generational trauma that contribute to feelings of powerless, emasculation and objectification, are further re-enacted in styles of parenting. Disciplining is harsh, largely in forms of beatings, put-downs, criticism and shaming. Love is expressed mostly in terms of ensuring provision of care, as opposed to showing loving tender care.

Fifth generation Gen Y, Generation Y or Millennials, is a demographic group of people born between the mid-1980s to late 1990. In this generation, cycles of violence are repeated and compounded, as trauma begets violence, with trauma re-enacted through increasingly severe and mindless black-on-black violence. The era of technological and scientific advancement, along with changing social practices, provide more opportunities and choices for black people to take their rightful place in the world. Paradoxically, progress gained in equality and inclusivity also highlights the crisis of race relations – what was endured over previous generations, and the losses therein. Fifth-generation progeny mourn the losses from the past through multidimensional modes of creative and intellectual expressions for celebrating reclaiming a proud sense of racial self. Recognizing the trauma trajectory of the past activates generational hauntings and the accompanying pain.

Sixth generation Gen Z or Generation Z, colloquially known also as Zoomers, is the demographic cohort of people born in the late 1990s to 2010s. This tech-savvy, pragmatic and open-minded population may relate in society with more integrated social awareness, responsibility and individualism being the children of Generation X. However, despite being the owners of full citizenship that promotes state membership pride, privileges and protection because they own a similar national identity as the majority white society, sixth-generation blacks may not be speared the activations of generational trauma, often triggered by experiences of unconscious racial bias, overt racial discrimination, unequal treatment in education and being held back in the educational and workplace systems. Place of birth may afford citizenship and ownership of national identity, but the lived experience in the birth home for many may not feel as secure.

Kai Erikson suggested that collective trauma is the 'psychological blow to the basic tissues of social life that damage the bonds attaching people together and impairing the prevailing sense of community' (Erikson, 1976, p. 233). Black collective trauma has cascaded down these six generations and its transmissions can still be identified in present-day functioning.

Trauma is passed on through:

- parenting practices *(interpersonal and multi-generational routes)*
- family scripts that shape thinking and behaviours *(spiritual and multi-generational transmission routes)*
- our internalized belief and value systems *(interpersonal, social, psychological and multi-generational routes)*
- culture-specific mental health challenges that we face in everyday life *(sociological, psychological and multi-dimensional routes)*
- re-enactments via 'the internal oppressor' (Alleyne, 2006), which refers to the workings of the internal adversary that operate as the enemy within *(spiritual and multi-generational route)*
- forms of abuse (sexual, physical, emotional/psychological, domestic, etc.) that lead to internalized negative messages being transferred to children and offspring *(interpersonal, sociological, psychological and multi-dimensional routes)*
- unresolved conflict continuing across generations (e.g. conspiracies of lies, silence and shame) *(psychological, spiritual, interpersonal and multi-generational routes)*
- family secrets that are tragic and destabilizing, which can erode a family, leading to disconnection and/or collusion *(psychological, spiritual, interpersonal and multi-generational routes)*
- belief in a 'family curse' – an affliction that leads to a mentality of helplessness (e.g. mental illness, physical differences e.g., albinism) *(psychological, spiritual, interpersonal and multi-generational routes)*
- being held emotional hostage to historical oppression/ marginalization and the psychological difficulties experienced in managing the challenges therein *(psychological, spiritual,*

interpersonal and multi-generational routes)
- through carrying the familiar presence of the burden and
  psychological ruptures from racial hauntings *(psychological,
  spiritual, interpersonal and multi-generational routes).*

The above list describes forms of trauma transmissions that are distinctly psychological (over-identification) interpersonal (historical enmeshment), sociological (re-enactments), spiritual and multi-generational (via 'the internal oppressor' (Alleyne, 2006) and identity shame). Additionally, trauma transmissions have been researched as being passed on physiologically via the epigenetic route.

Epigenetics

What is new in helping us to understand trauma is the emerging field of epigenetics. Epigenetics began over 60 years ago as a series of isolated observations in three disparate areas of biology. It picked up momentum during the 1970s, with the advent of molecular biology and, during the last 10–15 years, has emerged as a standalone discipline complementary to genetics. Recently, epigenetics has experienced a period of rapid growth and redefinition, particularly with advances in molecular technology for monitoring the biochemical features of epigenetic change.

Science is discovering that trauma can be passed to future generations through more than simply learned behaviour. One of the recent findings in epigenetics is that patterns of gene regulation can be transmitted across generations, adding a further complication to the story. It is suggested that trauma or its effects are being passed through our genes and could have major consequences for us as a species. Epigenetics is informing us that the influence of inheritance from the parents is not simply the gene types received, but also their influence on gene expression (called imprinting). Epigenetic research (Yehuda and Lehrner, 2018) reveal in their findings that multiple factors, such as traumatic environmental influences, can affect the body. Stress hormones in the body change the cellular structure of genes in ways that have an effect on the epigenetic quality of the genes. It is relatively easy to summarize that the obvious slave-captive stress hormones in black slaves will have had easy passage down the generations for the other obvious fact that the crippling poison of racism still persists, and the struggle still continues.

The imprints of trauma from the past have left indelible marks of pain on the black soul and a moral stain on the white soul. In Chapter 6, we will return to this concept of white fragility.

CHAPTER 4

The nature of hauntings

Discovering the concept of hauntings

In deciding on the subtitle of the book, I tested responses to the word 'hauntings' with a number of colleagues, friends and family members. The word emerged slowly during the intensely immersive process of writing the book, and I was quite struck and relieved at the affirmation that I had put my finger on and captured something unheeded about the black experience. My informal respondent group spoke of hairs standing up on arms and having goosebumps at the mere mention of the word in the context of the black experience, of something lingering and a presence after a racialized incident. It struck me that their automatic psychosomatic response could not be faked, and it is my belief that what has ceased to be a coincidence must, at some level, be a phenomenon. Their feedback was very reassuring, as it was a clear indication of a collective recognition of something within us that was real, still alive – and certainly still active. The responses suggested that such shared somatic reactions might also be evidence of the epigenetic transmission of something experienced and acknowledged as the pain of black generational trauma. It was clear that the concept of hauntings, which I further corroborated by my literature search, was an apt description of the silent impact of racism on black lives.

A trajectory: the analytic concept of hauntings

In the trajectory of analytic exploration of this intriguing concept, it is most alive for me in the significant writings of Professor Stephen Frosh (2012, 2013), in which he advances the concept of hauntings. His work speaks powerfully to one of the most traumatic silencing and hauntings of recent generations: the Holocaust. Before him on the path of discovering the workings of this curious phenomenon came Avery Gordon (1997), whose stunning sociological research studies aspects of life – reality, truth and presences – belonging to the human collective. Although both she and Frosh refer to the lingering impact of racial slavery, Gordon doesn't speak directly to any particular group's hauntings. Frosh focuses mainly on the Jewish experience and includes an important post-colonial critique of psychoanalysis in its treatment of hauntings.

The phenomenon of hauntings was addressed by Abraham and Torok (1994), who perceived it as the existence of a collective psychology in the unconscious mind of an individual or people. Their reference to 'transgenerational haunting' describes family pain passed down through generations that is too unspeakable or humiliating to be told and, as a consequence, leads to an unusual generational happening they termed the 'Transgenerational Phantom': 'an undisclosed family secret handed down to an unwitting descendant, and the intrapsychic secret or crypt, which bury an unspeakable but consummated desire' (p. 16).

These forms of uncanny collective occurrence were first studied by Freud (1919), in *The Uncanny*, whose interest in widespread forms of superstition led him to focus on old, animistic conceptions of the universe, where the dread of the evil eye, ghosts, spectres, omnipotence of thought and magical powers are manifestations of things repressed. The provenance of the concept goes even further back to Hoffman (1817), whose exploration of the uncanny, that which he saw as fearful and frightening, deliberated more on the *effects* and the aesthetics of the uncanny, namely those hard-to-explain sensations, particular types of strange and unusual feelings, which carry emotional impulses.

Freud, in a number of his works (1900, 1905, 1919), explored the repetition of experiences that troubled the mind and soul, even of the people and those generations who did not experience the trauma first hand and therefore could not lay claim to it as their experience. In this sense, Freud's patients' experiences did not belong to them and were concealed within the unconscious. He focused on dreams and the repressed in his analytical work with patients in his attempts to make the unconscious conscious. He emphasized the importance of the unconscious mind, as he saw it, governing behaviour to a greater degree than people suspected. The psychoanalytic world of Freud's time, however, drew on colonialist thinking, which labelled what it didn't understand about other people's psychic lives as primitive. Such was relegated to ghosts, the uncanny, occult ideas about thought-transmission, telepathy and possession by others.

Psychoanalysis has paid little attention to black generational trauma, only referring to and signalling it as something to be addressed, but really just touching the sides. I ask how can it be that a 400-year plus phenomenon, with all of its captivating, complex inter- and intra psychic workings, be left out of psychoanalysis's conscious recognition?

Psychoanalysis owes a debt of gratitude to the stimulating treatment of 'hauntings' by Frosh. S. (2012), in both his paper 'Ghostly matters: Haunting and the sociological imagination' and subsequent book, *Hauntings: Psychoanalysis and Ghostly Transmissions* (2013). In his writings, he acknowledges the original contribution of Gordon (1997), and credits her with having a 'clear idea that haunting is a social phenomenon, which is an index of oppression' (Frosh, 2012, p. 2). This is in opposition to Freud's reduction of haunting to unconscious repressions. Gordon defines hauntings in the following terms:

> I used the term haunting to describe those singular yet repetitive instances when home becomes unfamiliar, when your bearings on the world lose direction, when the over-and-done-with comes alive, when what's been in your blind spot comes into view. Haunting raises spectres, and it alters the experience of being in time, the way we separate the past, the present, and the future. (Gordon, 1997, p. 16)

Gordon gives credit to psychoanalysis for being the only human science to take hauntings seriously, but she feels that it has only scratched the surface – a critique that highlights the absence of analysis of hauntings in a wider and more diverse social context. Frosh's writing enters this forgotten space, focusing on what haunts psychoanalysis and the dimensions of hauntings that psychoanalysis struggles to address. He wakes up the discourse with a refreshing post-colonial critique on hauntings, as it relates to Jewish oppression but, again, these works allude only to the black experience, which this book advances with a more in-depth examination. The cue is taken from the questions he has raised here:

> psychoanalysis is also an active process of using the mechanisms of haunting ... The dimensions here are both 'vertical' (time) and

'horizontal' (space). The vertical refers to what gets transmitted from one time period to another, from one generation to another, so that those who have no direct experience of an event may nevertheless be affected by it. Much of the scholarship and clinical writing that has attended to this vertical dimension of hauntings has been concerned with the intergenerational transmission of trauma, and this of course is vital work. But it has other elements too, to which Freud was attuned, notably questions of the generational continuity of ethnic and religious identity. In more contemporary language, it is also what underpins much postcolonial critique: how the societies of today carry with them the active ghosts of previous times. How does this happen, how is something not-known-about nevertheless passed on, sometimes to the extent that it is obviously re-enacted? (Frosh, 2012, p. 242)

Racial hauntings: the black context

When it comes to racial hauntings in the context of the black experience, I choose to move away from Eurocentric explanations of European catastrophes and psychic trauma. These explanations focus on the subject and repression, psychic consequences of silence and the untold, and modes of remembering based on retrospective reconstruction and narration of unspeakable trauma.

Racial hauntings is the perfect bedfellow to the ever-present nature of the burden. Burden is the shadow side of black historical trauma, which is carried deeply in the unconscious, but not always easily identifiable within the self. Its relationship to generational trauma can be seen as a silent shame which is endured as an emotional weight and carried subconsciously in solitude. Burden is of our unconscious making, for we haven't yet separated fully from the enmeshment of black/white relational trauma. It is also what we are still left to hold and carry in the form of displacements, denials, projections and disavowed material from the white other – and other racial minorities who (consciously and unconsciously) position themselves higher up a perceived social and racial order. This is the nature of the enmeshed relationship of black/white dynamics. We may not always be aware of what we are carrying and what we are passing on to the next generation, but this phenomenon is very much alive.

The concept of hauntings is closely associated with the burden of black heritage. Burden relates to the thing that is left over from black history that is still being carried, and hauntings speak to the psychic rupture that is activated immediately but lingers long after racialized trauma. Unlike the silent, unseen burden, racial hauntings occur in the light of conscious experiences with the white other and their internal presence can be loud. Hauntings can be summed up as the mental burn that continues way after being stung.

The visitations of racial hauntings are embodied and feel like unwanted invaders lingering in the reverie of one's calm space. Racial hauntings occur *after* the actual experience of something injurious infiltrating or imposing itself on black people. This injury may come in the form of microaggressions, racism in any form, social injustice, and the continual displacements, denials, projections and disavowed material of the white other on to black others. The familiarity of these experiences for black people means that they also open up something that is supposed to be in the past, namely the pain of brutal historical black/white relations, that is experienced in the present. In other words, something that was always in the background gets triggered and comes very much alive in the present – and it haunts the soul. Some might say this is no different to post-trauma syndrome (PTS), but that would be a gross simplification. Furthermore, it would be a struggle to label racial hauntings 'a disorder' in the very narrow and strict psychiatric sense of mental illness. However, the concept and experience of black generational trauma could be fully recognized as integral and real aspects of a complex type III, complex post-traumatic stress disorder, as described in Chapter 3. These are lived experiences of emotional rupture causing identity wounding. They are ubiquitous and, therefore, inescapable as psychological trauma.

Racial hauntings: a fitting descriptor

As a concept, the two words can be used as a singular descriptor, as in 'the client was plagued by racial hauntings following his experience of blatant racism', or the plural sense, to refer to the concomitant effects of racialized hauntings, as in 'there is nothing primitive or paranoid about black people's experience of racial hauntings, for they arise directly from the silent impact of the dominant other's projections'.

As a descriptor, racial hauntings name the unheeded dimension in Mckenzie-Mavinga's very useful 'recognition trauma' concept (2009, 2016). This is the process that Mckenzie-Mavinga describes whereby powerful unconscious dynamics evoke 'powerful feelings in the bones', to the extent that they cause mental blocks and silencing of the voice when in the presence of racial trauma. I am naming Mckenzie-Mavinga's description of those dynamics evoking 'powerful feelings in the bones', as racial hauntings, for the ubiquitous resounding echo within the phenomenon suggests that this is undeniable interpsychic trauma.

It is important to understand that the term 'interpsychic' means between people, rather than 'intrapsychic', which means occurring within the psyche. The occurrence of racial hauntings is not in black people's heads. The occurrences are not paranoid imaginations or defences of a minority group, and therefore narrowed down to pathology (illness), as in Freud's (1937) defence mechanism of repression. This would be a gross disservice to a group's lived reality and would brand it with the Eurocentric interpretation only, as something uncanny – a repression suggesting something strange and concealed. Racial hauntings cannot be simply understood in these terms, as what I am talking about is known (not strange) and very familiar (not concealed) 'in the bones'. Black consciousness is troubled by this, as, if it has not been named, it cannot be pinned down and fully examined. In attempting to do just that, I have come to see racial hauntings as a relational dynamic with the white world, causing the activation of a familiar and heavy lingering presence for black people. These unpleasant and harmful encounters interrupt the quiet of black lives, leaving the affected wounded to the core. It is important to add that these reverberations may be felt by someone other than the recipient of the original trauma.

Racial hauntings and white ghosts

To illustrate how black society today still carries the active 'ghosts' of previous times, I wove the vertical and horizontal dimensions of the black experience together, illuminating the profound experience, relationship and nature of the burden of black heritage and its connection with racial hauntings. What evolved in the weaving process was clarity in the form of seeing burden as the vertical dimension of black oppression and racial hauntings as the horizontal dimension of the lived experience. Defining the dimensions of oppression in this succinct way enables us to recognize that the black experience of hauntings bore no resemblance to ghosts or the fear of what lay outside black awareness concerning our own history. We are conscious of a felt experience when something of the white presence interrupts our reverie, but the experience has not been fully examined and named. This does not make us ghosts to ourselves. Rather we carry the ghosts of others: the unconscious and unacknowledged eruptions that stem from the dominant other's secret longing for an (imperial) past, and the terror of losing status. One could say that any form of black emancipation haunts the colonial memory of a déjà-vu gone awry. For when you have had a privileged history, equality and independence for the oppressed will feel like your oppression. This is the uncanny nature of racial equality. The wish fulfilment for a secret nostalgia where power ruled supremely is no more.

Vertical and horizontal dimensions of hauntings are elaborated in Chapter 5, which focuses on shame and its vicissitudes and in Chapter 9, 'Healing from the burden of heritage'. Both vertical and horizontal impeding factors are the precursors to present-day racial hauntings, polluting the intrapsychic space of black life. What is activated are trauma responses of hyperalertness, hypervigilance and ruminations that leave a person with preoccupations such as *I should have said that when that happened; I should have walked away when that occurred; Why did that happen to me?* Hauntings are a relational concept, for the fact that they occur within the space of interpersonal interactions with the white other and in black people's general dealings in the white world. In short, both the burden of heritage and racial hauntings contribute to the absence of full mental freedom.

Racial hauntings in the collective

An undeniable example of the impact of racial hauntings in the black collective will perhaps always be the powerful and painful reminder of what was activated by the cold, bold and callous killing of George Floyd, aged 46, on 25 May 2020 in Minneapolis, USA. The reverberations following the televised live coverage of a cold and calculated act of brutality, carried out by one human being on a helpless other, opened up old pathways for the pain of racial hatred in its cruellest form to profoundly trigger black people and affect all of humanity. The spectre of that racial haunting lingered suffocatingly for so many to such an extent that every black therapist that I know in the UK was, and remains, inundated, two years after the event, with requests from black clients who wish to deal with the vicarious reverberations of this public trauma wounding experience.

The haunting evoked by George Floyd's murder created aftershocks that opened the doors to other racial hauntings and old personal traumas for black people. Many black clients who contacted me during the aftermath spoke metaphorically about not being able to breathe, meaning that they were finding it difficult to get on with their lives. Something had stopped them in their tracks, and the shock of such abject brutality caused distress and disorientation. My psychotherapy practice had never been so consistently full following this unforgettable tragic (and sobering) event. It woke up the world to the old reality of black life – one that every black person has always been aware of, but from which the rest of the world could no longer turn a blind eye. The aftershocks of this particular collective haunting for wider society was a brutal awakening to the reality of black lives. This reality orientation has since continued, compounded by the powerful counteracting force of the Black Lives Matter movement. These voices have positively shaped the current zeitgeist with regard to how society needs to view race, post-colonial thought, history, cultural practice, diversity and policy-making, to name a few of the defining changes following the George Floyd tragedy.

Adding to the experience of collective hauntings was the brutal murder of the 18-year-old black British A-level student, Stephen Lawrence, who was stabbed to death in an unprovoked racial attack by a gang of white youths on 22 April 1993. This tragic event, which is regarded as a landmark moment in British history, also evoked vicarious collective trauma for black people in the UK.

In comparison with the George Floyd killing, I would suggest that the collective haunting from the Steven Lawrence murder activated a deeper and more profound effect on black life in the UK. The conscious recognition of a black life murdered was deliberately overlooked by the country's supposed law-upholding institution. The lingering and pervasive impact of racial hauntings were unlike George Floyd's murder

– although equally impactful – as the latter case involved one active visible custodian of the law (and his complicit compatriots), who were all swiftly and judiciously punished for the crime. The Lawrence's efforts were thwarted and blocked at every twist and turn of this protracted and perverted case, by systemic lies, cover-ups and institutional corruption. The impact of racial hauntings was prolonged as an independent inquiry took 20 long years to uncover and pronounce the UK's Metropolitan Police Service to be institutionally racist, with only two of the six white youths being put in prison to serve time for this heinous act. The burden of pain was made greater by the collusion and corruption of an entire institution that failed to honour a basic tenet of their duty – to make all lives matter. Devastation, which was manifest on many levels and in different forms, took its toll on many, who spent several years recovering, repairing and healing in the wake.

Understanding racial hauntings in the black context

Hauntings in the context of racialized trauma are not about the occult, scary ghosts, spirits, shadowy apparitions or creepy paranormal activity that spook in the night. Racialized hauntings are the prolonged mental impact that remains in the consciousness of a black person after a racial impingement from the outside world. The unpleasant nature of hauntings lingers way beyond the racialized traumatic event. Over time, they have the impact of pervading the black psyche. Racial hauntings occur in the wake of these seven types of racism. Lisa Cole (2019) defines these seven forms of racism beyond the dictionary meaning:

- **Interpersonal racism**: occurs at close quarters in the interactions between black and white people and is expressed via: micro- and macroaggressions; workplace unconscious bias, practice and behaviour; racist assumptions, slurs and negative racial thinking, including stereotyping, marginalizing and having low expectations of black people.
- **Interactional racism**: hate crime; emotional and physical harm to black lives.
- **Discursive racism**: racial slurs, hate speech, code words such as 'urban' and 'foreign' to communicate explicit or implicit hierarchies that perpetuate inequalities in society.

- **Representational racism** (particularly in the media, popular culture and advertising): racial stereotypical depictions of black men mainly as criminals, thugs or athletes; black people depicted in roles in which they pander to, serve or caretake whites, and/or given secondary roles that can be easily dispensed with.
- **Systemic/structural/institutional racism**: racist beliefs that create policies, practices, behaviour, stratifications and biased representations built into the very foundations and structure of organizations that perpetuate white supremacy and privilege.
- **Ideological racism**: world views, archaic colonial, imperialist and Eurocentric beliefs, race-dominant biased thinking that are all rooted in negative and reductive stereotypical views and beliefs about black and brown people. This form of racism has a negative impact on people of colour and denies them equality of opportunity and respect.
- **Covert racism**: the knowing and, in some cases, unintentional forms of racism that are kept hidden from public view or covered up by dangerous actions and tropes such as 'we are a tolerant nation'. In the colour-blind policies built on such notions of national acceptance and general open-mindedness, this also includes the unfortunate perpetuation of racism occurring in examples such as the cock-eyed view that to notice someone's race is being racist in itself. Such notions may be intended to create racial affinity but, in fact, they do the opposite.

I would like to add to Coles' (2019) seven forms of racism, a key finding from my doctoral research that identifies a complex form of **internalized racism**. This aspect manifests as an antagonist or internal enemy that is within the self.

- **The internal oppressor** (Alleyne, 2006): the internal oppressor is distinct from internalized oppression, as it is an internal adversary that becomes part of the self and ego structure. It is constructed through the internalization of negative stereotypical societal attitudes and beliefs that are held about black people and coming to believe these perceptions to be true.

Inner workings of racial hauntings

As neither the therapy nor analytic worlds have attributed much research to the generational impact of black people post-slavery, as it did successfully with Jews post-Holocaust, little attention has been given to black people and their social ontology emerging from a brutal historical past. Ontology is the branch of philosophy that studies concepts such as existence, being, becoming and reality. When social, psychological, analytical and educative elements are applied to ontology, many questions about people and the nature of social groups can be explored and understood; in this way, differing worldviews between cultures can be interrogated and evaluated. Black ontology has generally been marginalized in psychology and psychoanalysis, so, unsurprisingly, the more ethereal and shadowy aspect of what impinges, lingers and threatens black ontology has not been addressed in any depth. Frantz Fanon (1986) argued in his chapter, 'The Fact of Blackness', that the study and interpretation of ontology was flawed, insofar as white people can, with their gaze, minimize people of colour as objects. By contrast, people of colour do not do the same to white people. Ontology's concept of existence, being, becoming and reality cannot be neutral, as the white group is free to objectify, and the black group is fixed into, and objectified in the unfree position set by the white Other. Fanon goes on to argue that those with dark skin have to confront the constructed histories about their cultures and origins dictated by the majority group in colonialist societies.

Black ontology would, first of all, question what silent damage is being done to the quality of black life, when it is constantly interrupted by the menace of racial hauntings, almost always without notice. It would be a most unusual situation to find a black person who does not recognize the phenomenon of having the peace of their everyday life interrupted (directly or indirectly) by some racialized incident that leaves an unpleasant presence that is harboured internally as thought, feeling or activated memory. According to Isaacson (2003), the limbic system is a set of brain structures that control the main emotions associated with fear, anxiety, happiness and anger. The functional relevance of the system is that it operates in ways to keep us safe, and is thought to be an important element in regulating high levels of cortisol. This is the main stress hormone in the body that becomes over-activated during trauma, for example, racialized trauma. Our bodies continuously monitor cortisol levels to maintain steady levels (homeostasis). Higher-than-normal or lower-than-normal cortisol levels can be harmful to a person's health. When racial hauntings are activated, the limbic system is forced into an overworked state to maintain emotional equilibrium. Black bodies go into overdrive to deal with the production of excessive cortisol, which is a necessary task for mental preservation. Over time, these constant silent internal goings on of racialized trauma impact the quality of black lives. The damage is silent, not only to our bodies, but also on our mental systems and, ultimately, our souls. Conclusively, racial hauntings change notions of safety and freedom for black people.

Racial hauntings as the relational third

The ubiquity of racial hauntings in a black/white enmeshed relationship is a destructive 'relational third'. The idea of *the third* has often been used in psychoanalytic thinking to describe the emergence of a new level of mental functioning that is essential for psychological development. Winnicott (1971) called this the third area. Ogden (1994) applied this idea to the analytic situation in his proposition of an 'analytic third' arising out of the intersubjective field between analyst and patient. For both Winnicott and Ogden, intersubjectivity has three components:

1. Shared emotions (attunement)
2. Shared attention
3. Shared intention.

However, racial hauntings as the relational third in a black/white relationships suggest the very opposite, that is something ambivalent, unfriendly and even hostile, which is activated in the intersubjective field. There is little to no sharing of conscious minds. In fact, the relational third is experienced as a total lack of understanding of cultural and race awareness in the cross-cultural encounter, which means that there is very little sharing taking place that could lend itself to Winnicott and Ogden's concept of the third, which they speak about as the helpful element enabling shared consciousness between conscious minds.

For black people, the relational third is experienced more as an interloper – a presence or spectre that invades the intersubjective field and ends up spoiling the atmosphere with something unpleasant and messy. The disturbances in these unnamed uncomfortable encounters can be fleeting, but they leave in their wake continual ruptures, which contribute to racial hauntings.

Hauntings: a black and white enmeshed condition

If we view black/white historical relationships as intertwined and enmeshed, then it would make sense to see the two sides as being affected by each other. Therefore, hauntings are present in both white and black people's psyche. The distinction for black people is that hauntings are experienced as attacks on their race, hence my reference to racial hauntings. The phenomenon is carried as a heavy presence when the menace of racism interrupts and threatens black ontology, which I have previously described as having a grounded sense of being in the world. For whites, I am suggesting that hauntings (perhaps without the 'racial' prefix descriptor) are the ever-present terror of retribution for the sins of the past. In this sense, hauntings from a troubled colonial and imperial history continue to spook the white conscience, leaving something in the white collective unconscious scared or frightened of the black other.

For white colonialist western societies, the spectre of payback time for a terrible past unatoned and unrepented continually lurks in shadowy spaces, where catastrophic fantasies create an ever-present hypervigilance for the possibility of an almighty uprising from 'the natives'. What I am describing here, conceptually, is a phenomenon I refer to as the 'white fright–guilt complex'. This is a repressed historical guilt that manifests as hyperalertness to a perceived danger from the black presence or from witnessing black equality and independence as an existential threat. The dynamics of this phenomenon can be observed in everyday instances where a white woman is seen to instinctively clutch her bag closer to her chest on sight of or being in close proximity to a black man, or the situation where two or more black males in conversation at an office water cooler may quickly stir suspicions of them hatching a plot or getting up to no good.

Black people's natural intuition of these regular occurrences is held within black folklore as shared stories to connect and bear witness to each other. Adding to our understanding of the 'white fright–guilt complex' an observance of a fast-growing extremist culture, inflamed by the impact of Trumpism, suggests a renewed agency to reclaim and protect the white position in society. America's relationship and recent reassertion of protection rights to gun ownership speak powerfully to what is going on in the white psyche. In this context and at this juncture, I see white hauntings as white America's hidden fear of a potential black revolt, activated by the powerful global impact of the Black Lives Matter movement. The abiding fierce relationship with guns appears to offer a reassured preparedness to protect white lives from possible black revenge. White hauntings suggest the white conscience working in overdrive, as self-protection gets bound up with the terror of reprisals and the need to maintain power in the face of the unknown. Self-protection in America is also bolstered by both the Second Amendment right to own arms and the Fifth Amendment of the United States Constitution, which honours citizen's rights to not be compelled to be witness against oneself, by being forced to produce evidence from one's own lips. These protection clauses have both become the automatic choices of reliance for defence in cases of race hate crimes and acts of racism.

It would not be a stretch too far to suggest that black minorities have developed an acute alertness to the racial impingements from the outside that do harm to the soul. Black people have learnt the art of adopting an amphibious nature, that is having mixed and twofold abilities to switch effortlessly into protection mode and back into relaxation mode. This is not unlike the simple activity of changing into one's 'going-out clothes' when stepping outside for social engagements and then changing back into one's 'house clothes' when we get home. This learnt skill is so authentically mastered that it offers two identities, that is to say, two selves; this is not meant in the schizoid sense, but it is rather an authentic adaptation to negotiate the impingements in the white world. This social dexterity allows us to know the ways of both worlds. However, although this twofold nature and skill is a blessing, it is also a curse we are forced to negotiate in the outside world.

Racial hauntings are so inextricably linked to having a full under-standing of the impact of generational burden that further direction is needed on how to manage its presentation in psychotherapy practice. I offer three examples, one hypothetical and two personal examples, to demonstrate how therapists can identify the phenomenon and address the psychological and emotional impact on black lives.

Example 1

Giles, a white male who prides himself on being 'woke' because he has done the work on himself, says, in a meeting at work where there is only one black member of staff amidst the predominantly white group, that he strongly believes there is a hangover from history for black men and their relationship with authority. He boldly goes on to back this up with what he claims he has read as evidence. He states that Jamaica was the chosen island for rebellious slaves and this legacy has left an imprint of rebelliousness in black Caribbean men's relationship with white authority. The implication in this arrogant claim is one of gross judgement, pathologizing of black men, biased uninformed thinking, and plain and simple racial offence. He also demonstrates a profound ignorance of black history and geography by implying that Jamaica is representative of the whole of the Caribbean, also known as the Island Countries. His lack of awareness of as many as 700 islands, of which 26 are countries (each one different culturally and unique), is an example of racial homogenization.

Understanding and interrupting racial hauntings

The unpleasant spectre of racial haunting will be heightened and compounded if what is claimed by Giles is met with silence and goes unchallenged by his white colleagues. It will raise questions about collusion for any black staff member present in this team, leaving them to work in an environment that feels deeply unsafe. It therefore requires white colleagues to own their outrage and challenge this male's cocky, offensive and overtly biased behaviour.

Feedback, however, must give value to the receiver and not release for the giver, and therefore some helpful challenges might be offered in the form of comments such as:

- 'I find your claims to be racially offensive and naive.'
- 'Have you considered the impact of what you are saying?'

- 'Put yourself in a black person's shoes – how would you be feeling after hearing that racist assertion about black men?'

It is important not to let such racist judgements go unchallenged, as it will implicate the whole white team with the charge of racial indifference. A racist work culture is judged by what is tolerated in its midst and therefore, if you are not a solution to the problem, you are colluding with the problem. Such an incident should not be left unchallenged and the offence should be pointed out, not in an overzealous way to shame Giles, but to educate.

The following is likely to happen to the black member of staff if this comment is left unchallenged:

- The lone black person will experience the incident as a microaggression or outright racist behaviour. (This is the initial impact of racial hauntings that cause interruption to black ontology.)
- Racial hauntings will be activated to linger and pervade the work environment long after the incident. (This is the unpleasant, heavy presence of the activated racial haunting.)
- The black staff member will be left to stand alone in their upset or distress during and after the incident. (This is the (internal and external) rupture – the dislocation.)
- The workplace will become a distrustful environment. (Hypervigilance is a product of the activated racial haunting.)
- The black worker will ask themselves questions such as 'Who can I trust?' 'From whom can I expect support in matters of race conflict in the workplace?' (Black worker experiences isolation in the workplace.)

Racial hauntings activated by such workplace incidents can pervade a black person's mental space and may often be compounded by other similar incidents. It therefore helps if the things left out of conscious recognition are given a voice. Thus it is necessary for white colleagues to speak up, own their own outrage, name the offence, challenge the offender and not leave black folks to do their work.

Example 2

Althea Gibson was the first African–American tennis player and professional golfer, and first black athlete ever to cross the colour line of international tennis in the 1950s by winning a total of 11 Grand Slam titles, at Wimbledon, the US Nationals and the French Championships. In a radio programme celebrating her amazing and talented life, a white English male interviewer was heard asking the sports historian brought in as an expert commentator whether Ms Gibson had been desperate to turn her hand to these many talents. My enjoyment in listening to this wonderful exaltation of a black woman's achievements through racial adversity was rudely interrupted by the use of the ungracious word 'desperate'.

Understanding and interrupting racial hauntings

As I was aware of the reasons for the dislocation and rupture, I made a conscious effort not to become hostage to what is all too familiar. However, the incident did not go unobserved:

- It caused me to physically bristle. This was the initial impact of ungracious bias that caused the violent interruption to my reverie.
- Spontaneous hot tears spurted from my eyes. This is the somatic response that arose from the heavy presence of the activated racial haunting.
- I asked myself where was the interviewer's sensitivity, tenderness and care? I wondered why does it always happen to us? This was my attempt to make sense of my dislocation and the rupture to my enjoyment.
- The impact of this incident lingers for the rest of the day. This is the racial haunting activated vicariously on behalf of another black person.

Through self-awareness, I avoided darting back to the past and hovering on the ways blacks have historically been treated by whites. I mentally tuned out my rage. The work of mending psychic ruptures caused by racial hauntings means finding ways to ritualistically engage in mental hygiene: de-escalate historic ruminations; take care of the mind through forms of relaxation, meditation, journaling; learn how to turn down the volume of the internal noise; shut out the interloper by smoking out the ghosts of the past (using incense), uplifting mantras and breathing in fresh air. Rituals of this nature are vital for restoring and reclaiming control of one's healthy mental space.

Example 3

I reflect on a very personal experience as a black Caribbean woman who had a cherished 20-year relationship with a white English family. I felt like a member of this unit and was embraced as such and, in many ways, they had become my surrogate family in England. The spectre of racial hauntings reared its head in an incident that not only ruptured the profound bonds between us, but severed all ties, never to be mended.

The incident unfolded when one of the family, who was in a relationship with a black man, decided to adopt a very young black mixed-race child. The child had suffered both emotional and physical abuse at the hands of their black biological mother, who herself had struggled with mental health problems and an abusive relationship with her partner. The child had subsequently developed an anxious/fear response towards black women and would become very agitated and distressed in their presence. With the appropriate and balanced corrective emotional experience, however, children's capacity for resilience enables them to respond well, repair well and thrive well.

The overzealous matriarch of this white family decided to take matters into her own hands in order to 'protect' the child. One strategy was to unceremoniously instruct me to avoid being anywhere near the child, as my blackness would cause the child distress. Another strategy that was implemented by the matriarch was 'flooding' therapy, which involved 'swamping' the child with pictures of my (black) face, so as to prepare them for an eventual meeting with me. I found all of this upsetting and ridiculously ironic, as the family resided in a multiracial inner-city area. Although I believe the measures employed were of good intent, they caused deep hurt, and feelings of being let down and pushed out. I also felt depersonalized – reduced to being just a black face for some psychological experiment. In this objectification, my feelings seemed to not matter; there was only an exaggerated 'white' desire to repair the 'black' damage the child had suffered.

I was bitterly disappointed that, after 20 years of a cemented relationship, there was no trust in me to exercise my wisdom to do the right things. I was left haunted by this breakdown which seemingly focused on one racial signifier – dark skin. The wound was deep and, vicariously, made even deeper as I was left with questions about how such a traumatized child would thrive in the real world, where there are people of every hue.

Understanding and working therapeutically with racial hauntings

If this story were bought to a therapeutic situation, above all, the therapist should facilitate the telling of the client's story, as is experienced in my case and circumstances. The therapist will learn that the spectre of racial hauntings was powerfully activated on many levels for the client in her painful experience. The therapist will come to understand that the event triggered complex dynamics of race conflict, overzealousness, power and privilege, which opened up generational conflicts of black/white historical relations. The story will also reveal how the dynamics had poisoned the relationship with the friend and damaged all closeness and trust with the family, known for 20 years. What was left in the wake of the client's experience was unprocessed hurt, a nasty atmosphere and unpleasant feelings that would keep racial hauntings alive for a very long time after the incident.

The following should be held in mind when working with a client in such a scenario:

- Explore with the client how the experience is affecting her and in what ways.
- Ascertain whether the experience has been a trigger for other difficulties of the same or similar nature.
- Be forthcoming in picking up, facilitating and exploring all references pertaining to current and historical material that highlight power imbalances and difficult race dynamics in black/white relationships
- Ask explicitly what role race plays in the experience of being hurt and the depth of feelings carried.
- If you are a white therapist, enquire how your being white may be impacting the therapy process.

- If you are a black therapist, enquire how being black may be impacting the therapy process.
- Make space for a range of emotions to be 'rinsed' (that is, expressed again and again).
- Allow expressions of anger and rage to be aired, and be careful not to judge these as scary emotions to withdraw from in the work.
- Related to this, be mindful that, rather than judging anger as potential aggression, it needs to be held therapeutically as a manifestation of profound hurt.
- Assess what the client wants to do with her feelings and to what end. Discuss her choices for dealing with the hurt.
- Respect and follow the client in her therapy, even if she decides to deal with the racial hauntings by letting go and ending the relationship.
- Facilitate mental hygiene healing work for the client so she can reclaim her control and mental realignment.

Can black people be free of racial hauntings?

It seems that one cannot escape the phenomenon of racial hauntings unless one chooses to exist in a racial silo. Racial hauntings are inescapable for the simple fact that they are part of the very nature of burden – the transmissions and impact of black historical trauma that are left out of the world's conscious recognition. In carrying this burden alone, black people can work at lightening the load but, whatever the nature of the trauma, as long as it is continually directed at one's racial identity – in other words, the core elements of self and being – the inevitable impact is bound to activate old whiplash-type mental injuries that will go on to ache and leave a presence: racial hauntings.

To end this chapter, it seems fitting to include the second half of my introductory poem 'Creole Hauntings' here, as it offers a resolve for dealing with the impact of this mental injury.

Creole hauntings are not just about the little boy
Whose disquiet drives him from pillar to post
Nor is it Freud's repressions
Cured by invocations of ghosts.
For us, these experiences are familiar and current
Regularly inhabiting the soul
When racial impingements annoy
Frequently destabilizing and threating to destroy.
The zeitgeist signals it is time to deploy
What the collective is entitled to enjoy
Reprieve and healing from these historical hauntings
That must NOT be passed on as inheritance by the current convoy

CHAPTER 5

Shame and its vicissitudes

'If you find the psychic wound in an individual or a people, there you also find their path to consciousness.'

Carl Jung (1964, p. 166)

Introduction

A major legacy of generational trauma is shame and its impact on black identity wounding. Through successive experiences of suppressed freedoms and adaptations to negative and stereotypical societal constructs, my venerable ancestors and those who followed were forced to wrestle with the ongoing struggle for equality, authenticity and autonomy. Internalizing the negative impact of racial oppression takes its toll and contributes to a genuine malady of the self. This quote from a black client in therapy sums up the nature of the shame malady:

'Shame told me there was something fundamentally wrong with me and those who looked like me. Society said so and I accepted that I was inferior; I was the Other; I was a mistake. Life then became a task to do rather than a journey to enjoy. I had bought into the lie.'

This astonishing and poignant quote sharply identifies the tenets of black identity shame and black identity wounding, illustrating how it penetrates the core of self and damages self-worth, self-esteem and the freedom to just be.

Meaning of shame

Shame is ubiquitous and is related to how we think others see and judge us. Its Germanic root 'skem' means 'to conceal oneself'. The emotion of shame can include feeling inferior, self-conscious, powerless, worthless and that we are different to others who will scrutinize and judge us. Shame is the loss of approval.

As a feeling, it is often confused and used interchangeably with its sister emotion, guilt, which is judicial in nature. The judging part of guilt makes us recognize 'I have done a bad thing', or leaves us questioning 'How could I have done that?', which are responses to moral transgressions (one's own standards). Guilt in this healthy regard allows for positive self-questioning and self-evaluation, which can lead to remedial action and remorse.

Shame is relational, involving scrutiny of the self and one's identity, and can lead a person to think 'I am bad person' or 'How could I have done that?'. Guilt is about action and *doing* wrong, whereas shame is about condemnation and *being* fundamentally flawed. It is associated with other emotions such as humiliation, disgust, disgrace and other self-evaluating ruminations, all of which degrade and pervade all aspects of the self.

The emotion of shame is what I refer to as a me-myself-and-I emotion. It is paradoxically intensely private, yet can feel so very exposing and overpowering. Shame can be felt in a here-and-now moment of exposure and yet be ever-present and part of one's psychological make-up. When 'normal' shame occurs, the immediate experience can be likened to 'la petite mort' or 'a little death', a French expression that describes the brief loss or weakening of consciousness . This is the kind of single-incident shame that is often felt in the moment when someone experiences or commits a shameful act. Overwhelming feelings arise from the consciousness of doing something dishonourable, improper or ridiculous, or from it being done to oneself. These are moments when the self is exposed or uncovered and leads to the feeling of wanting the ground to swallow you up.

A particularly painful form of shame is one that, if left unaddressed, can become toxic (bad for emotional health) and archaic (old and serving no current purpose). These aspects remain tied to the self, like grown adults who have outgrown their stay in the parental home. Unlike normal single-incident, shame-based situations, toxic and archaic shame stays buried within and becomes part of our self-identity. A person suffering from toxic shame will experience a chronic sense of worthlessness, low self-esteem and self-loathing – all connected to the belief that they are innately shameful or bad. Toxic and archaic shame can exist separately but they are more often inextricably linked due to the nature of the shame wound.

The most common precursor to this kind of shame is trauma. Trans- and intergenerational trauma both contribute to the crippling nature of shame and, when passed down the generations, it becomes toxic, with its poisonous transmissions reinforcing identity inferiority complexes. Toxic archaic shame can easily be triggered in our intimate attachments, in dysfunctional and abusive relationships, in our encounters with all forms of authority and in work settings where the workplace culture is non-inclusive and oppressive in nature.

Toxic archaic shame that stems from transgenerational trauma may be constantly aroused in the here and now through repeated experiences of rejection and betrayal by a society that relegates minorities to the margins of humanity. It is a powerful internal enemy that acts to diminish the self and leads to either the individual or the group becoming apathetic and compliant with the status quo. In my view, when apathy – which occurs when we are systematically worn down by impingements from the outside world – takes hold, it can lead to compliance, which is an acceptance of one's lot. These are the hallmarks of indifference induced by the reductive nature of shame.

There are major therapeutic challenges for therapists who find themselves working with clients who have given up the will to engage, and whose shame internalizations have led to a kind of emotional death by shame. It is my experience in working with shame that those whose psychological make-up and psyches naturally gravitate towards the life instinct (eros) for self-preservation will, when at rock bottom, carry a belief in and unfaltering hope of the light at the end of the tunnel. Such individuals have not been weighed down by toxic archaic shame and gravitate towards love, socialization, cooperation and full engagement in life. Conversely, those whose psychological make-up instinctively catastrophizes, because their psyches have been beaten down by trauma and negativity, may turn away from eros instincts and become stuck, dwelling in the death instinct (Thanatos). Such observations were made by Freud (1915), who noted that those of his patients who had repressed traumatic experiences had the tendency to repeat the repressed material as a contemporary experience rather than remember it as something belonging to the past.

What I am concluding about the challenge of working with chronic archaic shame is that the carrier who has made an unhealthy investment in it will find it hard to let go, move on and seek out the new. The work for therapists, therefore, frequently feels like an uphill struggle, with a need to maintain stoic perseverance. The work needs to be well paced and involves helping to increase awareness of self-destructive thoughts, the development of self-compassion, divestment from holding on to and re-enacting old wounds, and reparenting the inner child. Clients who have long been carrying inside an emotional death will need to truly mourn the loss of the old self, before feeling able to turn towards the new life-giving forces of eros. Working with toxic archaic historical shame is challenging principally because the practitioner will be working with both the individual and the collective aspects of shame trauma. For white therapists in particular, a mindfulness will be crucial in order to avoid the rupture caused by reshaming the shamed.

I suggest that shame-based individuals have difficulty in achieving healthy individuation, the process of coming into and maturing into one's full identity. The cycle only serves to lock the individual further into the damaging shame cycle and so it continues. I suggest that such a cycle has the following four steps:

1. Shame is induced in individuals through interpersonal interactions that lead to the production of shame.
2. Shame is internalized and eventually consumes our inner core.
3. The internalization of shame creates a process of internally disowning parts of the self. Kaufman (1992, 2004) labelled this splitting.
4. Splitting creates painful internal discrepancies that we attempt to correct without much success. That is because the self-hate associated with the disowned fragmented part creates repeated patterns and cycles any time shame is triggered.

The presentation of addictions, codependencies and enmeshments provide ripe opportunities for therapists to see the four-stage formation very clearly, as they all provide ways to avoid feeling the self-hate mentioned in stage four. As practitioners, we need to not only understand these stages for ourselves, but also help clients to develop a full awareness of their behavioural patterns. This is needed in order for them to gain an understanding of the work of letting go, reframing and utilizing new and more effective tools for healthier living. To see most clearly how this works in practice, I wish to share two examples of shame from my childhood in order to conceptualize this process.

Personal reflections on early family shame

The first is a strong recollection of my 6-year-old self, holding the humiliation of my father's shame experience during his very first ever visit outside of the Caribbean to a predominantly white western country, England. The second is of an actual shame experience that happened when I was 8, which is so embedded that it has left trauma transmissions familiar to me that I now quickly recognize and manage as a 'seasoned' adult (my mother's expression).

The (vicarious) shame experience of my 6-year-old self

This incident relates to my late father's visit to England and most of Europe in 1963, for a year-long sabbatical (his trip was undertaken with my mother and baby sister). This was his maiden overseas trip, having never taken leave from his post in Guyana (which, as already mentioned, became independent from colonial Britain in 1966). On arrival during winter to the mother country, Britain, my parents were picked up from Heathrow airport by family members and stayed with them in Harlescott Road, Peckham, London.

On a bitterly cold winter's day during the first week of my father's visit, he decided to get to know the area and set out with my baby sister towards the buzzing Caribbean market area in Shumont Road, Rye Lane, Peckham. The story goes that my dad did not dress my sister adequately for this expedition, having, of course, no previous knowledge or experience of winters in a western climate. He was apparently accosted by a group of white women who were outraged at seeing a baby in a pram without mittens and earmuffs. My father meekly recalled this experience of being loudly chastised on the streets of Peckham, with accusations of

Figure 5.1 *My parents' first visit to Britain in the early 1960s. Mother is holding my baby sister. Father is to the right of the picture*

child neglect, and being marched down the high street into Jones and Higgins[1] to purchase a new winter jacket, gloves and warm earmuffs for my baby sister. He recounted how the bunch of pushy women refused to leave the store until he had bought the items, dressed my sister in the store in the warmer garments, and finally listened to their last rebuke to never ever do such a thing again. The final humiliation came, I am told, when they decided to 'release' him from the store only when they were satisfied that he had passed the test for being a good parent and could therefore continue his walkabout with my baby sister.

While writing about this, I bristle with indignation at this missionary group of busybodies. I thought (and still believe) that, although the intent was honourable, and maybe even loving, the manner in which it was done was the height of humiliation to a black man newly arrived in England at that time. When I recall my father's retelling of this story, his grovelling gratitude and indebtedness to the white women infuriated me. His crawling humility was typical of his generation of black people and their relationship to the colonial *mother country* – a brainwashing into thinking and believing a superior morality and authority in the English. This is the mindset that leads the groveller to adopt an excessively

Figure 5.2 *My baby sister in her new woolly coverings held by our loving mother*

subservient attitude, to the point where they became the inferior, bad and stupid one. In my daddy's eyes, 'they' – the English – were always going to be right. In the excoriating shame experience, therefore, he gives away the currency that may have allowed him to negotiate a modicum of his dignity with the women and, instead, buries his own shame but, unconsciously, hands it over to the listener of his story: me.

Although I believe the grand gesture of the women was a good deed, the mob mentality of publicly exposing and shaming a naive black man was unforgivable. My father was not a wilful child abuser – he was just an innocent foreigner struggling to adjust to an experience unknown and unfamiliar. His lesson could have been learnt in a kinder and more sympathetic way. The mere recollection of this memorable shame incident is potent enough to arouse again the powerful and familiar presence of racial hauntings.

My postmortem examination of this early shame experience suggests that overzealous and dominant others are easily compelled into thinking they are right and virtuous in their collective moral stance, leading to righteous behaviour. This can be seen in the deeply embedded rhetoric, within the British colonialist mentality, which leads to a sense of duty to carry light and civilization into the dark and untamed places of the world. This narcissistic stance of teaching the 'natives' will always breed shame, as the other receives the projection of being the inferior one. This binary phenomenon is a critical theory of race dynamics, presenting an eternal challenge for white therapists working interculturally. Returning to my childhood shame experience, the discerning 6-year-old me would not have understood shame as a concept, but instinctively intuited the humiliation on her proud father's behalf.

Linking this shame experience to my treatment of the four-stage process of shame, it is important for therapists – especially white therapists working with black clients – to recognize that they will be working with some key elements of toxic shame, summed up as *relational, obsessional, cyclical* and *generational*. This means that the risks of reshaming the patient/client are high when trying to interrupt and break the cycle of the shame process. At the simplest level, the mere presence of the white face or the black face of the therapist might serve as a constant trigger of the client's shame, therefore the relational aspect of who the therapist is in their racial identity and what this represents for the patient/client in the transference will have to be addressed. At the more profound level of the work, the therapist will reshame and burden the client if the work falls short of an engaged attuned curiosity, an adequate working through and holding of the client's vulnerabilities. These vital elements for fostering an effective working alliance are key, and they guard against any unconscious dynamics being acted out in the therapy. It would therefore make sense to conclude that, for the work of addressing toxic shame and black identity wounding, the therapist needs to keep in mind that it is even more important to make the unconscious elements of the working relationship conscious, so that relational dynamics are not left unaddressed to fester and produce more shame that invariably reshames the shamed. As therapists, we will agree that the main aim in addressing the shame trauma cycle that wounds identity is to enable the client to disentangle from the familiar destructive patterns of internalized shame that keeps the burden of heritage (the historical past) and generational hauntings (present-day racialized triggers) alive and impactful.

Wearing my therapist's hat today, I can make sense of how my father handled the trauma. The proud black man removed himself from his humiliation and emasculation through the unconscious mechanism of disavowing – that is, denying its presence but, in the disavowal, unconsciously handing it over to me for safekeeping. It could also have been a case of conveniently dumping it where he felt it would do no damage. This story of my shame experience with my father highlights important themes of disavowed shame in the clinical setting, and how it works in the transference/countertransference relationship between therapist and patient/client. Who holds the disavowed shame for whom when it is too uncomfortable? Do black patients/clients pick up, hold and know the impact of such a burden when white therapists disavow their own triggered or activated race-shame in the work? What happens to the quality of therapy when the therapeutic relationship doesn't feel safe for the client/patient to open up and share their vulnerabilities? What are the consequences for the work if the shame is missed because there is no gatekeeper or no one addressing the shame? These are salient questions to explore in one's practice and in clinical supervision to deepen the effectiveness of intercultural clinical practice. I would contend that, as the dynamics of race and racism are so deeply triggering and uncomfortable for most, their impact in psychotherapy would be no different. Race-based shame exposes both blacks and whites, albeit in different ways. Black shame is essentially about identity-trauma (hurt and loss). White shame triggers identity-exposure (guilt and vulnerability). When these unheeded dimensions are lived out (consciously or unconsciously) in the therapeutic encounter, it is often the case that such fragmentation gets handed over to black patients/clients for safe keeping. This is the nature of the therapist's shame disavowal.

Whatever the nature of the shame disavowal, we must bear in mind that what is not owned by the shamed is usually vicariously picked up and held by the other. This vicarious shame experience compounded previously held childhood confusions about colonial black and white relationship dynamics. I feel that, as a result, my attunement to shame was sharpened to its presence not only in myself but, consequently, in all of my personal and professional interactions. Shame overarches much of what is difficult in black and white relations, and I believe the ubiquitous nature of shame is one key driving force that brings clients to therapy. Shame resides wherever there is psychological pain.

The second shame experience of my 8-year-old self

Although the first recollection of shame was the vicarious holding of my father's humiliation, I had my own experience of shame at the age of 8. I had been given the honour of being one of three flower girls to grace my uncle and aunt's white wedding. It was a lavish affair, with everyone dressed up to the nines and looking joyous and expectant. My aunt was resplendent in a huge white lacy gown, with a simple but elegant jewelled headband, and she held the most beautiful bouquet of pink and white sweet-smelling flowers. She wore white lacy gloves and the most radiant smile throughout. She had the cutest dimples and I remembered them making her face look even sweeter on her wedding day. I did not accord much attention to the men, but I remembered my uncle looking happy, and both he and my father cut dashing figures in well-cut gentlemen's suits. They were a colourful picture of beautiful people.

As an 8 year old, I was mesmerized and felt I was in a fairytale wonderland. As the white bridal limousine, festooned with ribbons, pulled up to take us from the church, the bride glided in first, followed by the groom, who only had eyes for his beautiful bride. I think I must have forgotten all the flower girl instructions, totally lost in my fairytale world, and I too glided into the bridal car, seating myself next to the bride and groom. Being so close to them was intoxicating and I remember staring up at the bride, as if hypnotized. The experience seemed to go on for ever in my 8-year-old mind but, quick as a flash, I felt someone yank my little arm. I turned and looked into the thunderous and angry face of my aunt (the one who had looked after us during my father's sabbatical), as she dragged me out of the car, shouting at the top of her voice in front of the wedding guests: 'That is not where you sit, you stupid little girl ... your car is over there.' (I remember the exact words all these years later.) I was then roughly pulled by the arm so fast that my feet could hardly make contact with the ground as she bundled me into the flower girls' car to the amusement of everyone. Some laughed, some pointed, whereas others just looked on with mouths open. I was consumed with shame and wanted the ground to swallow me up. For several hours afterwards, I felt deflated and exposed as the stupid one – the darker-skinned flower girl – who had got it wrong; this can be clearly seen in my expression in the photograph. I think I may have remained in a state of shock for the rest of the beautiful event, which no longer felt beautiful as I retreated into myself and quietly picked at the shame wound.

Figure 5.3 8-year-old me paralyzed with shame, standing
in front of my father (the tall man to the left on the back row)

This early shame event continued to leave a stain on my sense of
self until I was able to understand its impact and the power it had over
my choices in life. It led me to understand why I am punctilious with
time and being in the right place, for example the right platform for a
train or tube, or the correct bus to a destination. Changing planes has
always caused me anxiety and has since led to a firm decision to always
opt for non-stop flights, while still leaving plenty of time for eventualities
and obsessively checking departure times. Archaic shame would still
be triggered, after all these years, if I missed a plane, train, bus or tube.
The old wound would be activated, along with a mild feeling of getting
it wrong or looking stupid; this would also prevent me from asking for
help if I were stuck or lost. This is the potency of the original shaming
experience, several decades later.

Thankfully, the once hidden shame from being the dark-skinned
flower-girl, who was the only stupid one to get it wrong has long been dealt

with, perhaps because working with my internal (enemy) oppressor has soundly resolved all old negative scripts and conflicts regarding shadism/colourism, leading to profound pride and acceptance in being a black woman, intrinsically and fabulously beautiful, who has been blessed with a lovely shade of cocoa brown skin, from the rich and varied black colour palette.

Identifying the genesis of some of my shame has been therapeutic, the careful retracing of the origins and creation of the wounds has been both purposeful and healing. As Socrates' famous quote commented: 'To know thyself is the beginning of wisdom.'

I marvel at the 6-year-old me, who could feel her father's shame and hold it for safe-keeping, so to speak, and the 8 year old's shame, which I have traced back to make sense of some of the 'neuroses' I carried for a long time. The colourism/shadism wound is now completely healed through an acceptance that I do not *ever* need to feel ashamed or apologize for my race, my skin tone or my 'self'. Perhaps it is the early introduction to this ubiquitous emotion of shame that has attuned me to its powerful impact on the emotional, psychological and mental health of particular racial minorities – of all hues. I offer a challenge to all practitioners who wish to fully engage with the topic of identity shame in the consulting room to first do their homework, by tracing the genesis of their own shame for a deeper sense of its workings and impact. It is one of the areas of psychotherapy that I feel needs to be approached from an embodied place of knowing, as well as having the theoretical and conceptual handles to negotiate one's way in the clinical work with a client's shame wounds.

Working clinically with shame

Were I an adult patient/client relaying my 6-year-old first shame experience to a therapist, and specifically a white therapist, I would hope for several things to take place in the therapeutic processing that would make the experience an effective and healing intercultural encounter.

Here are some guidelines for therapists meeting this adult client in her early shame:

1. The intergenerational trauma dynamic is picked up, so that I can see what I was carrying for my father, where I might be burdening myself and how I may be caretaking unnecessarily. The following

interventions would focus the therapist's engagement with the client's shame experience and help to strengthen the relational dynamics:

- What kind of a man was your father – his values and belief systems? What were his views about white people before he visited England?
- Tell me about your relationship with him and you being his first-born?
- What is your role in your family and what do you feel you hold for them?
- How did the rest of your family respond to your father's encounter with the white women?
- What positive and negative traits/characteristics of your shame history/heritage do you feel you hold on to, and have reframed?
- How does it feel to share and reflect on these painful experiences with me, your white therapist?

A full exploration utilizing the above facilitation will signal the following to the patient/client: that the therapist is interested in them as a person and comfortable to engage, hover and be curious even when it is uncomfortable; that the therapist takes time to show genuine concern and offer encouragement for the full expression of feelings and experiences; that the therapist knows when to give primacy to important issues in the moment; that they possesses intercultural stamina to go where other white therapists might fear to tread; and that the therapist is comfortable in their own white skin to foster the transference at such close quarters and at a deep level.

2. The centrality of conflict in the shame experience is fully excavated. Clinically, this would mean that in terms of factors such as, timing, the therapist's attunement to the racialized shame burden being carried by the patient/client, and working with racialized oppression, it would be paramount to first give full space to the 'wounded' shame-teller to fully exhume, retell and exhaust the shame experience at her own pace. This retelling should be allowed for however long is needed, to spend time with the minutiae. The most important person in the story is the patient/client – not the colonial party. Therefore, a therapist who

strays from looking at the client's obvious race-wound in the eye and sees that it is necessary to allude to a good deed being done by the white women, or equate their act with strident feminists telling useless men how to get it right, would not be providing the necessary holding and containment. The patient/client would experience these interventions as deflection and an avoidance of where the point of maximum is at. To slide away from this focused and important vantage-point would definitely highlight the therapist's own discomfort, disinterest or even unconscious racial bias, and be damaging to the alliance and ultimately therapy.

3.   Although adequate space is therapeutically necessary for me (the client) to keenly feel the pain of my shame wound, the healing process can be achieved through being heard and understood by a holding and non-judgemental therapist. It is important, however, that the white therapist is able to listen without appearing overburdened, overly shocked, disgusted or overzealous in their wish to repair wrongdoings on behalf of their white tribe. The chances are that this will be picked up by the patient/client as 'damaging' the therapist or, worse, a prohibition – something that is not welcomed in the work. In such circumstances, the patient's/client's own shame will be heightened and become an added burden of hiding and holding in their own shame wound – and holding in unconscious servitude, the white therapist's shame-trigger and fragility. What is very clear in this analysis of who holds the shame in addressing the impact of racialized trauma is the fact that, when the client is left holding the therapist's activated and disavowed shame, the essential role of them *bearing witness* is lost – and may even cause further wounding in the trauma work. And returning to my 6-year-old shame experience, a therapist will fall foul of the shame disavowal dynamic by instantly jumping in and castigating the white women who shamed my father. Conversely, a therapist may feel the need to create a so-called balanced response, by trying to rationalize or prove the white women meant no harm and were being good citizens, while also giving space for the story to be told. Either of these responses on the part of the therapist is a therapeutic faux pas that has the potential to reshame the shamed. (See also point 6.)

4.   The therapist is able to show genuine curiosity and interest in

exploring the psychological impact on a child who is left to hold – or who chooses to hold – a parent's shame, and how this continues to affect the parent–child relationship dynamics in different ways.

5. The therapist sensitively, and in a timely manner, explores whether there has been the potential for shame resonances in my outside world. An example of this would be in my interactions with white authority, checking for triggers or the activation of pain when being told what to do by figures of white authority (for example the police, white managers, and so on). The therapist would actively be working with the activation of racial hauntings in this regard.

6. The therapist recognizes what are his or her own triggers and deals with what is activated in the rightful place, namely clinical supervision.

I see these six guidelines as, when taken together, forming a three-stage approach to working with the shame wound from any impact of racialized trauma.

(a) The first stage of the process is to allow permission for the exhaustive retelling of the manifest or immediate and fresh content of the shame to be told. Creating this space is important for the necessary replay of the shame experience. The process of replaying the minutia of events, which is often delivered as reporting to or talking at the therapist–witness, serves to unburden the shame-teller, validate them and ground their experiences in a safe space. This crucial first stage also carries additional importance and significance in black/white and cross-cultural encounters. People of colour who present with racialized shame trauma have a strong need to be believed in their experiences and, for the white therapist, this requires an engaged stillness to be able to empathize.

(b) The second stage of the work is to facilitate the processing of the manifest shame content. This is the active work that allows the therapist's enquiries and other facilitative interventions (similar to examples on pages 94 and 95) to be heard and emotionally engaged with for the purpose of making sense of the trauma impact.

(c) The third stage moves the patient/client slowly towards recovery from the shame wounds through the process of regaining their sense of mental balance from the dislocation of shame. I refer to this therapeutic facilitation as enabling the return to a state of ontological security – being grounded in our own skin and surroundings.

Shame leaves us with the exposing feeling of having no top skin and therefore being in a perpetual state of vulnerability and doubt. For practitioners of all clinical persuasions, it is worth remembering that the denuding impact of identity shame cannot be analysed away but slowly worked with as a process of realigning aspects of the self that have been degraded by humiliation. Our work as therapists is to help restore the patient's/client's experience of being defrocked and reduced in their humanity. Effective shame healing therefore is trauma repair. Therapy at this stage must focus on facilitating the recovering and reclaiming of one's human dignity for the restoration of personal pride and self-worth.

Language as the semiotic cover of shame

Our main access to patients and clients is through language, and in the talking therapies we communicate through a variety of ways, which includes our speech, tone, gestures, signals and body language, to name a few. Language as communication is essentially the main tool of our trade. Language bridges therapist and patient/client powerfully in the therapeutic encounter, and its close examination is essential for cross-cultural effectiveness. The old adage, 'sticks and stones will break my bones, but words will never hurt me', does not apply in this setting. Words (language) or the absence of its presence can cause hurt and even damage. The same is true for our patient's/client's experiences of racialized trauma in the external world. Racist language and oppressive acts (intentional or unintentional) will contribute to the shame wound. As therapists, we are all challenged therefore to examine this important and key tool of our trade and what we do with it when we are discomforted by the client's shame experiences. The consulting room has no special pass that removes it from social maladies of the outside world.

To make a link with my aforementioned therapist responsibility to facilitate the recovering and reclaiming of the patient's/client's human dignity for the restoration of personal pride and self-worth, it is important to include a note about pride in the treatment of shame.

As pride (false) is the first-born that gazes upon itself, its twin, shame, is the inevitable sibling who exposes what it is. They are mirrors of each other, as in the complex dynamic of black–white relationships. Pride looks for who is watching (*look at me – I am ok*). Shame watches for who is looking (*can I be me – I am not ok*). Both are inextricably bonded, but, in black–white dynamics, pride distances itself from shame for fear of holding its vulnerability.

Race semiotics is an important concept that offers critical understanding of the processes by which cultural participants preserve the status quo through upholding the symbolic meanings of cultural signifiers to manipulate the relations of power, dominance and subjugation in society. Stuart Hall's idea of race as 'floating signifier' (Hall, 1985, 1996) saw the application of semiotics as relating very much to society's way of dividing individuals into groups within the same society, and either connecting them because they share similar characteristics or judging and pushing them to the margins because they were different. This made Hall's definition a social construct. Critical semiotics highlight where ideological agendas divide, conquer and dominate, and language in all its written, verbal and symbolic forms, becomes one of the very interesting areas to study and analyse what is underneath the social cover, particularly in western privileged nations.

As mentioned earlier, healthy shame exposes us to the workings of our conscience. In the biblical sense of the shame-exposed nakedness of Adam and Eve, who it is said were punished for their transgression in disobeying a higher power – we can see the emergence of the linguistic covering society has cultivated in order to manage the exposure and guilt associated with shame. That is to say that language acts as the semiotic cover that gatekeeps or controls shame, so as to avoid the painful feelings that emerge. Pride gives primacy to the semiotics of language, while denying this right to shame. But we know that, if pride can allow its shallowness to be exposed, the achievement of humility and grace will lead to a healthy acceptance of shame.

I have a strong notion that the more linguistically sophisticated an individual or society is, the more developed the linguistic shame cover becomes, and the more acrobatically skilled language will be exploited to manoeuvre away from the impact of shame. This manifestation usually presents as having the ability to talk one's way out of a hole, having the gift of the gab, or intellectualizing and rationalizing when it would be more threatening to be vulnerable and humble. Language, linguistic prowess and pride all become powerful gatekeepers that guard against the shame-denuding experience. In my sense-making of the factors that make atonement a struggle for any abuser, it is the energy that is utilized in keeping the shame covers on, and the investment built up in holding on to the shallowness of pride, that prevent humility and grace from being let in to repair and heal.

Sublimation in black culture

As a healing concept, it is important to recognize expressions of sublimation that may be actualized in ways not familiar to one's own culture. In black culture, for example, sublimation may not only be frequently seen in the participation in sport and athletics (competitive physical activity), but also in all genres of music and the creative arts. But I also see sublimation in the most unlikely of places, for example the unconscious expressiveness in black male interactions with each other. There is the 'limp-drag' nonchalant gait that conveys an attitude that speaks to internal scripts: 'I am in no hurry to get to no one ... I come when I am ready ... you see me when I get there ... soon come' (Jamaican patois). I see this form of sublimated expression as a quiet rebellion against white western systems that celebrate signifiers such as deadlines, time control and conformity. The genesis of this limp-drag sublimation in a black subculture that also had its own unique dress sense, hair fashion, language and music may well have come about from a creative inventiveness to reclaim control over black bodies, time, space and expectations – history has shown it was the opposite. Men were objectified as creatures of physicality, with no other use or purpose than being studding machines for human plantations and the labour force for the cotton and sugar industries. Black men were literally a unit of currency. Obedience was rewarded; rebellion was brutalized. Sublimation in the midst of this tyranny can understandably be seen as a positive move, turning negative emotions into something that can be owned and celebrated. In the limp-drag example, the sublimated gain might seem inconsequential, but the inventiveness of creating a unique subculture for good or bad reveals the hallmark of creativity, ingenuity and self-rule.

A further example of sublimation can be drawn from the black shame experience of being 'linguistically muzzled', that is not accorded a rightful place to have our voices heard (and, if they are, for our protestations of inequality to fall on deaf ears). Sublimating this aspect of shame can be seen in urban black performers who have achieved global influence through the merging of lyrics, rap and music into an art form. Many variations exist of these expressions of freedom, in musical poetry, art, song and more. Especially striking about rap music is the insistent recurring beat patterns, which provide the background and counterpoint for rapid, slangy and often boastful rhyming patter intoned by the vocalist.

The workings of these sublimated expressions are culturally distinctive. The strategies highlighted in the examples have evolved over several generations, as a way to creatively manage the residue of historical trauma and the burden of society's negative projections. It must be noted that, for the very reasons these distinctive acts of reclamation are uniquely characteristic of this group's shame recovery process, misappropriation by another group by dint of privilege is akin to a re-enactment of pillage that adds to black identity wounding.

Sublimation as healing

'Shame is a soul eating emotion ... it is one of the scars of trauma, but shame shrinks as healing grows.'

(Jung, 1989)

Sublimation is perhaps the single most important concept in understanding the work of healing and managing shame. Because shame cannot be analysed away, it has to be managed. As previously mentioned, shame is internalized badness or infantilization of the self, with the emotion residing internally as a me-myself-and-I conflict. Shame has no object, as there is no object to fight against, that is, there no one to blame – shame is what we do to ourselves. Like the internal oppressor, shame is an internal adversary, an inner enemy that inflicts wounds on its own self. Shame is punitive, beating up the insecure self.

Sublimation is the act of utilizing the energies that stem from this place of deep shame, rage, chronic anxiety and negativity, and redirecting them towards a creative endeavour, as in artistic creation or intellectual enquiry or pursuit. Sublimation is therefore healing and the act itself can be a transitional shame cover – not to hide under, but to use creatively to look after oneself in a compassionate way. We can cover up to hide the exposed self or we can cover to look after and protect our health. Freud's idea of sublimation originated while he was reading the story of a man who tortured animals as a child and later went on to become a surgeon. Freud believed that the same energy that once drove the child's sadism was eventually sublimated into positive and socially acceptable actions that benefited others (Freud, 1992).

The most dynamic stage of healing from archaic shame and the shame wounding is through the transforming process of sublimation. In this phase of therapy, the practitioner facilitates movement towards the integration of the disrupted selves by creating an encouraging and proactive environment for effective restoration, leading to hope and empowerment. The patient/client will be stronger for having had the opportunity to create straighter lines of narrative about their experiences, instead of holding on to split, disjointed and untreated areas where pain resided. Through the healing powers of therapy, clients can be helped to reframe negative internalizations of their trauma to reshape and build a more meaningful existence through vulnerability. The therapist actively encourages the client's sublimation through their engagement in their choice of activities for healing. Sublimation in this context will translate as the process of utilizing the energies that stemmed from the trauma and redirecting them towards some form of creative pursuit or intellectual endeavour, for example writing, poetry, singing, retraining or meaningful activism.

I choose to share an example of my own sublimation process while writing on generational trauma. It is a spontaneous creative activity I had not personally visited or engaged with before. However, the process was ignited by a fluid energy that took on a form that brought restorative calm and pride.

Trials of belonging here

My father told me to go to England
It is the mother country, he said
I believed his words to mean
That's where you'll work and earn good bread

So I travelled to the UK to make here my bed
And engaged in a good profession that allowed me to get ahead.

Leaving Heathrow for the first time about 46 years ago
I am struck by the strange houses I see
Are these the English abodes where people sit and drink tea?
They look like factories to me, all joined up in rows
With chimneys billowing smoke, amidst the grey atmosphere and
winter snow.

White people flash brief smiles, lips contract as quickly as they
appear;
Are they being genuine or is it something they fear?
Such strange behaviour leaves me perplexed
Did I make a mistake? Or was I making them vexed?
It's difficult to know, so I keep my head low and focus on my career.

I study and work as a nurse, first bathing white bodies
Then tending to their minds
Some react negatively, as though I had no right to such intimate
finds;
Professionals ask, how come you speak so perfect English
Your grammar doesn't match with what we see.

Who does this alien think she is?
Some overseas imposter or a colonial devotee
I question the claim *we are very accommodating*
It's ridiculously hard to reconcile such paradoxes in my own
contemplating
I quickly recognize to remain grounded
 In an environment where the experience is constantly being
confounded
That I'd have to work three times as hard,
Not to feel mentally hounded
I also realize there is no need to engage in constant apology,
When I can make sense and understand my own ontology
Being black is not my raison d'être
For I am tired of just being a colour

My existence is not to please or appease
But seize the opportunity to be my own devotee
Shining and delighting in my own luminescence.

ADDENDUM

My original idea for naming this chapter 'Shame and its vicissitudes' was
to look at the mutations of the universal emotion of shame over time and
examine its applications and presentations in many places and spaces. I
also wanted to highlight the race thread, which includes the human race-
identity thread, and ethnic-race identities elements.

To this end, I coined my BBCCT zeitgeist phenomenon, to address
social vicissitudes of shame that identify other elements of identity shame
in our social and political worlds. Although the 'BBCCT' addendum strays
into the outside world, I need to remind myself that what affects the outside
world impacts clients' mental health and psychological functioning. My
psychotherapy practice, like many others, has been majorly challenged
over the past four years in finding an ethical framework for holding
tensions of the outside world drifting into the consulting room. These
manifest as clients' preoccupations, existential fears and worries,
depressive moods and helplessness, from an overwhelming sense of the
status quo and quality of existence of humanity's future.

Shame and the BBCCT zeitgeist

The BBCCT zeitgeist is a term I have coined during the period of writing
this book. It is an acronym that represents five phenomena that have
emerged over the past four years to impact our lives powerfully and shape
our lived experiences:

- Brexit
- Black Lives Matter
- Covid-19
- Climate change
- Trumpism.

The BBCCT^2 zeitgeist has presented us with many life-changing
challenges. It has opened up and generated many discussions about

identity and, perhaps with the exception of climate change, has ignited conversations specifically about race and identity. These have intensified feelings of instability, loss of control and shame. I will specifically highlight identity shame-based issues related to each of the five phenomena.

Brexit

The United Kingdom's withdrawal from the European Union (EU) is, from a psychological perspective, akin to a sibling wishing to leave home in order to individuate from its close-knit family members. During Britain's negotiations with the powerful 27 [sibling] member states of the EU, English identity was put through one of its greatest tests, and the challenges continue. White identity shame surfaced in myriad ways at each stage of the protracted and difficult process and, often, the negotiations resembled a desperate fight on Britain's part to not lose its once celebrated imperial identity. Churchillian adages were resurrected, accompanied by a constant harping back to the British bulldog spirit; there was much evidence of the semiotic cover dynamic at play in the form of English bombast and linguistic posturing. Identity shame was the constant enemy when Britain was put on the backfoot at every twist and turn, in an attempt to leave on its terms only. The incompleteness of the individuation process has remained an exposing and shaming phenomenon that has not been named and owned.

Black Lives Matter (BLM) movement

A common expression in the black community since the BLM movement gained traction is that, in the minds of the oppressor, the movement must feel like a war, for, when you have been privileged all your life, equality feels like oppression. The success of the movement continues to be championed by mainly young black and white people to reveal the bare awful truth that the past is still powerfully present in today's race relations. The tragedy that was George Floyd's murder woke the world up to the scourge of racial inequality, and galvanized nations into action to right the wrongs of racism. The BLM spirit swiftly developed to shift the status quo and generate loud articulate voices that spoke out about inequality and injustice. The trend towards questioning old establishment norms also created a genuine fear of fragmentation. The anxiety and terror felt by sections of the majority society could be clearly detected in the following questions and laments heard, and seen on social media, at the time:

- How far is this BLM thing going to go?
- What else do these people want?
- They want to take down our statues and heroes, change our street and pub names, decolonize our school and university curricula – whatever next, when will it end?
- Should Nelson Mandela's statue be pulled down? He wasn't a saint!
- This will end in a huge cry for reparations – and this country is already stretched financially.
- Don't white lives matter?
- All lives matter.

Other threats to white identity were observed in new phrases and descriptors, which seem to have settled permanently into the English Lexicon: cancel culture, social justice warriors, the current climate of hypersensitivity, Liberalism, those snowflake liberals, being woke, wokism, Wokeville, The Woke Mob, The Woke Brigade, virtue signallers.

The weaponization of woke

It feels important to say something about the origins of the word 'woke', which seems to have been not just hijacked, but weaponized. Woke is inextricably connected to race.

The origin of this overused – and now misused – word was, once upon a time, simply the past tense of the verb to wake. It then appeared in a *New York Times* article, published in 1962, about 'phrases and words you might hear today in Harlem' (Butterworth, 2021, online).

In 1972, a character in Barry Beckham's play, *Garvey's Lives*, which was the first play ever written about Marcus Garvey, the pan-Africanist, uses the term. He says, 'I been sleeping all my life. And now that Mr Garvey done woke me up, I'm gon stay woke. And I'm gon help him wake up other black folk' (Butterworth, 2021).

This innocent, but enabling, term then became part of the BLM movement and has now broken into the white mainstream. It has been politicized and weaponized to use against people (black and white) who aspire for inclusivity and equal rights, racial justice and social justice. Like political correctness, 'woke' has now become a way of shutting up folk both black and white who try to walk on the right side of humanity. The word has become the opposite of what it originally meant, and this is a quintessential example of the working of the defensive nature of white fragility.

The timing of woke becoming part of everyday parlance coincided with Trumpism and fake news. Woke has become synonymous with the derogatory slang term 'to be a snowflake', which implies that someone, usually from the Left with liberal views, has an inflated sense of uniqueness, is oversensitive, fragile and easily offended. Again, this disparaging term snowflake has confusing connections with race at its roots: in Missouri in the early 1860s, a snowflake was the term given to a person who was opposed to the abolition of slavery, implying that such people valued white lives over black lives. But in today's political world, 'snowflakes' usually wear their heart on the right side of decency. My sense-making of both the abduction and mistreatment of these two current and ubiquitous tropes is that they highlight the strange madness in black–white dynamics and, most curious of all, the use of unconscious defences to manage white identity shame.

Social shame consequences

The resurgence of the BLM movement has threatened white ontological security. The vulnerability resulting from the public shame and realization that one of their own could be capable of such cruelty and violence to another human being, witnessed by the world in real time via social media, was overwhelmingly destabilizing. Although solidarity was created in the obvious sense of shock and outrage at man's inhumanity to another man at its most base and primordial level, the witnessing of this tragic event seemed to divide racial group responses: profound disbelief and shame on the part of whites, and rage and empathic vicarious traumatization on the part of blacks. The accompanying emotions of shame and its sister, guilt, were promptly dealt with by a flurry of reparative activity to deal with white shame and guilt. Questions such as 'What can we do to change things?' and 'We hope you might be able to tell us what we need?' became familiar to organizational consultants like me. Many of us found ourselves in great demand to facilitate constructive shame coverings in the guises of diversity workshops, unconscious bias trainings, talks on race, mental health and racism – all to assuage white shame and guilt.

Many organizations had not clearly thought through and identified their organizational needs, but went into a flight into action-type shame response mode to meet the challenges.

There were, however, a few exceptions to this frantic knee-jerk response, and the following is one such example from a predominantly white company.[3] It is, to my mind, an exemplar of a well-thought-through consultancy request that conveys authenticity, humility and clarity amidst a clear recognition and acceptance of the shame exposure of not realizing their ideals.

> We've been recommended to you, Dr Alleyne, as someone who might be able to help us explore issues of Diversity and Inclusion within our company. We've arrived at a point where we are looking for a way to do a reality check on where we are when it comes to unconscious bias, diversity, inclusivity and all that goes with that. We thought we were doing well, but think there is room for improvement.

> Historically, it has been our collective and individual desire to be as conscious and aware as we can possibly be, and to keep looking. We have actively wished for a diverse company. I think there were times when we prided ourselves that we were doing it right, and doing it well, and to some extent I think we were. However, there is always room for improvement.

> After the George Floyd killing, we had a company-wide conversation about Black Lives Matter, racism, unconscious bias, white fragility, whether we as a company had blind spots, and if so what are they.

> We discovered there were people in the company who felt they had experienced unconscious bias, who had experienced carelessness, who had not felt able to voice their experiences. We discovered that maybe we need to look into some kind of mirror in order to see what we cannot see and raise our awareness to enable us to see where and how we can make better choices and improve our behaviours.

> Looking at the work you do, we think you might be able to help us with that.

Acceptance of white shame exposure and the recognition of the need to purposefully engage in meaningful acts, in order to redress and repair, is constructive and beneficial for all concerned. Guilt that produces feelings such as 'we are getting it wrong, therefore we are bad' can leave white individuals and collectives feeling implicated by their whiteness, and lead to fears of condemnation, and accusations of colluding with racism – this is less constructive. The arousal of white identity shame as a direct consequence of the reverberations from the BLM movement has been described by white clients in therapy as very exposing for them as individuals but, paradoxically, bearable enough to be met without resistance because it was also held by the collective. The feeling was 'We are in solidarity with this shame'.

The BLM movement exposed the excluding and damaging nature of archaic organizational and societal structures, systems and practices that have gone unchallenged and disregarded for decades. People were rudely awakened to action, in the midst of guilt that limits strength, to build stronger race relations. They were called on to transcend the race shame that covers the weakness to act.

Covid-19

Winston Churchill's famous quote has kept alive a British sense of pride in being invincible. It is regularly revisited to reignite the bulldog spirit in preparation for any perceived threat to Britain's sense of its own greatness. The stirring quote protects this island's literal and psychological borders:

> 'We shall defend our island, whatever the cost may be, we shall fight on the beaches, we shall fight on the landing grounds, we shall fight in the fields and in the streets, we shall fight in the hills; we shall never surrender.'
>
> (Churchill, 2008)

Unannounced, the coronavirus, with its ferocious and infectious nature, sneaked across the borders of Britain like an invisible intruder in March 2020. Britain, like the rest of the world, was caught completely off guard by the stealth of this silent danger, whose destruction was unprecedented. The big disease with a little name (Covid) remains the apparent enemy that no volume of Churchillian bombast can defeat.

Regrouping from the devastating impact of the last two years remains society's most obvious pervasive challenge.

Initially, I observed a nonchalant approach from the government. Perhaps propped up by historical and imperial internalizations of being an unbeatable power, it casually assumed it was going to be like the tale of David and Goliath, that is we would be unbeatable in the face of this new virus. The proliferation of a kind of rhetoric revealed the Blitz spirit: *It will not defeat us; we will not be beaten; we will not surrender; we will not kowtow to this microscopic virus.* This semiotic bravado appeared to reveal the shame covering those in power, as fatalities grew into their thousands. Rather than lose face, the shame of defeat was managed by returning to an investment in old colonial scripts that promised *world-beating* methods in managing the rapid virus spread.

Covid created a particular brand of psychic rupture and psychological injury to this island-nation people and, when the defeat by the virus was numerically indisputably evident, further linguistic shame covering was employed; this time it spoke of *all of us [the world] being in this together.* Turning to the rescue of collectivism conveniently allowed shame to dissipate into a false unity of togetherness. Previous exalted claims about world-beating solutions had to be toned down and, where previously bombast had prevailed, a collective pain, shame and mourning were revealed in the process of healing. A more humbled national pride could now allow the collective to emerge from the dislocation and give way to humility, the process aptly described in this quote: 'narcissism unbridled is the enemy of integrity' (Wurmser, 1981, p. 48).

Climate change

Society's shame cover seems permanently exposed as we are continually reminded of our unhealthy relationship with the environment. Climate change has left our world in crisis, from the lack of protection of our wildlife and habitat loss, to the increase in greenhouse gas emissions, and the havoc wrought by deforestation. Climate change committees and other independent bodies around the world have had to become the shaming parents who need to remind us to protect our planet home. The symbolic fig leaf that hides transgressions from a particular societal morality has slipped to reveal the biggest culprits in the mistreatment of planet Earth. At the risk of sounding tiresome, it would be true to say that the offenders are dominant industrialized societies whose ruling structures are predominantly white, male and western.

Trumpism

The exact terms of what makes up Trumpism are controversial, and the term is sufficiently complex to overwhelm any single framework of analysis. Nevertheless, what stands out as incontrovertible in the shaping of our zeitgeist is clear – Trumpism as a movement and ideology has disregarded and, in some cases, evacuated all elements of healthy shame to make space for the following: strong hierarchical and ethnocentric social orders, tribalism, evangelical support for an omnipotent saviour, right-wing authoritarianism, social dominance, like-me biases and collective narcissism.

Society has become split, divided and attacking. Shame about sociopathic behaviour was jettisoned by one side, only to be held with shock, resentment and anger by the other. The lack of shame became currency guaranteed to attract and maintain attention. The downward spiral and lack of morality, empathy, shame and guilt have all contributed to a global experience of civilization reverting to a regressive phase of social evolution.

The societal impact of the BBCCT zeitgeist has been inescapable for the obvious reason that each of the five phenomena has emerged within a recent four-year period. They have overlapped each other, layering the impact of society's shame and exposing our vulnerabilities as human beings. Additionally, these phenomena, which highlight the major psychological themes of national and racial identity crisis, human disconnection and loss of empathy, all powerfully contribute to the arousal and familiar presence of racial hauntings.

CHAPTER 6

Shame and its role in black identity wounding

Introduction

Identity shame arises in many contexts: when we are not seen or appreciated for who we are; when we feel the absence or loss of the positive gaze from loved ones or the outside world; when we are denied the positive mirroring of who we truly see ourselves to be. Identity shame is connected to historical wounding, which is the genesis of this original wound. At its deepest level, however, identity shame results from the loss of not having a rightful place in the human world.

At the time of writing, the Euro 2020 football final had whipped the country into a celebratory and good-natured mood. High spirits and a patriotic fervour were infectious, and there was something palpably refreshing, celebratory and unifying about the warm embrace that was openly given to England's racially diverse team. Yet it was quite striking, but not surprising to many of Britain's minorities, to see how swiftly the three black strikers' race became the target of so-called fans' anger and rage when England lost to Italy. A tweet in response to the harassment captures the identity-shaming phenomenon: 'When you score, you're English and a hero. When you miss, you're other and an immigrant.'

In this example, the subtext would translate thus: if the team is not 'us', then 'we' didn't lose. It wasn't the nation, or 'my' people who prevented football from 'coming home', it was 'them' – 'they' failed us. It would seem that, within an instant of England's loss, ALL players of colour were designated the label of 'other' and quickly relegated to the status of being more 'physical' and less 'strategic'; they were not 'clever technicians'. The disappointment seemed to be couched in the silent chorus of 'the other failed us'.

The apparent worst online social media insults that were hurled at the black players reduced them to the subhuman category of animal (namely monkey, ape or gorilla) and Neanderthal. How is it that in the beautiful game such ugly gestures are the chosen forms of insult to black players? Within the collective unconscious of the white antagonists lie these learnt, aggressive behaviours. They are often exhibited by baying crowds with snarled and hateful-looking faces, who, paradoxically, appear to be the more feral and rabidly wolf-like in their stance, rather than the humans at whom they direct their hatred. It forever remains one of humanity's strangest ironies in race relations that a person or group, feeling powerless with their lot, can seemingly simply elevate their position by projecting their disgruntlement and unhappiness onto the 'other' or group whom they perceive to be inferior and below their rank. Blacks are usually relegated to the bottom of this hierarchical human chain, where their humanity seems not to matter.

Every incident of brutality on black lives adds to the silent shame wound, a wound that deepens the perennial question *What is this hate all about?* How can one explain the astonishing facts of black men being shot by more bullets than white men or tasered with higher voltages for longer periods, and being physically restrained by three times the number of officers that are necessary to uphold the law? How does it stand to reason that an experienced American Special Weapons and Tactics (SWAT) team, normally made up of police skilled in military hardware, and trained to manage a host of highly dangerous situations (such as threats of terrorism and hostage taking), utilize this level of expertise on unarmed black men? SWAT teams and their comparable units in the western world are trained precision marksmen and women; yet, when these experienced law enforcers are faced with the black male, something primordial in their collective make-up seems to be activated, which makes normal fear quickly escalate to a terror of being engulfed by something savage and inhuman. When we are privy to the news that a total of 50 rounds of bullets were rapidly deployed by the New York Police Department (NYPD) in both plain clothes and undercover on three unarmed black males in the New York borough of Queens on 25 November 2006, where one was killed outright and two severely wounded, and all white officers were found not guilty, the irrationality of such a regular occurrence leaves the shame wound question *Don't black lives matter?*

The answer must lie somewhere in my concept: **What ceases to be a coincidence must be a phenomenon**. And what is the phenomenon? I posit the notion that, at an unconscious level, black people are still not perceived as fully actualized human beings, and the black male not only subhuman, but dangerous and to be feared. The unspoken nature of this dimension of race means that, at a collective level, the dominant other holds this irrational belief somewhere within the collective psyche. And, as with all unheeded phenomena, there is an element of acting out which thrives (namely the perpetuation of racism and identity shaming), and acting in, which continues (namely the shame wound and ongoing feelings of incompleteness and feeling not 'normal').

No other racial group is linked to the category of mammals – a subhuman species – like the black race. Jews are perhaps the closest minority group to blacks, only in the sense that a major aspect of this group's racial discrimination arises from their supposed 'different' biological characteristics. Alongside biology and in the ugly face of anti-Jewish racism is the old charge for their execution of Christ, and their purported position of world domination in finance and business, all presenting a triple whammy complex discrimination. As with black transgenerational and intergenerational trauma, similar consequences have faced this people and their progeny. The ability of the Jewish diaspora to heal from its brutal past and negotiate the vicissitudes of collective trauma is, in my view, an exemplar of collective healing from historical wounding and identity shame.

Identity shame

Identity shame is perhaps the single most important variable that overarches so much of what is seen in the psyches of wounded people – a bold statement that can be backed up by the phenomenon of its constant presence in clinical practice. Just about every black therapist found themselves with a full therapy practice following the reverberations of the BLM movement, suggesting that, in the area of generational trauma, the complex threads of shame remain deeply woven into black people's internal systems. The trauma triggers that brought black people into therapy following the murder of George Floyd was particularly disturbing, yet easily understood.

Identity shame is observable in black clients where, even when successes are achieved on full merit, there seem to be deep and troubling doubts about personal entitlement to such accomplishments. It operates in ways that make black people feel that they are not allowed the simultaneous privilege of being both masterpiece and a work in progress. Shame in this context can lead to imposter syndrome (also mentioned in Chapter 2).

Black identity shame scripts

All of the black identity shame scripts mentioned below, whether internalized or externalized, are examples of a complex phenomenon that requires some further explanation. According to the *Oxford English Dictionary*, the definition of shame is a painful emotion caused by a strong sense of guilt, embarrassment, unworthiness or disgrace. In psychoanalytic terms, it resembles emotions like jealousy, envy, spite, love, hatred, and pride. It might be related to feelings such as, 'I cannot see myself as I want others to see me' and, in this sense, would become an introjection (Rycroft, 1972), that is the taking in or internalization of external influences, such as judgement by others, with a resultant defensive structure. Jacobson described it as 'a reaction formation to exhibitionistic wishes' (Jacobson, 1964, p. 100). In this sense, it is a rigid defence structure built into the character and used against the risk of being humiliated, a risk viewed as continually present in racial and cultural oppression.

Black identity shame indicates the presence of narcissistic wounding, which is about wounding to self-esteem that triggers self-doubt and self-hate – not self-love, as narcissism implies. The narcissistically wounded self turns shame inwards, where it has no capacity to grow and, eventually, it has to project it outwards, most often in a critical, blaming or damning way of the self and others: these responses can be seen in the horizontal axis in Figure 6.1. In this sense, the disenfranchised self can assume positions of being, for example, **the martyr** ('Nothing gets done unless I step in and take over'), **the over-achiever** ('I must do that degree to bolster my CV before I even think about marriage and children'), **the victim** ('I can't change things, so why try'), **the scapegoat** ('If things go missing I know I'll get blamed – the black one is not to be trusted'), **the**

loser ('It makes life easy for everyone, so I do what people want'), the unfortunate ('Life seems to leave me at the back of queue ... never to be chosen').

Conversely, shame responses on the vertical axis may be categorized as withdrawal and avoidance, and can be identified in comments such as 'At 49, it is pointless attempting a tenth round of IVF to become a mum ... it is too dangerous to bring a black kid into this racist world' and 'After 20 years of being invisible in the eyes of my white peers, why should I bother applying for the senior post'.

The Compass of Shame (4 general responses)

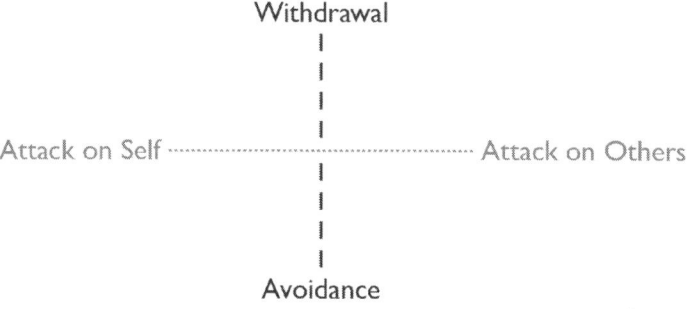

Figure 6.1 The compass of shame

Identity wounding can be perpetuated when someone positions themselves in life in a way that limits expectations and denies entitlements, for example not speaking up for what one wants or needs means not allowing one's voice to be heard, or an individual using language to describe their world in limiting ways, for example through the use of 'we' ('We don't do that in our culture' or 'That's for white people'). Identity shame can also be fostered through personal scripts that become codes and a conduct for living. The pessimistic negative mindset will adopt a particular position in their world; the following verbatim statements from my 2006 doctoral research highlight the unheeded emotion of identity shame, both internalized and often externalized:

- 'As black people we don't seem to come together and sustain our collective effort for any length of time.'
- 'We give lousy service, and we are not patient, no wonder we

are not good in business ... we expect to get rich quick ... we are not like the Asians who seem to struggle for years in their little corner shop ... and before you know it, they own the whole block with their food shops and restaurants ... we always want it to happen today.'

- 'We get too familiar with each other [as black people] and short-change our own ... it's like we expect so little of each other and for ourselves, that why we end up giving and receiving little back.'

- 'I had to catch myself the other day ... I was doing just the same as my white colleagues, thinking he [the black manager] was up to no good ... and there was no real reason for this.'

- 'I know I am driven ... no matter how much I do and achieve, I always feel I need to do more ... always going that extra mile ... giving just that little extra to be noticed ... it's so neurotic.'

- 'Sometimes in meetings, my voice feels so out of place ... I can't describe it ... it's deep ... and the difference sets you apart ... alienates you ... you know what I mean. My family think I sound like the powerful Maya Angelou [respected black writer and poet] but at work people make you feel odd ... you are seen as aggressive, intimidating, and scary ... it's enough to give you a complex.'

Carrying identity shame leaves a person with the 'struggle script' that says, 'I must always wear the badge that honours suffering and hardship'. This script might prevent a client in therapy from rightfully gaining the status of worthiness and entitlement to triumphs. The unconscious wearing of this mark of oppression presents a false notion that wins that are achieved too effortlessly are not legitimate; only transcendence through suffering is worthy. These 'I must prove myself' shame scripts can be crosses to bear and make it hard for a person to be compassionate and loving towards themseves. Even when accolades and praise are offered by others, such compliments may seem hard to accept or they may fall on deaf ears, perpetuating feelings of not being worthy of receiving anything good.

Black identity shame often covers the pain of trauma and feelings of inadequacy. The following verbatim scripts highlight a defensive (and protective) mindset and value system that try to deal with pain:

- 'I am not interested in theory – I go by my instincts.'

- 'What's the point in trying – you'll only get no for an answer.'
- 'Promotion is not for me – it forces you to conform to the system – I don't want to lose who I am as a black person.'
- 'I don't do deference where white people are concerned.'
- 'I can never trust white people – I have a healthy disrespect where they are concerned.'
- 'You can't afford to show vulnerability – people will walk all over you.'
- 'When things get too much, I just walk away.'
- 'You take me as you see me – what you see is what you get – like it or lump it.'
- 'This is who I am – I say what's on my mind – ain't changing for no one.'
- 'I don't trust anyone but myself.'

William Grier and Price Cobbs (1968) coined the term 'healthy paranoia' and it is clear that the more defensive scripts are usually rooted in a lack of trust. Grier and Cobbs described this concept from the adaptations observation among blacks in trying to function effectively in a predominantly white society. They caution, however, practitioners to be aware of distinguishing healthy paranoia from psychopathology, since it acts as a defence against an oppressive environment that has been hostile to the interests of black people. However, as seen in the aforementioned scripts, the protection adaptation limits trust, but should nevertheless facilitate the therapist's understanding of this mechanism used for survival in black life.

The internal oppressor

Much has been written about black internalized oppression (Akbar, 1996; Freire, 1970; hooks, 1996; Lipsky, 1987; Lorde, 1984), which is the process or action of absorbing (consciously or unconsciously) the values and beliefs of the oppressor and subscribing to stereotypes and misinformation about one's group. Such a process leads to low self-esteem, self-hate, the disowning of one's own and other minority groups, and other complex defensive interpersonal behaviours that influence and impair quality of life. Although this concept has been fully explored by the writers mentioned above and many others, the phenomenon of the **internal oppressor** is still understudied and unappreciated and thus largely unknown in the field of psychology, counselling and psychotherapy. Only a few (Lorde, 1984: Alleyne, 2004c) have dealt specifically with the concept of the oppressor within the self. I maintain that the internal oppressor – an aspect of self that becomes the inner tyrant or enemy – is distinct from internalized oppression, which is essentially the internalization of external shaming experiences that invalidate our authenticity and inhibit our personal agency.

The internal oppressor and generational trauma

Like shame itself, the internal oppressor is an aspect of the self that holds on to historical and intergenerational baggage and re-enacts the trauma transmissions through the generations. I use the term 'baggage' in this context to describe all that that people of colour carry around within ourselves unwillingly and, sometimes, unknowingly. Shame is inextricably linked to the internal oppressor; shame says, 'I am bad, unworthy, not good enough, not lovable'. The internal oppressor is my internal adversary, my own enemy, my discrediting-self.

In terms of black–white relations, the internal oppressor creates a post-slavery/post-colonial mindset that colours black people's dealings with the white other. It influences our interrelational dynamics and attachment with this other and may even collude unconsciously with the prevailing external difficulties. Crucially, the internal oppressor seems to be ever present but lies dormant for the most part; it is only when it is in contact with an external oppressive situation – real, perceived or a mixture of both – that the historical memories are reawakened, opening up old wounds that can lead to silent, invisible rewounding of the self and identity. Prejudices, projections, intergenerational wounds and the vicissitudes of our historical past are all aspects of this inner tyrant. They are kept alive within the transgenerational transmission of trauma, suggesting a degree of a persistent post-traumatic syndrome in black people's existence.

Alongside these historical aspects of the internal oppressor are other factors, such as our narcissistic injuries, personal unresolved difficulties where power and control predominate and painful unresolved family dynamics. The nature of the internal oppressor appears to be the sum of these characteristics, which rest in the shadow of the self. The legacy of black people's historical past, along with the burden of internalized oppression, both seem to play a crucial part in shaping pre-transference relationships and attachment patterns to the white other.

The picture being created here is one of the past and present, as well as internal and external factors, being inextricably linked and fused. This can lead to forms of codependence which I refer to as cultural enmeshment. Enmeshment in a broader sense is the subject of the next chapter.

How black people manage this aspect of the self is a key factor in achieving ontological and mental health security. For symbolic emphasis, I am inclined to borrow the current semiotic race symbol of the killing knee. Although it is important to reclaim the right to black life by claiming the solemn ritual of taking the knee, we must also not forget the important work of dealing with the internal oppressor, which behoves us to remove the knee *from our own necks*, so that our negative internalizations and shame-based traumas can be released and allow us full breadth – and breath – to heal injured souls and archaic historical wounds.

Impact on relationships

Black identity shame has the potential to threaten individual relationships within the black community, whereby we act out feelings of indignation, anger and frustration at other black (and brown) people who 'show us up' (Lipsky, 1987). Lipsky noted that this acting out is often taken out on those closest to us and destroys our relationships with each other, leading to divisions and divisiveness among ourselves and also in relation to other minority ethnic groups.

Black identity shame can have an impact on our relationship with our children, who may face fierce criticism from black mothers and fathers whose honourable intention of 'disciplining' gets mixed up with notions of obedience, submission and compliance (paradoxically, these were the very requirements that slave owners imposed on their slaves in order to maintain order and the state of subjugation). The need to control, and the fear of being 'shown up' in front of others, invariably leads to aspects of parenting that destroy the development of autonomy, self-assurance and confidence in black children. From my therapeutic observations of black Caribbean, African and Asian (extended) family dynamics, both of the psychological separating out processes needed for autonomy and individuation seem to develop at a slower pace in comparison with white British/Eurocentric (nuclear) family dynamics. This latter point raises key issues for practitioners regarding what they might see as constituting a healthy, 'normal' individuation process, and by what and whose yardsticks it is measured.

Black identity shame has played a large part in creating difficulties for black groups in sustaining combined and collective efforts. Many a group's efforts have ended prematurely and/or been aborted because of an apparent loss of faith in the power of groups. I have witnessed many black groups, business and social ventures that were birthed with great purpose and impact, only to dissolve and disappear within a short period of time. Longevity seems an elusive reward. This may be related to how life is viewed as influenced by the internalized scripts set out on pages 117 and 118.

Related to this, black identity shame can lead to cultural isolation, which is the withdrawing from other black people and other minority ethnic groups; consequently, we act out our hurt, embarrassment, fear, dislike and mistrust by dividing ourselves among each other and creating hierarchies. Such divisions can be seen to occur among African–Caribbean people, British-born blacks, black African nationals, mixed-heritage individuals and Indians/other Asians. Further divisions are created in the way we label each other within these minority ethnic groups – terms such as 'house slave', 'coconut', 'field nigger' and the very recent 'having brown privilege' are all used among black and brown people and divide and rank us within a social order. Shame has left us with complexes about skin colour (colourism or shadism) and ethnic ranking, as summed up in the Bill Broonzy song 'Black, Brown, and White', first recorded in March 1952 which strangely became a rhyme adopted by both black African and black Caribbean children (and one which was familiar to me in the school yard):

> If you are white, you are right
> If you're brown, stick around
> If you're black, get the hell back.

White European enslavers, including the British, manipulated human beings into a pecking order of ethnic groups, races, and skin colours and tones acceptable to them. History and contemporary life both testify to the fact that lighter skin tones are more acceptable at the front of society's stage: brown people are tolerated as providing key services and seen to cause less trouble; black people are objectified and/or rejected as inferior and less able. I refer to this human ranking system as a 'hierarchy of oppression', one that perpetuates these divisions and identity shame wounding. Its impact has left a lasting legacy of complexes and divisions among black people, people of mixed race and those of south Asian backgrounds and ethnicities to this day.

Identity shame and its resultant tendency to isolate us from our cultural and racial roots also find expression in our semi-conscious and unconscious choices in so many aspects of life: our choice of partnerships and close friends; social pursuits; the way we dress; the accents and mannerisms we adopt; the choice of names for our offspring; our racial positioning that situates us closer to white ideals; and in our sense of identity as a whole. Cultural shame and its complex manifestations are a major theme that presents both the white and the black therapist with immense challenges and, in order to work with this central and important psychological injury, one must understand the historical and intergenerational contexts, along with the structure and nature of the trauma.

Black identity wounding in practice

Personal experiences in training

Being black in Britain in the early 1970s was a character-toughening experience, but nothing was as difficult as the emotionally challenging occurrences I experienced during my training as a counsellor and psychotherapist, and subsequent (but aborted) journey to train as a group analyst. The following two examples tell the story of the kinds of shame experience that trainee counsellors and psychotherapists of colour will endure at some point during their training.

An experience of black identity wounding as a trainee psychotherapist

In one of my psychotherapy trainings, where the programme was based on a three-part structure of lecture, group supervision and experiential group, a personal experience of shame left painful memory imprints and marred what should have been a safe and positive journey.

I attended a weekly one-and-a-half-hour experiential group, consisting of approximately eighteen white students, one person of colour and a white group facilitator. The therapeutic aim of the meetings was for us to therapeutically engage with whatever evolved naturally for us from week to week. The facilitator's role was to 'field' the dynamics with the main purpose of enabling us, the students, to learn from the intimate engagement of sharing, caring, taking risks and baring souls. Being the only visibly black member of the group was not an issue for me (this was quite common in my life) but my 'differentness' was made even more visible in a shaming turn of events.

In one of the earlier formation sessions of the group, a white group member who had twice referred to me as 'coloured' was gently corrected as I explained that, outside of South Africa, the term was defunct and that I would prefer the term 'black'. Encouragingly, I went on to say that I was OK with being seen as a black woman and elaborated that I was not embarrassed by the term, nor felt I needed to apologize for being black. I was gentle and respectful without compromising on something deeply important to me. I was not surprised, however, when it was revisited at the following group session. In the check-in, the white group member whom I had challenged the previous week chose to share a dream when it came to her turn to check in. With a very woeful demeanour, she told the group that she had found her dream extremely disturbing and did not know what to make of it. She then proceeded to tell the dream, avoiding all eye contact with me but somehow seeming to catch the eyes of everyone else in the group. She described being chased by a big black gorilla that 'chumped' bits out of her arm. This snippet was all that she could remember, and she proceeded to look visibly distressed before bursting into tears. The dream-teller finished her story, concluding that it was the most terrifying experience she had ever had and, with wet doe eyes, looked pleadingly at the facilitator asking *What is it all about?* One group member immediately piped up to say that it sounded like a very scary nightmare. Nothing else was said thereafter and a deathly silence ensued for what seemed like a very long time.

What stunned me about this group experience was that, in the moment the word 'gorilla' was vocalized, seventeen pairs of eyes swiveled, in unison, in my direction; some looks were sheepish and embarrassed, some darted uncomfortably between the floor and me; others, emboldened in a knowing way, stared with looks that said *Yes it's you she is referring to – you were the aggressive big black gorilla chomping bits out of her arm.* My swift understanding of the situation told me that the nature of the dream content was significant material from the unconscious realm of the white dream-teller. My analysis of what the heck was going on could be summed up thus: my challenge the previous week was not appreciated. It exposed the dream-teller's naivety and ignorance about black people and race. It played on her mind to the point that when it reached the unconscious realm, it terrorized and threatened her personal pride. The unconscious shame resistance then functioned in a stereotypical way to diminish, dehumanize and relegate the black me-attacker to a savage, mauling beast.

Seventeen pairs of staring eyes on hidden faces proved to be one of my most core-shaming experiences during training, and a particularly informative one that taught me more of the powerful workings of deeply buried unconscious black–white race dynamics at play. I had hoped for this powerful experiential group experience to be a rich source of processing and deep learning on many levels for all of us, namely the opportunity to process shame experienced by the shamer and the shamed, but the opportunity was roundly killed off by one of the most powerful dynamics in race relations – indifference – lack of genuine interest to learn and stay with the discomfort of this powerful learning.

Postscript: how shame is compounded and protracted

The long and uncomfortable silence that followed this astonishing group dynamic was an additional wound, on top of being marked by the gaze of my seventeen white peers and the white facilitator. Other wounds were reopened: the intergenerational shame wound of my 8 year old self, at being in the wrong car and in the wrong place, was triggered; the overarching transgenerational wound was activated in the re-experiencing of a familiar hurt by white people. What compounded the whole painfully wounding experience were two additional facts: the white facilitator, who seemed impotent and pitiful in that situation, did absolutely nothing about the loud silence in the group. My peers chose to leave *the accident* and me, *the victim*, unattended and unsupported, dying a silent death of shame in the middle of what was meant to be safe, holding space during my training.

This experience has stayed with me and shines a very bright light on what I know to be the experience of many other black and brown students as they negotiate their counselling and therapy trainings, even to this day.

My shame experience and my identity wounding could have been helped in so many ways, if the group facilitator had been able, confident and competent enough to hold, contain and field the underlying tenets of this powerful exchange. It would have also helped if the facilitator had interjected with an enquiry about what was in the group silence. He could have facilitated by asking where each group member retreated or disappeared to within themselves, and whether they felt able to share their findings. He could have issued a gentle challenge for the group to give voice to the unspoken issues in the dream, and used the powerful dream symbols to explore the manifest elements and latent content of the dream. He could have also done all of aforementioned, while attending to the very important point that shame issues require careful therapeutic holding and space to repair.

An aspect of this holding and repair would have been to ensure that all further group dynamics were contained, so as not to run the risk of reshaming me (the shamed) and the dream-teller (the shamer) whose particular dream content was an attempt to manage their shame by unconscious expulsion (sharing it in the group to fellow white peers) and dehumanizing the attacker (me). A very competent intercultural facilitator, who bravely integrates the importance of 'unorthodox teaching' (my term) in experiential groups, might have concluded that what had been powerfully and painfully experienced in the group was one of the most primitive (basal) ways that fear is processed in specifically black–white race dynamics.

An experience of black identity wounding in group analysis

Especially difficult was my analytic group experience where, as the only black person in a group of eight white members (including the facilitator, known as the 'conductor'), I felt subjected to repetitive microaggressions that left me feeling completely traumatized and unsupported. Throughout, the facilitator seemed completely impotent and sightless to the phenomenon of subtle and not-so-subtle intercultural dynamics within the group. As a consequence, the painful experiences of being 'marked' and targeted as a repository for the group's negative and unwanted feelings slowly induced a crippling emotional effect. It was as if I truly understood the word 'trauma' for the first time, especially in relation to my race and my black identity. The experiences were subtle yet powerful, and culminated in a profound feeling of isolation, invisibility, not belonging and being an insignificant anomaly. Conversations happened around me where I was not included, nor felt I had room to join in. I gradually sunk into a dark and lonely place of becoming a selective mute.

On one of the rare occasions when I spoke, I offered a perspective on customs which was the topic being discussed. I shared that it was quite common in the Caribbean, where I was born, to mark the birth of a baby or christen a new home before moving in by pouring libation (rum on the ground), to bless ancestors and the gods. I remember loud laughter erupting in the predominantly white group following my contribution, which felt mocking with the intent to shame. When one group member dismissed my contribution as sounding like native witchcraft, and another asked if the activity was tribal, I bristled with indignation. With a polite smile, however, I explained that I thought my cultural ritual was absolutely no different to the ritual the Queen performed at ceremonies where she is invited to smash a bottle of champagne on the bow of a new ship before it sails. I added that I saw both activities as similar rituals to mark rites of passage, only culturally expressed differently. I recall sensing a palpable stiffening discomfort within the group and, if the group energy had had a voice, it would have said *How dare you align your crude native ritual with the tradition and pomp of our royal ceremony?*

Both the group shame language and shame behaviours worsened after I had dared to demonstrate that I had a voice and was entitled to share and contribute. But my attempts to be included were silently and brutally taken away. I felt as if I had been 'sent to Coventry'.[1] Having endured months of this exiled treatment, I was further confused by the actions of the white facilitator who gently placed a hand on my shoulder and quietly confessed to being 'very sorry for what was happening'.

I still think about how much it would have helped me and the group to name, explore, understand and work through these difficult group issues if the facilitator had had a fuller understanding and ability to hold and field the virulent nature of race dynamics. Instead, they were all left well hidden in plain sight to die a death with no name. My (white) clinical supervisor, who was very supportive in my psychotherapy practice throughout the whole of this experience, kept asking why I was choosing to stay in the group – and I did stay, for three painful years. My justification was that I needed to be sure that I was not running away from an important life-enhancing challenge; furthermore, I sincerely hoped things might change. Towards the end of this twice weekly, three-year long experience, I sat simply staring at the floor. I became mute.

Wounding in the workplace

Over the years, the cumulative experiences of these unheeded forms of oppression have resulted in a strong desire in me to be free from its chokehold and participate in the liberation of others (students, counsellors, psychotherapists, trainers, group facilitators) on both sides of the black and white divide. It is the main reason I engage in my work as consultant to organizations, specializing in addressing race and other diversity conflict in the workplace. It is why I facilitate workshops on themes of race and cultural diversity at various therapy training bodies and why I regularly give talks and lectures in these areas.

The nature of workplace difficulties regularly discussed in therapy led to my acute interest and research into understanding the particularly devastating way that stress was affecting black people in the workplace – a place we spend a good chunk of our lifetime. The phenomenon of workplace stress for black and minority ethnic workers that I observed was insidious, and took its toll on black psychological health in destructive ways, mentally crippling the lives of many by damaging confidence and self-esteem. It made some workers ultimately lose their livelihoods, as many could not face the workplace again, whereas others emigrated back to the Caribbean and Africa for an easier life. A few developed severe stress-related illnesses that ended their lives, leaving loved ones behind.

Over the course of my 30 years as a psychotherapist and my work with black identity wounding, I have come to explore the phenomenon in quite some depth. It begs some serious questions: do black people hurt differently? If they do, how is that hurt manifested and why is it different?

As I explored these questions in clinical practice and my own academic studies, I started to see the emergence of a series of events, a set of interpersonal interactions and dynamics that lead to a miserable entrapment in the group and consequent expulsion from the group. These dynamics, akin to a mental deportation, take place in a number of different settings where black and brown people find themselves the minority in predominantly white groups.

This Spiral of Events (Alleyne, 2004b), which will be explored in detail below, can be clearly seen in the following account of one worker's experience of shame and black identity wounding in the workplace.

Case study: Mavis

Mavis was a 37-year-old black woman who was born in Jamaica and came to this country as a child. She worked as ward sister on a unit for elderly people and managed a predominantly white female staff group and one black nursing assistant. Mavis had cherished a previous reputation for being proficient, professionally capable in her senior position, a conscientious worker and well respected. She was known for speaking her mind and was sometimes seen as difficult for this reason. Mavis noticed that her management strategies were constantly questioned and debated, that her instructions to staff were deliberately disregarded, and she frequently faced subtle challenges by some staff who appeared to support white patients' complaints and requests to not be touched by Mavis or the black nursing assistant.

On one occasion, Mavis reported overhearing one of the white nurses saying that she (Mavis) was too qualified for her own good and that if she wanted to boss people around, she should go back to where she came from. This was very upsetting for Mavis and she felt terribly betrayed. When she challenged her team, she was met with a collective silence. Such situations continued and the lack of intervention from management began to eat away at her. A once confident and competent manager, Mavis started to make mistakes at work, take time off regularly for emotional stress and depression, and felt less generous in her duty to care. Over the eight months following the betrayal incident, relationships on the ward broke down further and management stepped in and acted against Mavis's ability to manage. During the next nine months, she remained on long-term sick leave suffering with the following: high blood pressure; hair loss due to obsessive hair pulling (trichotillomania); obsessive skin picking (dermatillomania); poor sleep; loss of appetite and menstrual cycle; irritability; obsessive and paranoid thoughts of being targeted; agoraphobia and deep mental stress – all of this while being embroiled in a bitter battle to fight her case. Mavis was eventually dismissed from her job at the same time as deciding to retire on medical grounds aged 40, due to a diagnosis of clinical depression and severe stress. She then developed late-onset diabetes and neuralgia (nerve pain), and attended twice-weekly therapy with me for four years.

The initial work in therapy primarily paid attention to the manifest content of Mavis's workplace trauma experience. This work required a here-and-now focus on the issues and distress that were the result of Mavis's emotional injuries in the workplace. As she had become so wounded by her deeply distressing experiences, it made sense for the therapy at that stage to just be about providing a holding and containing space where she could feel heard, held, understood and believed. The therapy later moved into the latent content of her trauma, by dealing with older traumas that had been activated by the workplace trauma. An intergenerational aspect of Mavis's trauma was painfully reopened as she was reminded of her mother's and father's experiences of racism in the NHS. They had both given many years of dedication to the institution, while enduring similar experiences of racial discrimination and hostility in the workplace. Therapy was the mainstay to Mavis's recovery and, with renewed mental energy and a determination, she fought a bitter battle to seek justice to clear her name. Mavis reopened her workplace grievances and she finally won her employment case for workplace race discrimination and unfair dismissal. The Tribunal's ruling awarded her substantial compensation for the workplace injustices endured over a long period without support.

The postscript to this case study is one of the saddest I have encountered in the whole of my clinical practice. Following the outcome of her mental ordeal, Mavis and her family decided to emigrate to the Caribbean for a less stressful and easier life. They built a bespoke home and relocated soon after the house was completed, saying goodbye to family, friends and the UK, the place where their children were born and the country they had called home for most of their lives. After one blissful year of life in the sun, Mavis suffered a heart attack and died.

Many readers will identify with the fact that, generally speaking, the workplace can be very stressful for a variety of reasons; what is particularly significant for a minority ethnic person, however, is the extent and impact on every aspect of the self – physical, emotional, psychological, mental, spiritual and racial. My doctoral research indicated that this was widespread for minorities. Like tinnitus (constant ringing in the ear), the experiences of the marginalized are distressing for the sufferer, but silent to those around. The quiet acts of oppression such as those experienced by Mavis remain an unheeded dimension of race relations and, although subtle and seemingly insignificant initially, their effects are insidiously powerful and damaging. In some cases, these unconscious and conscious biases increase in intensity to become blatant racial assaults, for example the case of one respondent who reported that a picture of a gorilla was drawn on his coffee mug by office workmates who brushed it aside as something that was done 'just for a laugh'.

Underpinning the title of the book are the inescapable themes of identity shame and identity wounding, which add to the trauma and burden of heritage.

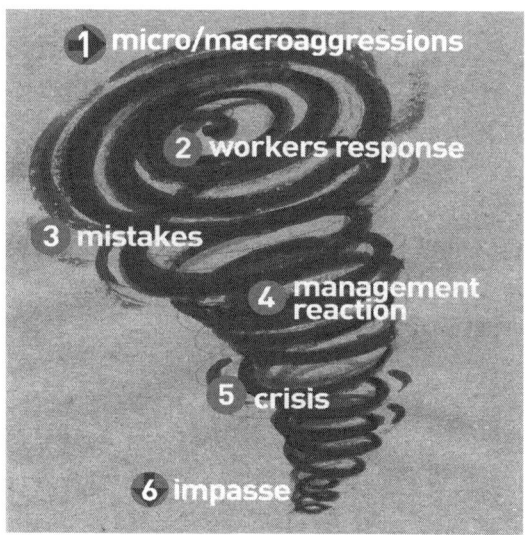

Figure 6.2 Spiral of Events (Alleyne, 2004a, 2004b, 2004c)

I present my Spiral of Events (Alleyne, 2004a, b and c), to illustrate the downward trajectory of Mavis's story and the damaging workplace experience endured. The pictorial example clearly lays out the situation for further understanding of the wearing down and destructive processes of the phenomenon of workplace oppression.

Stage 1: Micro- and macroaggressions of the Spiral of Events, had started with Mavis having to deal with seemingly minor incidents that cause offence and upset:

- her management strategies were constantly questioned and debated
- instructions to staff were disregarded
- subtle challenges by white staff who appeared to support white patients' complaints
- white patients asking not to touched by Mavis or her black nursing assistant
- overhearing gossip that she (Mavis) was too qualified for her own good
- she should go back to where she came from if she wanted to boss people around
- shamed by being publicly corrected by seniors
- white staff seldomly making proper eye contact with her in her capacity as senior staff in charge
- being ignored and excluded from normal pleasantries expected in professional interactions during the course of a work shift.

These are all acts of microaggression (Russell, 1998) and, although they are seemingly minor events, the impact on the individual over time is considerable. As former president, Bill Clinton, publicly acknowledged in his 29 March 1997 weekly radio address, Federal News Service:

> ... racism ... is not confined to acts of physical violence ... Every day [black people] and other minorities are forced to endure quiet acts of racism – bigoted remarks ... job discrimination ... These may not harm the body, but ... it does violence to their souls. We must stand against such quiet hatred just as surely as we condemn acts of physical violence.

> William J. Clinton, The President's Radio Address Online by Gerhard Peters and John T. Woolley, The American Presidency Project www.presidency.ucsb.edu/node/224472 (accessed 1 June 2022)

Violence to the soul causes deep wounding, shame and feelings of infantilization. The black person becomes cautious, vigilant and hyper-sensitive to future possible wounding or hurt; meanwhile, the microaggressions continue. There may also be examples of macroaggression (Russell, 1998) alongside. These are seemingly minor attacks on the person's group or culture. Such examples can be the over-usage of adjectives such as 'aggressive', 'threatening' and 'difficult', when referring to black people, or viewing black men only in terms of the physical and as dangerous. Such words and narrow perceptions of race can eventually 'mark' the individual and wound them. When these situations occur, they are experienced simultaneously as a collective assault and an assault on the individual that highlights their difference in a negative and reductionist fashion

The relentless oppositional blocks from the micro- and macro-aggressions Mavis experienced, together with the impact of racially biased reactions to her seniority, left her feeling deeply wounded, and further betrayed by her managers, whom she received no help from when she complained about her plight.

Stage 2: Mavis responds to her terrible treatment at work by asserting her responsibilities. Her challenges were met with collective silence, which had the effect of disregarding the importance of her workplace reality. Comments, such as, 'You are being too sensitive', 'You have a chip on your shoulder', 'You are being difficult', led Mavis to try even harder to rescue the situation. Her hurt was mostly not recognized and, when they were, her feelings were dismissed. Mavis began to turn her pain inwards with damaging effects to her professional and personal self-esteem. Over time, she became more preoccupied and felt herself resigning to a state of professional impotence and a feeling that her suffering was invisible to others. Being not seen and believed in her distress added greatly to her initial experiences of the workplace trauma.

Stage 3: Mistakes and slip-ups become the visible signs of the onset of Mavis's depression – a clinical state of desperation, despondency and loss of control to change her circumstances. Mavis becomes obsessively preoccupied with her situation, leading to a loss of the concentration necessary to function well and maintain her high professional standards.

Stage 4: Management's reaction – from having initially adopted a complicit role in managing Mavis's workplace difficulties, which leaves Mavis feeling unsupported and undervalued, management's response is now swift, harsh and excessive. They overreact, showing a great lack of skills in dealing appropriately with Mavis's first outward signs of not coping and they act in an unfair and incompetent manner. Her mistakes and slip-ups are immediately noticed and highlighted in a shaming and exposing manner, often in the presence of Mavis's rebellious white staff. Her shame is compounded. Her 'penalty' was to be given an increased workload, which, when challenged by Mavis, was met by a threat to transfer her to another department. Following these events Mavis described a change in the workplace culture, described as 'conspiratorial', otherwise experienced as management closing ranks. As Mavis's situation at work continues to spiral downward, where she is convinced she is being set up to fail, she finally accepts that she is a victim of workplace bullying, harassment and victimization. She is forced into a corner of much ego-justification, which becomes her defence against being devalued and made to feel powerless.

Stage 5: Crisis – at this stage, Mavis's workplace difficulties have spiralled to a crisis. She feels stuck and desperately unhappy. Both sides have become entrenched in their positions. Mavis's manager issues a formal warning and instigates unusually quick actions for disciplining procedures to be brought against her. Mavis thinks through the three responses she has at her disposal:

    (a) withdraw and accept the powerlessness of defeat
    (b) become indifferent by working the minimum standards and withdrawing all generosity
    (c) fight back or overreact, possibly making a louder case of 'racism!'.

Mavis is forced to take a long absence from work lasting nine months because of both mental and physical ill-health.

It must be noted that, in the last case of fighting back, even though racial discrimination is clearly evident in Mavis's experience, in some other cases of workplace oppression, racism is not the whole story. Often when racialized trauma in the workplace is activated, it activates conflation with personal experiences of trauma (where bullying, isolation and all forms of abuse have occurred within the individual's life, such as in their family, the church, school and experiences through education). The black worker may blanket their problems with the accusation of racism, which only serves to create more entrenchment.

During this crisis stage, Mavis's attendance at work is erratic, with more and more time taken off for sickness. She is advised to see her GP and prescribed sleeping tablets and antidepressants. Mavis also begins to experience a pervasiveness of other medical conditions, which include:

- chronic fatigue syndrome, very similar to myalgic encephalopmyelitis (ME)
- late onset of diabetes
- hypertension
- mood swings
- loss of libido.

For black workers trapped at this crisis stage, despondency further sets in, as there is usually no other alternative then to consider the following actions:

- retire from work on medical grounds
- be dismissed from work and/or
- fight the battle legally via a protracted and expensive employment tribunal.

Stage 6: Impasse – psychologically the impasse signifies complete loss of control and for Mavis this meant her situation had ground to a halt, placing her and management in complete deadlock. Worn down and totally exhausted by her eighteen-month ordeal, Mavis decided to retire on medical grounds, at the same time as her employer elected to dismiss her unceremoniously from her senior post as Ward Sister.

With little recourse to receiving the right kind of treatment in these all too frequent situations at work, many black and Asian minority staff feel entrapped within the impasse that is illustrated by the Spiral of Events. Workplace oppression is prevalent, yet unrecognized and formally acknowledged as race trauma in organizations with their human resources departments and workers' unions' structures. This leaves many therapists picking up broken people who are psychologically ravaged by the enduring events of the Spiral of Events. The focus of therapy unquestionably becomes trauma, loss and grief work, often at the intersection of race, gender, age, class, religion and sexuality dynamics.

Working with invisible injuries and race-related stress

In the earlier stages, when clients report incidents of micro- or macroaggression, they may be unaware of the full impact that these incidents have – or might have. However, if they are in therapy at this point, they already have a place where these incidents can be named and processed, and options for responding can be explored. Those who come into therapy at a later stage, and possibly as a result of the stress they are now conscious of, may well have already presented to their GP and be experiencing a number of medical and psychological symptoms. In addition to those already cited, we should be alert to the following experiences:

- having dreams or nightmares about going to work
- feeling ground down
- feeling oppressed
- feeling as if work has taken over, hijacked one's internal sense of self and become a source of emotional terrorization.

Clients may present with post-traumatic symptoms, such as replaying painful and difficult work events over and over. They may have low-level or clinical depression, headaches, sleeplessness, tearfulness. They may also present with psychosomatic symptoms such as vague and recurring pains in the stomach, head or body generally. One respondent from the study was convinced that she had terrible bad breath because, as she put it, 'Every time I opened my mouth, I was shut down'. When clients are caught up in this spiral, above all they need to talk, be heard and be believed. Many people may choose to stay in their situation because they are worried about getting another job and meeting financial commitments. It is important that they receive support for their experience, their sense of self and to develop a critical awareness in order to feel empowered.

Postscript: shining a light on black people's experience in the workplace

Although social science research has acknowledged the debilitating effects of workplace stress generally (Markham, 1995; Rick, 1998), my literature research indicates that not much analytical attention has been given to black people's experience in the UK workplace. Although American research has excelled for many decades in assessing racial identity attitudes and African self-consciousness, and in researching race and psychological functioning among African–Americans in many contexts (Hacker, 1992; Hughes & Dodge, 1997; Locke, 1992), it is glaringly evident, by comparison, that fewer research projects have been conducted that analyse race dynamics in the UK workplace. It would be wrong to suggest that nothing is being done to improve racial diversity in the workplace in the UK, but the kind of literature that focuses on the analysis of unconscious dynamics of race in this context is scarce. There is some British literature from around the late 1990s that addresses the mental health aspect of race and trauma, namely from the works of psychiatrists Fernando (1991, 1996), Burke (1984) and Bhui (2002), who have dealt with race and mental health. There is also the work of psychologists Maxime (1993, 1994) and Banks (1992), who have focused on black identity and children, and Cross (1971, 1978), who has addressed racism and identity.

Fortunately, in the last decade, the proliferation of social media platforms and the abundance of online information has led to a brighter light being shone on the subtle areas of race dynamics in the workplace. Two recent examples of black identity wounding as a direct result of indignities in the workplace, are described below.

'I'm not the defendant': the trials of a black barrister

Alexandra Wilson, a black female lawyer, made headlines when she was mistaken for a defendant three times in one day. She remains determined to tackle racism in the courts (Wilson, 2021).

Forced out by Kevin Maxwell review – prejudice between police

Colin Grant, a former black detective, recounts in shocking detail how he was abused by fellow officers for his race and sexuality and the dangers he faced in fighting for justice (Grant, 2020).

I include, with the full permission of my client, Dr Tulika Jha, her poem to share in this space. Her experiences, not unlike those of Mavis, have been helped by the support of regular psychotherapy and creative ways to manage her healing process. The poem is an exemplar of sublimation in the context of workplace oppression and its activation of generational trauma and racial hauntings.

MAD, BAD or SAD?
The 3 phases of Activism

Once you have seen it
You cannot un-see
Yet survival in this state
Takes up all your energy
They tell you, you are mad
Some support maybe?
From the very people who are trying to oppress
Really?
And you better not get angry
Because then you are acting like a child
Emotional Intelligence
Something you need to try, try and try
Until you learn to silence
What your anger has to say or
You will be silenced
Because that's no way
For a lady to behave
A lady of colour at that
You are then deemed 'bad'
Excluded and shamed
Because you can't be tamed
Made to believe
Your fundamental aim
Is to deceive

But once you see, I tell you, you cannot un-see
The ones who look like you mainly
Do not have a voice
Those who do
Have got there by
Years of gagging it
God forbid, if they speak
Their precarious positions will shift

Then, there are some like my little boy

Who just wants to believe
That people are not treated badly because of the colour
Of their skin
He wants to preserve
That safe place in his heart
Of the only country he knows
His homeland
He asks if it can contain him?
His skin, his parents' protests and his grandparents' compliance
After all he says, each generation faces less
Racism
No one calls me a Paki at school
It's not like that
And I get irritated
Flesh and blood of mine
Would rather believe in the goodness of the oppressors
Than I?

I later realize
That my son and some friends of mine
Are turning a blind eye
Not because they are bad
But because they don't want to be sad
To contaminate security, even if it is a false sense
It's important
for their existence
It's a PPE against enormous pain
That annihilation, betrayal and repeated oppression
Tends
When you are being abused
You don't want to admit
It shames you for letting yourself be
A victim

By this point
I have crossed the first two stages –
Mad and bad
Now they say, you are sad

This one you cannot deny
You feel it in your heart, body and mind
Sadness – so much easier for all to point
It doesn't have the force that anger can afford
Because the fire has been suffused and now it burns out

Self-care they say
Self-care
You can't pour from an empty cup
But my cup you filled with poison
That you made me make
Stewed over days of betrayal, exclusion, micro/macro aggression
My cup is not empty
It's very much full
Now you want me out of your face.
Because it makes your guilt feel responsible
Go spend time with your 'loved' ones
That's the most important thing

Even hubby says it's not important – this fight
And I surrender my phone to my boy
Who doesn't want to believe that racism exists
He wants his mummy back
Whilst at work they breathe a sigh of relief
The voice that holds them to account has ceased
Mission 'sadness' achieved
3 steps of Activism complete
Mad, Bad and Sad.

Reproduced with the kind permission of Dr Tulika Jha

Shame and identity

Identity is a central theme in counselling and psychotherapy, and shame
is the natural bedfellow of identity. The theme of identity includes
looking at our history and the collective development that extends across
generations.

Questions I consider to be at the heart of the work with identity shame are:

- Who am I?
- Where do I come from?
- What experiences have marked and shaped me?
- What is my relationship with my history?
- Which parts of my history have I absorbed knowingly and unknowingly?
- What have I developed for myself that is independent of my race and culture?
- Where can I engage in healthy critique and evaluation of my collective?
- How do world events involving identity, race and culture influence my subjectivity?
- Where do I re-examine and adjust my biases and personal scripts?
- What is my recollection of my first-ever experience of shame and its impact?

These pertinent questions are also necessary for therapists to explore for themselves, to deepen their awareness and facilitate intercultural competency in their work; this is necessary in order to provide clients with the right therapeutic space in which to restore themselves from their shame-based trauma issues.

Black identity development

One of the most cited works on identity development is that of Erik Erickson. According to Erickson (1963), identity formation consists of two components: ego-identity (experience of connection, belonging and recognition) and self-identity (who I am, the core of who I am). Essentially, the formation of these two anchor components (the latter of which includes racial identity) results in positive outcomes for healthy ontology. Racism and its impact on black identity erode these anchors and make it difficult to maintain a healthy experience in the world and one's ability to navigate the extra hurdles and obstacles in society.

Madan Sarup (1996) takes the analysis of identity a stage further. He suggests that identity is a mediating concept between the external and internal, the individual and society, theory and practice. Identity, then, is a convenient concept from which we try to understand many aspects of our lives – the personal, political, racial, gender, class, sexuality, and so on. Sarup (1996, pp. 28–43) refers to the 'it is' and 'I am' aspects of identity, which can become entangled when there is continuous discord between the two. Sarup suggests that the 'it is' aspect of identity is a public identity, created out of a set of misinformation, misinformed perceptions and stereotypes, which is put on to an individual or racial group. In the case of black people, this social construct of identity is usually negative. Society generally tends to relate to black people from this social template unless closer connections and attachments prove the opposite. The 'I am' aspect of identity is the private part that most accurately resembles and represents what we feel, think and know about ourselves (this is Erikson's self-identity, explained above). The stark contrast between how one is perceived in public and how one sees one's private self can differ widely and contribute to confusion, an inner state of insecurity, and dis-ease or distress.

Societal perceptions of blackness carry many negatives and the impact on black people is varied. Some have come to expect this negativity and have adjusted to it through a process of transcendence. Others are constantly triggered into angry responses and act out their feelings. For others, the discomfort of living with this ever-present split (discrepancies between public and private identity) takes its toll and leads to inner disturbance, particularly if compounded by other present or latent personal difficulties and life struggles. A therapy client who worked as a senior psychologist summed up her feelings about this experience thus:

> 'My private reality plays a very important part in creating my identity. It's how I see myself and what my proud parents taught me. When the terrible racism at work punctured that, I was shattered and depersonalized ... this is the way I have been left.'

The puncturing of a black person's private identity, that is, their truth about how they truly know themselves, and the contrasting negative way in which society sees and treats them, can destabilize a person's ontology, that is, their mental balance and rootedness in being in the world. This suggests that, when it comes to race relations, the battleground is twofold – both personal and political.

Other respected writers and educators (Akbar, 1996; Cobbs and

Grier, 1968; Ellis, 2021; Fletchman Smith, 2011; hooks, 1996; Lorde, 1984; McKenzie-Mavinga, 2009), who address the theme of black identity issues, emphasize the task for black people to educate themselves for critical consciousness. By this they mean the ability to show independence of mind by reasoning for oneself and having emotional literacy to be more culturally and racially competent. In hooks' (1996) *killing rage, ending racism*, she reminds people of colour not to see blackness solely as a matter of powerlessness and victimization, but rather that there is a need to have a deeper understanding of institutional and systemic racial oppression in all its facets, which over-determine patterns of black–white social relations. She reminds us of the challenge for educational discourses and in race conversations, to 'insist on theorizing black identity ... from other multiple locations, not simply in relation to white supremacy' (hooks, 1996, p. 248). Hooks challenges the notion of a stereotypical monolithic black culture, which is perpetuated sadly in both black and white sectors of our society. She firmly suggests the point:

> ... narrowly focused black identity politics do a disservice to the complex and multiple subjectivity of black folks. While I am deeply committed to a politics of black self-determination that seeks to maintain and preserve our unique cultural [heritage], I know that the project of cultural conservation need not negate our diasporic wanderings into worlds beyond traditional blackness. The nationalist insistence that black identity must be 'saved' by our refusal to embrace various epistemologies (ways of knowing), cultures, etc., is not a movement away from a Eurocentric binary structure [Euro-scepticism as we know it in today's Britain].
>
> (hooks, 1996, p. 247)

Psychic interruption and collapse

Fanon (1986) also comments on difficulties for black identity development thus:

> When the negro makes contact with the white world, a certain sensitizing action takes place. If his psychic structure is weak, one observes a collapse of ego. The black man stops behaving as an actional person. The goal of his behaviour will be The Other (in

the guise of the white man), for The Other alone can give him worth.

(Fanon, 1986, p. 154)

Although Fanon first wrote his views in 1952, their relevance to today's circumstances is just as poignant. Black people operating in predominantly white settings, for example the workplace and education, seem to develop a certain kind of healthy awareness – a 'sixth sense' – for the presence of racial prejudice and discrimination. This extra-sensory perception creates a preparedness to manage the negative effects of microaggressions in general social contexts, microinequities in the workplace and the more serious impact of racial prejudice, racism, institutional and systemic racism in one's daily living environment. However, it has been my experience that the individual whose sense of self is validated only or mainly in terms of their being black will have a different sense of personal consciousness activated when in the presence of white people. The psychic structure may be more prone to being upset or knocked off balance by racial affronts (subtle or overt), and consequent emotional states of hyperalertness and hypersensitivity will be developed to cope in these encounters. My vast clinical experience suggests that such mental states are capable of causing interruptions to 'coherency' (the feeling of being at one with oneself) and 'continuity', both of which are related to Kohut's (1977) grounded sense of self. When environmental stress deriving from racial impingements is superimposed upon such individuals, they can experience a psychic collapse.

It has struck me that when Fanon (1986) wrote '... if his psychic structure is weak, one observes a collapse of ego. The black man stops behaving as an actional person. The goal of his behaviour will be The Other ...' (p. 154), he was thinking in a deep and analytical way about this very phenomenon of black ontological security in an unequal world.

It is my belief that the issues discussed, when seen to be continually impinging on the racial self, and internalized over time, can lead to a sedimentation of hurt – an intrapsychic process that can contribute to deep identity wounding and unheeded forms of mental distress.

Psychoanalysis tells us that a person can potentially contain the experience in their own mind as unconscious phantasy, memory or, alternatively, as some distorted defensive version of their experience of psychic catastrophe. Shame and its vicissitudes are largely held as troubled memories and distorted defensive trauma mechanisms in the context of racial identity. However, these psychological factors can be ignored and, consequently, contribute to the burden of heritage.

Shame and narcissism

As already seen, shame is deeply interwoven with issues of narcissism, though the two realms are by no means identical. In the context of black identity, shame is the veiled companion of narcissism – a healthy self-love that is related to self-esteem, self-worth and delighting in all things lovable about oneself. Shame in this context stems from the internalized conflict that arises when the self finds itself having to deal with aspects of external authority (society) and the need to protect the innermost and vulnerable parts of the self. The function of this shame is to defend against anxiety that threatens to destroy an integral image of the self but, in so doing, shrouds full actualization and integration of these positive aspects of the self.

Psychoanalytic theory suggests that narcissism in adults is related to defences against shame and that narcissistic personality disorder is connected to shame as well. This is a generalized view that needs deconstruction. According to the psychiatrist Glen Gabbard (1989), there is the 'oblivious' subtype, whose characteristics are grandiosity, arrogance, boastfulness, and who demands to be in the spotlight because they are right. In terms of racial oppression and black–white dynamics, I attribute these character traits to dominant groups and aggregate power structures that invest much energy in maintaining positions of world power, ownership and control. These elements can be seen operating within Britain's historical class system, a structure that is designed to maintain the status quo of a social hierarchical order. This was famously and wittily portrayed in the iconic 'Social Class' sketch on the satirical comedy series *The Frost Report*, 1966, featuring John Cleese, Ronnie Barker and Ronnie Corbett:

But, according to Gabbard, there is also the converse to this grandiose 'oblivious' category. This is the 'hypervigilant' subtype who is self-effacing, carries a deep sense of shame and who is fragile (further explored below) and oversensitive. I am proposing a notion that white identity shame in

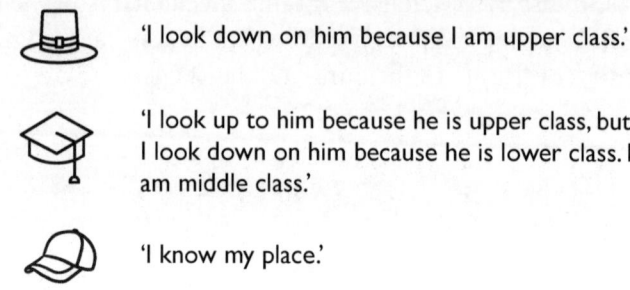

'I look down on him because I am upper class.'

'I look up to him because he is upper class, but I look down on him because he is lower class. I am middle class.'

'I know my place.'

Figure 6.3 *Social class as depicted on* The Frost Report

the context of white Britishness contains elements of both the oblivious and the hypervigilant, when it relates specifically to colonial identity and the past. White identity shame seems to be managed by a harping back to the accomplishments of Empire or propped up by 'world-beating' blustering, which has become the current default political stance. These posturings provide immediate gratification, while insulating the self from any aspect of narcissistic injury, which might come from criticism of that past. This is the genesis of the shame resistance that blocks open engagement in race conversations.

The impact of the absence of self-objects in society

Kohut's self-psychology has broadened my understanding of not only the relational aspects, but also the intrapsychic experiences of shame and narcissistic traits in the make-up of the black psyche. I see black people's intrapsychic experiences of self as contingent on the interpersonal events of their history.

Heinz Kohut's (1977) contribution of the idea of self-object to psychoanalysis led him to believe that the self could survive and prosper only in the context of experience with others. He called these experiences self-objects, that is having the sense that one is appreciatively responded to, experiencing affinity and inclusion by others, and having society mirror back positively and equitably. In such a merger, the self is maintained and allowed the capacity to grow in ways that cannot be achieved in a vacuum. Self-objects therefore remain essential throughout life. A lack of twinship with positive mirroring self-objects in society leads to an inward dwelling and the causation of shame and narcissistic wounding in black people. These lived experiences can contribute to an ongoing self-negation that keeps both the individual and the collective stuck and forever trying to prove a rightful place in the world.

In this sense, narcissism is about a preoccupation with a self that longs for the acceptance from cultural self-objects. The narcissistic wound occurs, therefore, in the space of longing to actualize the wish fulfilment. According to Freud (1997), wish fulfilment occurs when unconscious desires are repressed by the ego and superego. In the case of minorities, this repression often stems from taboos imposed by society and struggles to gain an equal and entitled place in civilization.

Martin Luther King's wish fulfilment first appeared in a dream that led to the iconic speech where he envisioned a 'new world' in which people were 'not judged by the colour of their skin, but the content of their character'. Martin Luther King's famous 'I Have a Dream' speech was delivered on 28 August 1963 and it speaks powerfully to the shame wound of humanity.

As I see it, the vicissitudes and complexities of white identity shame and narcissism remain one of the most unheeded areas of pathology, one that continually escapes diligent and systematic investigation from analytical elite societies. In my view, this silent sickness is one of the most disregarded areas of mental ill-health.

Shame and narcissism for minorities must not be confused with the same kinds of defence structures of white identity shame and narcissism, but must be clinically viewed as deriving from the true, lived experiences of non-white people or people of colour, which create different kinds of vulnerability and particular forms of neurosis. Both black- and white-identity shame contribute to mental health instability, but their aetiology is different and unique.

Differentiating black and white identity shame

Although a universal experience, shame has different dimensions when applied to the black and white context of history, heritage and identity. The dynamics of this 'soul-eating emotion' to the self-system (Jung, 1989; Mayer, 2017) are complex and complicated when it comes to differentiating. I will try to highlight some of these differences, making use of Gabbard's (1989) two subtypes, which might be particularly useful for therapy practitioners.

Gabbard's oblivious narcissist subtype is so called because it has no awareness of the reactions of others and is apparently impervious to their hurt feelings, and is generally unaware of their impact on others. I have stretched this concept to include dominant others, for example groups, races and nations who, by virtue of the positions they occupy in society, create not only inequalities among subordinates and minorities, but also attract feelings of envy and jealousy from the less fortunate or privileged other. These elements contribute to the shame-inducing dynamics for black people who are usually in the minority position in society, as previously explored in Chapter 2 (Cycle of Events, Alleyne, 1992, 2009).

Closely examining the underbelly aspects of Gabbard's oblivious subtype, the manifest behaviours and qualities of superiority, privilege and power inherent in this subtype are, in fact, the antithesis of a fragile self-identity – one that hides a multitude of historical, political and reputational sins and consequent repressed shame. This explanation leads to my summation of the key difference in black identity shame and white identity shame:

- Superiority and dominance act as masks to cover the exposure and terror of white identity shame and white fragility.
- Black identity shame is the burden of carrying deep-rooted wounds and ongoing struggles, which are borne in relation to the dominance of the white other.

White fragility

The term 'white fragility' was coined in 2011 by Dr Robin DiAngelo who, in her critical analysis of race, defines the concept as 'a state in which even a minimum amount of racial stress becomes intolerable, triggering a range of defensive moves' (DiAngelo, 2011, p. 54). In her earlier paper on 'White Fragility' she argues that

> ... white people in North America live in a social environment that protects and insulates them from race-based stress. This insulated environment of racial protection builds white expectations for racial

comfort while at the same time lowering the ability to tolerate racial stress, leading to what I refer to as White Fragility. White Fragility is a state in which even a minimum amount of racial stress becomes intolerable, triggering a range of defensive moves. These moves include the outward display of emotions such as anger, fear, and guilt, and behaviors such as argumentation, silence, and leaving the stress-inducing situation. These behaviors, in turn, function to reinstate white racial equilibrium.

(DiAngelo, 2011, p. 56.)

Despite its mixed reception in the UK, this concept has a rightful place in race conversations today. It is a useful concept that provides a steadying handle to explore a well-known phenomenon in black–white dynamics. Many minority ethnic readers will agree that they have, for decades, been the recipients of white fragility through not being listened to, believed, supported, included. At the same time, there has been a blatant lack of empathy for the real suffering caused by the impact of racial inequality, but our voices have barely been heard when we have tried to raise the level of consciousness about its destructive presence.

Ironically, it has taken a member of the 'white fragility group' to name the phenomenon in order for it to be given credibility. The impact of white fragility causes wounding to black identity and the collective has always known this. As I have observed with most race dynamics: what ceases to be a coincidence is a phenomenon – and that is the remarkable fact. Racism is not a fluke or accident. It is not a freak of nature. It is the way one race of people are taught and nurtured to think about themselves in relation to others.

The challenge for white liberalism in race conversations[2]

White liberals, who typically feel a combination of guilt for white history and empathy with those who are oppressed, may often be encountered in the psychotherapy world as practitioners or clients. Being a 'white liberal', of course, does not mean that person is devoid of racism (if we assume that racism is so insidiously embedded in white culture that no one escapes contamination). Rather, the white liberal is someone who struggles against racism, because they know that this is in their best interest – because the shadow of racism on the white psyche makes them ill. They will conduct their struggle imperfectly, unable to fully grasp the lived experience of what it means to be black, just as men who identify as feminist can never enter the lived experience of female oppression. White liberals are an ambiguous, hard to define and indefinite group of people, and often traumatized in their own right. They can get in the way of change, by leading rather than following, by creating the discourse around equality rather than listening. They may be simply virtue signalling, while keeping a comfortable distance from the fray. What one can be sure of, though, is that there are white liberals who seek to understand, who care about living in a racism-free society with the possibility of affinity between people from all backgrounds because they see that as in their best interest too. They are imperfect friends, but not the enemy.

Reaction formation

The analytic concept of reaction formation refers to a defence mechanism that is primarily concerned with how our instincts express the very opposite of true feelings, actions and thoughts. These are basal instincts and our attempts at self-preservation when they threaten to expose us. As conflicting or fearful feelings surface, there is a strong drive to abandon or jettison the sense of threat engendered. Reaction formation is therefore about the strategies employed in managing these conflicting feelings. In black–white dynamics, where the potential for losing face is great, they are abundant. Reaction formation is an exaggeration of the directly opposing instinct, making it a neurotic defence mechanism. It is easily spotted in the exaggerated reactions of intellectualization (a lot of explaining), displacement (moving away from the subject), regression (crying) and projection (dumping and blaming).

It is very relevant when applied to the thorny area of black–white dynamics, because, when we think of dominant groups and serviceable others, the other is always to some extent within. The minority other mirrors and represents what is deeply familiar to the dominant's centre, but this is projected outwards. So, for instance, a white male who feels insecure about his masculinity may extol the virtues of his intellectual capacity and objectify the black male as just being physical. Primitive anxieties triggered in a race conversation may instinctively lead a white person to move away from engagement, by cleverly steering the black person into the spotlight so that they can hide their shame exposure in the dark – like a parallel to the myth of Dracula's terror of being destroyed by sunshine and light.

The back-pedal shuffle

In black–white encounters, conflict can occur when, for example, white people feel that they have put their foot in it and/or caused racial offence. The semiotic covering (morality) slips to reveal the race transgression and the private and vulnerable self that feels the shame of getting it wrong. The proverbial stiff upper lip is one such semiotic cover that is worn in English society. The semiotic code dictates never being without this covering, and race conversations particularly highlight the dynamics in action.

Reaction formation is particularly observable in what I refer to as 'the back-pedal shuffle'. The back-pedal shuffle is manifest in expressions such as 'I feel I need to make myself clear', 'I must cover my backside here', 'I must explain myself', 'I didn't mean to ...', 'It was just banter'. In these frequently heard statements, there is much exaggeration and insistence – almost a plea to hide what has been exposed. In some instances, the shamed might inadvertently push their discomfort back onto the other (a form of projection), with accusations such as 'I feel you might be overreacting' and the proverbial 'Are you implying that I am a racist?' or 'I think you have a chip on your shoulder'.

White shame arising from this defence mechanism leads instinctively to mental dams being built and fortified to defend against the terror of the shame exposure. As previously discussed, this intense internal activity invariably interferes with the quality of engagement in race conversations, as the shamed person becomes self-absorbed and overly concerned with protecting themselves. These dynamics stymie race conversations and they suffer constant ruptures. The challenge is to learn the art of self-regulation when these primitive fear responses are triggered and, equally, to feel the fear and do it anyway. Strengthening cross-cultural and cross-racial competence will most likely lead to a performative wellness that reassures the catastrophic worry of dying of shame. However, the instinctual fear of disintegration from white identity shame may prove too great a risk and some may choose to desist from further engagement with matters of race. A retreat to old social scripts leaves the great weight and heft of race work to the be carried and held by the black other. A key take-away message here for understanding the workings of reaction formation in black/white dynamics is for the white other to OWN the primitive in YOU.

Reaction formation as a Freudian concept is said to be more marked in anal characters. To put in context what I mean, Freud's 1908 classification of character types which trailed off in popularity, and reappeared in contemporary personality psychology, identified the overarching trait of the anal character as *holding back* a pleasure that originated in the childhood fascination with shit. Orderliness, obstinacy and miserliness (ways of being in control) were reactions against filth and sublimated as acceptable social ways of dealing with the fear of making a mess. I advance the notion that if race is internalized as that which threatens to expose, and thereby create inadequacies that reveal our messiness, it would account for Freud's holding back anality in making some sense of the real fear for white people to engage in matters of race and particularly black issues. Race symbolically exposes all that is private, intact and lily-white, daring individuals to let go and not disavow responsibility to the others.

I would also add, from observation, that anality, more politely referred to in British culture as the British reserve, is more prevalent in cultures where being stoic and linguistically skilful is given high primacy. To maintain the stiff upper lip keeps emotions in check – a holding back that dignifies situations demanding the show of raw emotions. These cherished semiotic symbols are awarded high value, for they are guaranteed to deal with the threat of white identity shame when the semiotic cover slips to reveal the messier sides.

White identity disclaimers

A more recent phenomenon has come to my attention following the emotional and mental aftershock of the public murder of the black American, George Floyd, by a white police officer. Essentially, white identity disclaimers protect white comfort.

The trend for whites to begin their every conversation with what I term 'white identity disclaimers' has reached the point of being vapid and burdensome to the listener. Examples are:

I'm embarrassed to be white.
I know I was born white and privileged, and I feel ashamed of that ...

I realize I'm speaking as a white male ...
As a white woman ...
After all I am white and therefore can't know anything about being black ...
I must confess, I am completely ignorant of these issues ...
I don't think I can comment on that.
"That's very interesting" or "That's terribly interesting", employed as the standard economic response to the race challenges.
"I really don't see colour, I treat everyone as human beings".
"I don't care if you are black, yellow, green or purple, I treat everyone the same."

It would now appear that every view on race and engagement with race-related matters requires a white identity disclaimer. Although pardoning oneself might bring comfort, and even ward off the threat of shame, the trending activity is paradoxically a disavowal, that is, it offloads a burden for the other to hold. Why so? Because disclaimers are distractions from the self which, in other words, are plain old excuses. Disclaimers are a swift way to negate responsibility, accountability and risk-taking in race conversations.

To fully understand white fragility in the context of white identity shame, readers might find an exploration of these four key questions helpful:

1. What is your story? Your story is your background plus your life experiences.
2. Who taught you that story? What values and belief systems were imparted to you about your race and culture?
3. Which cultural scripts from that story do you now hold dear that have shaped your racial identity?
4. How does your story influence your thinking and behaviour today?

Here is a personal example that illustrates the importance of the above work in managing shame-based issues. I recall a piece of diversity consultancy I facilitated for an all-white group some years ago. To open, I asked the attendees to respond individually to the following: Share two values that you hold quite dear to your own culture and why. One participant immediately raised her hand and timidly asked, 'Is this exercise for us?' I deliberately allowed a pause to indicate my incredulity at the question. The silence seemed to create a quiet panic that led her to ask a supplementary question: 'What do you mean by *our* culture? We are all white and English here.' This exchange, from which the following subtext can be extracted, speaks volumes:

- The question of culture is irrelevant to us white people.
- If this is about discrimination, we don't have that problem.
- Culture is for and about minorities.
- Your question is for the wrong audience.
- You should know better than to ask us such dumb questions.
- Whiteness and Englishness transcend race.
- This training could be a waste of our time.

Leon Wurmser (1981), in his book *The Mask of Shame* distinguishes three major types of shame effects: simple shame anxiety; shame as a complex affective and cognitive reaction pattern; and shame as a character attitude preventing dangerous exposure. In making distinctions for shame in the black/white relational context, one can conclude that white shame is a complex affective and cognitive reaction pattern that shapes character attitude to prevent dangerous exposure. On the other hand, black identity shame can be seen as a complex affective and cognitive reaction to black identity wounding.

CHAPTER 7

The chokehold of historical enmeshment

Only you can free your mind to be your own self

Introduction

Historical enmeshment speaks to the entangled relationship between the black race and the white race that creates psychic burdens, which continue to weigh on black lives in the present. The work of separating from this enmeshment will always be made harder if the dominant other fails to recognize the unfinished task of atoning for the means by which inheritance was gained and heritage bolstered. It is my view that, until the progeny of Britain's imperial colonialist past accept and deal with what is left out of conscious recognition, the disowned white hauntings will be carried vicariously as a burden by the black other. This unheeded dimension of black–white relations is the essence of what I see as perpetuating the phenomenon of historical enmeshment in black life. The perpetrator and the wounded are intertwined.

Separating from historical enmeshment and transcending the pain of heritage cannot be achieved only by black people engaging in individual healing work for themselves. There is also the inescapable need for the other side to engage in some form of national atonement and reconciliation with an ugly past. This missing link keeps the enmeshment alive but so obviously, as in the connecting analogy of a symbolic bridge, which, if crossed, could potentially bring about healing for both black and white collectives. South Africa, an exemplar of such restorative work, achieved its aim of collective healing, to a large extent, through the 1995 Truth and Reconciliation Commission and reparation in the form of payment to victims of Apartheid. Something brought into consciousness and dealt with collectively began the process of freeing white South Africans of their mortal crimes – this was necessary for black and white healing alike.

Other forms of historical reckoning have involved the most senior personnel at the highest levels in the land. For example, Germany, another model representative of honouring mortal debts owed, has engaged prodigiously in its repentance and atonement efforts to deal with its past – the Holocaust and its antecedents, namely its colonial history in Namibia, Tanzania, Rwanda, Burundi, Togo and Cameroon. These white colonialist settlers engaged with an important and necessary rite of passage in order to deal with their past and exorcize their mortal hauntings. However, Britain continues to exhibit a collective forgetfulness that unwittingly keeps its shame and guilt disowned in the nation's identity and very soul.

This chapter will add to the post-colonial critique discourse by answering some tired old questions from well-intentioned people:

Why can't they get over the slavery lark?

Can't they just accept the fact that history was then and this is now?
Why did you choose to come and live here, a predominantly white society?

Isn't it time to focus on the future and stop looking backwards?

What is it that you people want from us – what will satisfy you?

How much money do they expect this small island to hand over?
I had nothing to do with it – what am I expected to do?

Whether such discourses take the shape of these unhelpful and defensive questions, or they occur within the midst of genuine analysis that seeks to understand the nature of generational trauma, my intent in this chapter is to show that historical enmeshment is a chokehold and thereby contributes to the aliveness of this trauma in black lives. Again, I wish to reiterate that the burden is *not* static, but continually in flux as a direct result of present-day racial hauntings. These have the impact of keeping the past very much alive in the present, as their presence loiters just outside the door of black consciousness, when triggered.

The context for black/white relations

Black people's enmeshment with the white world is unique, because black bodies have always been regarded in terms of *engagement with, connection to and providing service to* the other. This objectification of a people leaves scars and hauntings in the collective psyche of those who are still viewed and treated as beasts of burden without souls or humanity. Why have they become so disposable as to be regularly placed as vanguards on so many fronts – conscripts positioned at the coalface of other people's wars, the human pillars and lifeblood of the NHS,[1] fitting hosts, biological specimens and test subjects for harmful medical and clinical trials, chemical tests and social research? The wound of being historically objectified is the original trauma that creates the unique ambivalent codependent and enmeshed relationship between black and white.

When it is argued that slavery had more to do with human greed than racism, it is hugely problematic. This naive, one-dimensional statement about British colonial history completely overlooks the true nature of greed, which is inextricably linked with the despotic nature of man's inhumanity to man in jousting for top position in the social order. The historical and present-day construct of the black body as naturally built for servitude plagues and haunts the black soul, for it speaks of black identity being one-dimensional and limited. These hauntings, in turn, contribute to the psychological impact that I refer to as the chokehold of historical enmeshment. There can be little argument about how well established this stigmatization, carried in the experiences of the black collective, is. Why else, I ask, would so many artists (poets, storyteller rappers, musical performers and so on) speak about enmeshment in their own inimitable and creative ways? Many acknowledge the phenomenon in ways that remind the collective to take heed to disentangle from its chokehold.

One of the most famous pioneers of reggae, Robert Nesta Marley, aka Bob Marley, exemplifies the collective experience in his powerfully poetic lyrics: '*Emancipate yourselves from mental slavery; None but ourselves can free our minds.*' This poignant and stunning line in the famous 'Redemption Song' is Marley's quintessential encapsulation of the work of healing from mental slavery. The first verse, below, speaks powerfully to this chapter's theme. I believe 'Redemption Song' is one of Marley's most powerful acts of sublimation. The haunting strings of his single guitar and profound poetic wisdom of his Jamaican creole lyrics exemplify the act of sublimation.

> Emancipate yourselves from mental slavery; None but ourselves can
>   free our minds.
> Old pirates, yes, they rob I;
> Sold I to the merchant ships,
> Minutes after they took I
> From the bottomless pit.
> But my hand was made strong
> By the 'and of the Almighty.
> We forward in this generation
> Triumphantly.
> Won't you help to sing
> These songs of freedom
> 'Cause all I ever have:
> Redemption songs;
> Redemption songs.

'Redemption Song', Words and Music by Bob Marley

Historical enmeshment, in the context of black/white relations, is the unrecognized and dysfunctional opposite of marginalization. It highlights difficulties in black people's relatedness to white people, for the obvious and undeniable fact that the relationship with colonial history is still alive. The ongoing psychological impact of traumatic transmissions also exists for many other racial and cultural groups, such as Jews in relation to the horrors of the Holocaust, indigenous American Indians recovering from the oppression of white federal regimes and Aboriginal people's marginalization and discrimination by Anglo-Australian states.

For black people, this has resulted in an attachment dysfunction – a mental over-involvement with the white race that causes hyperarousal and hypervigilance in black/white interactions, hindering reciprocity of trust, empathy, kinship – and respect. Such interpersonal engagement leaves black people seemingly psychologically entwined and stuck with an unconcerned parent-type colonial figure, whose indifference can be experienced as neglect and abandonment. The relational enmeshed dynamic is then experienced as one where blacks are a mere unit of currency, and convenient objects used to boost white privilege.

At this juncture, it is important to make a distinction between the two terms **codependency** and **enmeshment**, which are often used interchangeably. The fact is they are not the same, but linked, and it is important to clarify the difference in order to deepen our understanding of how historical enmeshment functions.

Codependency

Codependency is defined as being psychologically influenced by another person to the degree that personal needs are suppressed and ignored. This is a state of being held back in personal development; autonomy and independence are severely impeded and can sometimes be lost in the process of being reliant on, controlled by, and needing the other to fulfil one's own needs or to complete oneself. Codependency as a concept originated in Alcoholics Anonymous (AA), where codependants were defined as those dependent on or stuck in a relationship with someone addicted to alcohol or drugs. In this codependency, there was an unhealthy need to be needed by each other or stuck with the difficulties of the dependency.

Relationally, codependency creates addictive relationship patterns, where self-worth is gained from helping, fixing and rescuing others, even though it may be clear that the other is capable of doing these things for themselves. Self-worth is then measured by doing rather than being; validation is only gained from an external locus of control, rather than internal, leaving codependent people trapped in abusive, unfulfilling and unhappy relationships. Existence then feels purposeless and can never be enjoyed when separate or separated from the codependent other, for the relationship is the only place where they can feel useful, needed and wanted. Codependency is, essentially, over-reliance on the other.

Enmeshment

Enmeshment is a merging of identity so that neither person functions like a whole independent person. In merging with the other, the two identities become one or pathologically dependent on each other for survival. More simply put, enmeshment is present when our sense of wholeness comes from another person. It is, in short, engulfment. Enmeshed romantic couples are likely to say things like 'You complete me', 'You are my everything', 'I am nothing without you', 'You make me whole'.

Enmeshment is also a concept used to describe families whose personal boundaries become diffused and subsystems undifferentiated, and where an over-concern for, or preoccupation with, others leads to a loss of autonomous development. The concept was introduced by Salvador Minuchin (1974) who described how children in such families lose their capacity for self-direction and development of distinctiveness; under the weight of parental needs, such children may find themselves trapped. When family pressures and conflicts increase, the child may end up becoming the identified patient, that is, the one with the problems and, consequently, the family scapegoat.

Enmeshment dynamics elaborated

Dysfunctional enmeshment according to Minuchin (1974), is a disorder resulting in developmental arrest that leads to a difficulty in disengaging from internal objects, for example, one's mother or father. Relating Minuchin's concept to the dynamics of historical enmeshment, the internal object for black people could be the white colonizer. Dysfunctional enmeshment would be the psychological difficulties involved in the colonized disengaging from this bind that impedes personal growth and the individuation process. Such enmeshed states and relational patterns may come to resemble parent–child and codependent attachments, where both sides end up continually seeking mutual advantage through each other. For the parent (the colonizer) it may be the need to exercise power by forever keeping the child (the colonized) in an infantilized position. For the symbolic child, there may remain lingering needs to be fully seen, appreciated and respected. The 'child' may feel the need to have the object present to fight against, while, at the same time, craving equal opportunities to exercise full independence. Inherent in such codependent relationships are the workings of projective identification previously addressed in Chapter 2.

Black people's relationship with the architects of their colonial histories bears a resemblance to the many complex dynamics and tenets of

Minuchin's family enmeshment theory (Minuchin, 1974). His use of the term 'psychic incest', which represents the chokehold of family pressures, bears similar resemblance to the chokehold of historical enmeshment for the colonized; in this context, the relationship dynamics may be termed 'historical incest'.

This seems an appropriate conceptualization when we consider black/white historical enmeshment. The genesis of this phenomenon, for the black diaspora, started in 1562 and ended in 1834. Not only did it create burgeoning economic industries in the west for dominant white nations, but it also left in its wake the trauma of economic and psychological destruction. The resultant unhealthy symbiotic attachment created pathological dependencies of black nations on white colonizers – and corresponding pathological desires to keep the black in the convenient role of 'object-currency'.

History has shaped the relatedness dynamic between the colonizer and the colonized, where the identity and national history of the former keeps white identity alive and still relevant. The Colonial Empire was not benevolent and, in Minuchin's concept of the parent–child entanglement, where abuse and dependency leave child and parent toxically enmeshed, the same can be said of the relationship between colonizer and colonized. The level of power and invincibility that arose from imperial conquest would have been bound to create dominant and narcissistic parent-like qualities that would not have questioned the ability to subordinate others. Were it not convenient, gratifying and rewarding for the parent–colonizer, the toxic codependent relationship with colonies could not have lasted for 400 years.

When Minuchin's concept of enmeshment is applied in this context, the black minority becomes the identified patient. Blacks are frequently infantilized and straitjacketed in the role of the delinquent – criminal, untrustworthy, limited, not capable – and consequently the scapegoat for all of society's ills. Kovel, (1970) and White (1989) describe this racist dynamic as operating through the process of projective identification, where disowned aspects of the idealized white self are deposited into black people. It is then the minority group who are forced to carry the aggression, hostility, rage, greed, sexual voraciousness and impurity from which the white civilized person prefers to dissociate.

The reverberations of the colonial era have clearly left its mark, creating forms of codependency with an identification through the other. This state of affairs has left black people with more struggles to negotiate when it comes to the important process of differentiation: an analytical term used here to describe the process of separating and emerging gracefully autonomous. The effects of colonialism have much to answer for in this struggle.

From an analytical perspective, such codependency can interfere with the task of becoming autonomous, a process underpinned by catastrophic fantasies of individuation (Jung, 1923). The tendency would therefore be to settle for what is safe and comfortable – a state of dependence and waiting to be given opportunities – while feeling dissatisfied, frustrated and even enraged with one's stuck position. From a cultural object relations perspective (Segal, 1982), this point was borne out in my doctoral research by a powerful comment made by respondent no. 30, who felt that 'as black people, we seemed unable to initiate and be self-governing unless validated and monitored [kept in check] by the white man'. Enmeshment (Minuchin, 1974) breeds dependency (and inexperience) due to the developmental deficits arising from this unhealthy union. The way out of enmeshed states is to separate, and seek autonomy and self-sufficiency. Separation in the black–white context, however, is not to be interpreted as separatism, isolation or alienation from the white other.

Codependence and enmeshment would clearly suggest then that there is a propensity for us as black people to seek self-definition through the white other, while also being extremely critical of this other. This tricky ambivalent situation can lead ultimately to difficulties in experiencing oneself as separate in one's own identity. Dependence of this kind, coupled with the angst arising from carrying around historical baggage, can create a focus and preoccupation with the white other that can lead to merging (both cultural and spiritual), with the individual self becoming more elusive. Enmeshment and codependence in this context can become a disease of lost selfhood. Utilizing one's personal energies in continually tracking the parent (the white other) creates a dynamic that heavily influences pre-transference connections in any given situation. It can also lead to an oversensitivity and anticipation of racial and cultural conflict, even when they are not present. Another respondent, no. 4, from my doctoral research demonstrated this point by the following comment: 'I always carry a healthy disrespect for white people because I can never trust them.'

For the colonized, the merging of the historical past with present-day re-enactments can often lead to a mental replaying of the civilization/

savagery binary. This experience is ever present on many levels and feels unavoidable for many ethnic minorities as they interact in the course of daily life. Experiences that activate shame, pain and the wretched tiredness we feel when forced to deal with the impact of the civilization/ savagery binary, include the following:

- experiencing racial prejudice in public interactions and in the world of social media
- hearing negative generalizations made about one's race
- having assumptions made about one's identity or capability because of one's race
- experiencing microaggressions, that is, casual off-the-cuff remarks that cause offence to you, **the individual**
- experiencing macroaggressions, that is, intentional and unintentional discrimination against a whole **marginalized groups** because of its racial characteristics and/or culture
- experiencing racial prejudice and harassment in the workplace
- experiencing unconscious bias and discrimination in the workplace
- having dreams, hopes, opportunities and entitlements crushed and denied full actualization because of systemic, structural and institutional racism.

These experiences threaten the balance of black ontology and keep people intertwined in an unhealthy bind with the dominant other. Being enmeshed with the one who has dominion over you is one of the unhealthiest attachment bonds there is. It keeps one caught in the bind of being hypervigilant of anticipated threats, longing for the freedoms enjoyed by the privileged other and simultaneously stuck in semi-permanent states of arousal from the activation of injustice and outrage. Arousal by undesirable provocation is, at best, an infernal nuisance; at worst, it is injurious to the balanced harmony mental health.

Life scripts

The chokehold of enmeshment can influence a person's life scripts in ways that become mandates for living in an unfair world. In the following examples, the right to self-determination is motivated by an external locus of control. The codes of conduct for living a more reactive life (first set of scripts) or through disavowal (second set of scripts) are all in response to the dominant other, even when they appear to be about reclaiming control and exercising personal choice. Both forms of adaptation – 'acting out' and 'acting in' – are the inescapable signs of historical enmeshment.

Reactive scripts ('acting out')

- I must be always on the lookout for racism and challenge it whenever it arises.
- Under no circumstance will I let them get away with unacceptable behaviour.
- I will call you out at every opportunity and expose your racist thinking.
- I will not stop until I make them pay for what they did to me.
- I will show them.
- They need to be taught a lesson – slavery is over.
- I will work three times as hard, so they have no excuse but to accept me in this firm.
- I will say it loud, and I will say it proud, and I'll make myself a nuisance until they take notice.

Defiant scripts ('acting in')

- Too bad if they can't handle my disposition or temperament – I am not brown nosing for anyone.
- I am not going to get my blood pressure up for the cause; others can take up that fight.
- What you see is what you get. Like it or lump it.

Each type of script contributes to the bind that sets the trap for being in either reactive mode or disavowal mode. However, there is another, often unheeded, middle position. Relating in the white dominant world may lead to adaptation that manifests in posturing that I refer to as *fawning*. In the presence of a white person, fawning will be the behaviour that the black or brown person adopts with the sole purpose of seeking acceptance and inclusion. Fawning is a strategy or behaviour learnt and is used as a way of moving away from negative stereotypes that the majority society has imposed on certain minorities with impunity, for example, 'They are unreliable', 'They are not trustworthy', 'They are aggressive'.

Some racial minorities may subtly engage in the toxic activity of using some of these stereotypes to 'other' fellow minority groups as a way of gaining acceptance and closer membership to the majority white group. This fawning trauma-reaction tends to provide the illusion of comfort, when the inner belief is 'the flies are not on me or my group'. Racial minorities can unwittingly separate themselves from other minorities in these subtle ways in the hope of an easier life via the appearance of being exceptions from other troublesome minorities. Behaviours, views and more must now all change in accordance with the dominant group. To the keen observer, fawning can be detected in behaviour that possesses some or most of the following: excessive flattery and idolization of the white other, bootlicking, cowering, crawling, humbling the self, showing excessive servitude, pandering to Eurocentric principles and values, and slavishly following a particular status quo that earns white approval.

Fawning scripts

- If I change the way I speak, adopt similar values and behave like them, I might gain membership and acceptance.
- I don't want to end up being the black sheep, so I had better toe the line.
- It's easier to keep my opinions to myself; that way, I don't rock the boat.
- I mustn't make demands or ask for help, for I might be seen as struggling and not capable of doing the job.
- I cannot afford to shine too brightly and show them up, for I might be seen as an 'uppity nigger' who doesn't know their place.
- I am very grateful for being accepted in this country; therefore, I have no right to complain about inequality or racism.
- I know I won't be fully accepted, so being tolerated is better than rejection.

Fawning elaborated

A powerful example of fawning, in my assessment, can be observed in this problematic statement: 'I don't have to accept membership of any minority ethnic group, for I can rely on my brown privilege.'

The term 'brown privilege' thankfully only sustained a flicker of life during the Trump era. People from every corner of society felt emboldened to claim what they felt were their personal and group's rights, mostly for worse, and this phrase seemed to hitch a ride on the back of Peggy McIntosh's (1989) concept of *white privilege*. The term was first coined by the famous black civil rights activist, William Du Bois, in the 1930s and then came into prominence after anti-racism activist and writer Peggy McIntosh published her ground-breaking essay 'White Privilege: Unpacking the Invisible Knapsack' (1989). As a white person, she shone a bright light on how valuable a currency white skin was for white people and its oppressive consequences for the black other. The excerpt below encapsulates her powerful essay:

> I have come to see white privilege as an invisible package of unearned assets that I can count on cashing in each day, but about which I was 'meant' to remain oblivious. White privilege is like an invisible weightless knapsack of special provisions, maps, passports, codebooks, visas, clothes, tools, and blank checks.
>
> (McIntosh, 1989, pp. 10–12)

It is troubling when particular minorities, although possessing knowledge and understanding of what white privilege is, choose to co-opt the term (knowingly or unknowingly) for its benefit. This seems to be an unthinking way to explain differences among black, brown and mixed-race people. McIntosh, through her concept, was indeed addressing the privilege of white skin, which is the forerunner to superiority in the bald reality of lived experiences. 'Brown' minorities claiming this same term, by simply reworking the phraseology, strikes me as devastatingly naive and divisive, as it colludes and contributes to the ugly legacy of both black people and brown people's colonial history. Hijacking conceptual race handles, however tangential, seems only to contribute to further divisions, and help stoke fires of hierarchical oppression among minorities. Such inaccuracies create damaging consequences for racial cohesiveness in all contexts, particularly those of pedagogy and politics.

The above example explains some of the essential tenets relating to re-enactments of historical enmeshment. They depict intergenerational trauma, often coupled with the impact of personal and other conflictual issues, all becoming entangled in the theme of trauma. Fawning as a consequence of historical trauma is, therefore, the withdrawal from the pain of history by unwittingly enlisting the oppressor to avoid the shame of owning one's own oppression.

The role of the internal oppressor in the chokehold

It is a sad fact that it is not only the social mechanism within our divided society that keeps the bind of historical enmeshment alive, but also the invisible mechanism of the internal oppressor (Alleyne, 2004). This is the internal enemy which, in many ways, is a more dangerous adversary than external forces because it resides within. The fight with the inner enemy parallels battles with the chokehold of identity shame. Neither the internal oppressor nor shame has an object, meaning that there is an internalization that invariably becomes an internal fight with the self. We create the inner enemy intrapsychically, that is, by ourselves within ourselves. To win this fight we must face our internalizations (negative scripts), where fears, anxieties, catastrophic thoughts, paranoia, shame, naivety and negativity all reside.

For the therapist, enabling clients to separate from historical enmeshment is an important task in the healing from intergenerational trauma. It involves the work of replacing unhealthy internalizations with new scripts that can redirect self-determination towards the goals of healing, revitalization of the ego and transcendence from racial hauntings.

Burden and racial hauntings in the context of historical enmeshment

In Chapter 4, we explored the distinct difference between 'burden' and 'racial hauntings', which I see as the ever-present but not always conscious weight of trauma that is passed down the generations. Burden is shaped by both the past and the present. The past element is the latent content of black oppressive history and the consequent trauma transmissions passed down the generations. The present or manifest content element of burden is kept alive by having to deal with all forms of racism and being impacted by the silent wounds of racialized trauma. Racial hauntings are part of the present and manifest. Both latent content of oppression (burden) and manifest content of oppression (racial hauntings) are active dynamics of historical enmeshment.

Burden in this sense is traumata – the pathological wound carried that keeps enmeshment dynamics alive and is the index of black oppression. This burden can be released or lightened, which is part of the healing process. Racial hauntings reopen historical wounds and therefore deepening critical consciousness for self-awareness, self-regulation and self-protection is crucial in order to separate from historical enmeshment.

Racism: furthering an understanding of historical enmeshment

To further understand historical enmeshment, one needs to have an overview of race and I present the following views and theories of psychoanalytic thinking on the subject. Much written material on race and, specifically, the focus on black–white relations, still has the tendency to address external issues such as cultural imperialism, social and political inequality, forms of racism, crime, mental health, and education. In counselling and psychotherapy; where it is expected that such discourse will also focus on the internal, material is still wanting. The existing literature has given attention to familiar themes on race, through the repetition of debates and counter-debates to the point where we can now expect any current discourse to include recognizable themes along the following well-worn lines:

- 'a racism which does not have the pseudo biological concept of race as its main driving force has always existed' (Balibar and Wallerstein, 1991).
- Racism as the colour-blind position, which allows white individuals not to see difference, and avoid the shame involved in owning their own racist thoughts (Morgan, 2008).
- Racism as a borderline issue, which presents as avoidance and

marginalization of race in psychotherapy (Lowe, 2006).

- Racism as splitting, projection and projective identification (Dollard, 1938; Gordon, 2004; Hinshelwood, 1989; Money-Kyrle 1960; Rustin, 1991; Timimi, 1996; Young, 1992; Ward, 1997;). These texts follow arguments and counter-arguments that suggest the above-named concepts are ways by which individuals may sharply compartmentalize people and relationships in the external world into good and bad, and polarize their responses accordingly. Corresponding processes of idealization and denigration are inherent in these racist attributions. Additionally, any unwanted feelings and responses are placed outside of the self to protect against fear and anxiety (usually irrational).

- Racism as concerned with dynamics of the Oedipus complex (Chasseguet-Smirgel, 1990) – Nazi genocide is referred to here as a clear example. This concept is concerned with a Freudian notion that all revolutionary conflict in society stems from feelings of desire (a wish to possess the other) and hostility that are acted out in sibling rivalrous groups.

- Racism as an irrational process and therefore a form of neurosis if held on to (Rustin, 1991). This belief suggests that irrationalism derives from preconceptions about others not observed as facts. Such feelings can form judgements, strong opinions and corresponding actions in the face of the truth. Such destructive narcissism could lead to pathological organizations of the personality with the corollary of irrational thinking and neuroses.

- Racism as sibling rivalry (Sterba, 1947), which presents a way of understanding how and why black people are made to represent sibling rivals and be infantilized in the presence of white people.

- Racism as a manifestation of sexual jealousy (symbolized by historical lynching practices and present-day black male disempowerment) and a concept also associated with the objectification of black people as primitive, the physical, shit and evil (Berkley-Hill, 1924; Fanon, 1986, Vannoy-Adams, 1996).

- Racism as a response to modernity (Frosh, 1989; Sarup, 1996). In this context, racism is cultural imperialism and exploitation and therefore highlights issues of power and the powerless and the dominant and dominated.

- Racism as boundaries and boundary drawing – 'a way to fix the other, to assert and maintain sense of absolute difference between self and other' (Gordon, 2004). As an exception, this perspective has struck me as a refreshing addition to the body of available text.

Separating from the chokehold of historical enmeshment

Separating from the chokehold of historical enmeshment is an ever-present struggle, as it challenges black people to stay grounded in the midst of constant racial impingements from the outside world. These struggles are a fact of black life and, for the fact that in a multi-racial society races have to work and live side by side, black–white relationships often resemble, and cannot escape, these codependent states. Both sides are reliant on each other, but often feel separate from each other. For example, it would be a national crisis, and a critical state of emergency for this society, if we paused to think what would happen if all frontline workers, carers, transport workers, nursing personnel at all grades, shopkeepers, hospitality staff and other ancillary workers at Britain's 'coalface' all dared to go on strike. The catastrophe that would befall us all would be devastating. Society would grind to a halt, for the unarguable fact that the jobs identified in the list above are mostly occupied by black and other European ethnic minorities. Ethnic minorities are the vanguards and providers of society's basic needs and yet their services are poorly rewarded and underappreciated. On the other hand, ethnic minorities need to live, work and earn, and so cannot avoid being part of society and, sadly, the inevitable infringements of racism and prejudice that accompany this.

Problems encountered in separating from the chokehold

I return to my doctoral research studies of 2006 and current private psychotherapy practice to highlight some key observations that contribute to problems encountered in separating from the ever-present phenomenon of historical enmeshment. The particular dynamics chosen are by no means the exhaustive list, but feature in both black research respondents' stories, and clients' presentations. These dynamics underscore the unique difficulties faced in the process of separation and individuation.

Ego justification

Ego justification becomes a natural defence mechanism against being devalued:

> *Back home I was very respected and always looked up to. Here, you are nothing – just another black face.*

> *got this far because I am well qualified with lots of experience – God only knows how some of them got promoted to these high positions.*
> (A black worker lamenting being overlooked for promotion)

These are just two examples from my 2006 doctoral research project, but sadly they echo similar comments from my clients today, 2022, who turn to psychotherapy to help them through the devastating emotional, mental and psychological impact that race difficulties in the workplace can have. Being devalued at work pushes the minority ethnic person into situations where they constantly feel they have to justify their actions in order to maintain integrity and self-worth. The implication here is that elements of transgenerational trauma are activated, which compound the here-and-now experience of feeling diminished and not being treated as equal in terms of skill and capability. Ego justification becomes the work of having to constantly explain and prove oneself, making it difficult to separate and enjoy the privilege of just being one's true self.

Black-on-black dynamics

My doctoral research findings highlighted black-on black dynamics as a further factor that complicates separation from the enmeshed relationship with the white other. Black workers described concerns and their criticism of some black managers who use the same template as white managers to manage black staff. It was felt that the template carried all the stereotypes, unconscious biases and discriminations that are based on the 'norms' of white institutions in their dealings with black people. These black managers were seen as 'selling out', a term used to indicate a process of being transformed into the white system. One black client who herself is a senior mental health professional, and who is currently in private therapy because of workplace harassment and unfair dismissal, explained to me that she felt her black manager 'was identifying with the [white] aggressor'. Her understanding, after many occurrences of this treatment, is that it is a displacement of black people's own historical experience of abuse that gets repeated or perpetuated through acts of abuse on others. She cited this phenomenon as one of the reasons that some black parents dish out excessively harsh punishment to their children in the name of teaching them a good lesson.

The implication here is that re-enactments of abuse keep generations entangled in a web of historical trauma, making it difficult to separate with relative ease.

Blackness, class and enforced homogeneity

Class dynamics present in curious ways when they are applied to black people. Class as a word meaning a social system where there is a pecking order of rank, level, grouping, caste and social status seems to create problems at the best of times, but especially during social and economic crises. However, when class is applied to race, both black and white sides seem to have difficulties embracing the obvious diversity that exists among black people. As a racial diasporic group with a common history, black people are as diverse as the diversity that exists in the plant kingdom. Yet, for whites, there seems to be no space created for these clear differences, as it appears much easier to relate to black minorities as a monolithic mass. The same struggle seems to present among black people. For blacks, difference and being different within our own group seems to invite sibling dynamics of jealousy, envy, rivalry and competition, where we replicate the very same ranking system.

Class issues clearly create divisions on complex levels for different reasons on both sides of the racial divide. Some obvious differences can be found in personal background, family status and ease of access to life opportunities. Both my black psychotherapy clients and my black research respondents of a particular background have described class loosely in terms of having particular opportunities that allowed them benefits in life. These may have been character building, which was gained from having a stable family background, where positive internalizations of the parental imagoes (idealized mental images of a parent or parents that influence behaviour) contributed to an in-built confidence to meet the world. For others, it was the gratitude of being given a good education from a young age that was given high primacy in their family culture. For others still, it was parents' financial abilities to travel with their families to see more of the world and have minds and perceptions broadened. These differences, while affording some black people opportunities, better prospects and comforts in life, paradoxically seemed to act against them in their own racial group. Many have reflected on these positives as acting in ways that made them feel that they did not fit in either the black or the white community. One respondent said she felt like 'an anomaly' because she did not fit the commonly held stereotypes white people have of black people – and the generally held views black people have of the 'typical' black person.

In private practice, black clients for whom class was an uncomfortable signifier of their identity, spoke of times when, for instance, they were called 'uppity black' because they spoke a certain way, held unusual interests and had good deportment. In one memorable therapy session, I recall a black client describing a situation where it was even assumed that she must have had a white partner to be the way she was – an implication that she was *refined* by this white other.

Other dynamics relating to blackness, class and enforced homogeneity were described in terms of such black individuals being singled out by white people in positions of power and 'used' against other blacks – a divisive dynamic that creates an obvious hierarchy and a kind of sibling rivalry among blacks. Four black research respondents who worked in the NHS spoke about being singled out and made the subject of harsh envious attacks. They were accused of being 'too qualified for your own good'. These four women spoke about the unconscious attempt to homogenize black people, that is, 'they see us all the same ... only to serve at a particular level'.

All of the examples and experiences described above raise issues for class diversity and the uniqueness of black individuality to legitimately coexist in all its differentness. Unconscious bias can activate people's preconceived notions of whom and what they want you to be, and such dynamics create negative reactions on all sides.

Blackness, class and enforced homogeneity are a constant burden black people find themselves having to shake off and, as explained, this dynamic can come from both sides of the racial divide. When such racial hauntings are activated by jealousy, envy, rivalry and competition between blacks, it is a sad reminder of work still to be done in our own backyards, as they indicate re-enactments from our history that are still at play. When they are activated by white racism, they add to the painful reminders of inequality and injustice, and further reasons to separate from the chokehold of historical enmeshment.

Personality types and workplace difficulties

I return to a specific focus of my doctoral research, which provided an in-depth psychotherapeutic understanding of black identity in the workplace. The workplace seemed a particularly important environment to focus on for several reasons. First, it is the place we spend most of our waking hours; secondly, the workplace replicates family units, where it is hard to be both an individual and a member of the family group, yet we know both are required for wellbeing and success. The dynamics of people working in these family-orientated groups can sometimes do harm to personal wellbeing which, in turn, could damage the reputation of the organization/family. Misunderstandings in cultural and racial difference, for example, could exacerbate tensions in the family/workplace, leading to possible breakdown.

Apart from race, I was interested to discover whether typologies played a part in workplace difficulties experienced. However, the findings did not indicate a specific kind of black person who was more prone to experiencing workplace difficulties of the kind described in the study. However, two 'character types' (the term used loosely and not in the clinical psychological sense) were found from opposite ends of the 'personality-type scale'. At one end, there was the very articulate, challenging and assertive black individual who was more likely to be singled out and branded aggressive, scary, problematic or the difficult one. Such an individual was more likely to be vocal in their complaints about the presence of real (or perceived) racism operating in the workplace and would often speak up for themselves and on behalf of others. They were frequently seen as a threat, 'a thorn in the backside of management' and 'a headache' to control. Management appeared more likely to use draconian methods to silence such individuals, rather than engage in collaborative and constructive ways.

At the other end of the scale was the more quiet, compliant, unchallenging, fawning 'I will do whatever it takes for a quiet life' type, seemingly easier to manipulate, overlook, be seen as the 'good black' and marginalized in the workplace. Whatever the personality of the worker, the research findings revealed a clear point: the nature of workplace difficulties for black workers were often subtle, insidious and heavily veiled with civility and complex defensive political postures and manoeuvrings from the other side.

The inclusion of personality types in workplace contexts as contributing to the chokehold of historical enmeshment suggests that blackness, as a signifier of identity, will often attract undesirable attention in complex ways that are hard to avoid or ignore. The reality of these often-hidden race dynamics is that they inevitably activate racial hauntings that contribute to, and keep alive, enmeshment dynamics.

All of the aforementioned difficulties that contribute to the enforced homogeneity of blackness and class can be worked through, reframed and transcended. I will be addressing these aspects of healing and transcendence in Chapter 10, 'Healing from the burden of our heritage'.

Enmeshment doesn't allow for individuality, wholeness, personal empowerment or healthy relationships; rather it leaves the enmeshed individual not knowing where they begin or end. In the context of black–white relationships, the toxic dependency that was actively fostered and manipulated in the past in order to keep the subordinate group in a position of 'knowing their place' can lead to similar dynamics in the present, where unhealthy psychological dependency on, or merging with, the dominant other may continue. Facilitating awareness of these dynamics in a timely and sensitive way in therapy can enable black clients to gain deeper understanding of their struggles with imposter syndrome and other difficulties relating to shame, identity and self-esteem.

Being caught in the chokehold of historical enmeshment tends to leave individuals with carried feelings whose constant presence can function to shape aspects of personality and disposition. These feelings can weigh heavily enough to aggravate and create reactive temperaments and character traits. This is the extent to which harmony in the limbic system for black people is eclipsed. The calm enjoyed by those who do not have to worry about race discrimination becomes an elusive privilege that is hoped for but not easily achieved.

CHAPTER 8

Intersectionality and racialized trauma

Freedom is our divine 'right' to showcase the many selves society chooses not to recognize

Introduction

'Being black is not my *raison d'être*.' This is my French for explaining the fact that blackness is not my only reason for being, nor the factor that justifies my existence – it is just one aspect of my make-up. This terse response expresses my annoyance at society's general tendency to create black homogeneity: 'Their body type is best suited for sports'; 'You are much better at dealing with anger'; 'Are you from Jamaica?'; 'Sciences might be too much of a stretch for you; perhaps hospitality might be a better choice?'; and so on. These are some of the ways in which racial homogenization plays out – through racial stereotyping, via unconscious bias communication, having low expectations of black people or the group, racial infantilization and creating lower ceilings through the act of racial levelling (that is, being made to 'stay in your lane'). See also Chapter 7.

My pithy response and opening quote also defend the obvious fact that we are not just one self, but many distinct and integrated selves. In my case, these include: my womanly self, myself as part of a family, my educated professional self, my independent and autonomous self, my middle-ageing self, my slightly lower than average height self, my sapodilla-brown complexion self, my Guyanese–Caribbean self, my naturalized British self, my self-employed self, my unorthodox self, my childless self, myself as empath ... and, in this long list of selves, my black self. All of these are overlapping parts of a hybrid identity. As black people, we strive to reach the fullness of our many selves, but this work is often hampered by society's tendency to minimize, homogenize and dehumanize black lives.

Homogenization is the opposite of the interconnected nature of intersectionality, and leads to marginalization – reacting against this requires an effort that involves explaining, justifying and defending one's entitlement to a full existence. All such responses demand energy that interrupts the rhythm of black life and threatens to take away from its vitality and privilege.

There is no monolithic black in black identity, for we are a hybrid of blackness personified.

The concept of intersectionality

Broadly speaking, intersectionality is the idea that disadvantage is conditioned by multiple interacting systems of oppression. However, the term has been interpreted in many nuanced ways during our changing times, and as viewed through the different lenses of many feminist and non-feminists writers.

Kimberlé Crenshaw is the African–American lawyer, professor and civil rights activist who coined the term in her paper (1989), using it to explain the multi-layered oppression of African–American women. Much has been developed conceptually and written about intersectionality since then: hooks (1981); Lorde (1984); Brooks Higginbotham(1992); Lewis, Mendenhall, Harwood and Huntt (2013); Hancock (2016); Hill Collins (2019, 2020); and Turner (2021) are just a few who have added to the literature. It must be noted that the term had already been addressed by black women's rights activist Mariah Stewart, the first African American woman on record to lecture publicly on women's rights in the 1800s, and in Sojourner Truth's, 'Ain't I A Woman' speech, delivered in 1851 at the Women's Rights Convention in Akron, Ohio. The activism of social reformer Savitribai Phule in India in the 1850s also led a campaign that promoted education for the socially oppressed. Education in the subcontinent at that time was limited to males of the Brahmin[1] caste, and she worked to include all girls and women – and marginalized low-caste men. Although in essence her work was about women's rights, and she was a true feminist, her work encompassed the intersectional issue of caste.

Over the last thirty years, the term has been at the forefront of many discourses, as a way to think about inequality, often dealing with – but not limited to – race, gender, class and sexuality. Rather than view inequality as relationships where there is a dominant centre and subordinate other at the margins, feminist writers have extended the focus: through the concept of intersectionality they have mapped the various ways in which race defines gender, and how it serves as a live wire, conducting the charge for other hierarchical social relations, including class and sexuality. Intersectionality in our contemporary times is a global analytical framework for understanding issues of social justice and human rights. It can be seen as a tool that provides a lens through which we can understand how identity politics create power and oppression in the areas where race operates as a hidden dimension.[2]

Intersectionality as a tool

Other scholarly writers have extended Crenshaw's concept, addressing previously unseen race dimensions. This has included other areas of inequality, relating to power, racial justice, pedagogy and the shaping of legal discussion. Patricia Hill Collins and Valerie Chepp (2013), for example, address the wider impact of oppressive structures as they affect other people who are subjects of discrimination:

> Intersectionality consists of an assemblage of ideas and practises that maintain that gender, race, class, sexuality, age, ethnicity, abilities, and similar phenomena cannot be analytically understood in isolation from one another; instead, these constructs signal an intersecting constellation of power relationships that produce unequal material realities and distinctive social experiences for individuals and groups positioned within them.
>
> (Collins and Chepp, 2013, p. 58)

Their broad-brush treatment to intersectionality seems particularly pertinent to our contemporary times, encompassing various tenets and focal points, which may be summarized thus (2013):
- Intersectionality is a tool that can be used to identify where

policies fail to fulfil the needs of marginalized groups, and where they contribute to oppression, marginalization and identity wounding.

- Intersectionality is a theory that breaks with the essentialist view of identity (social and individual) as static, and is rather one that changes and evolves within the existing context to produce distinct lived experiences.

- Rather than adopting a purist essentialist stance that sees identities as having intrinsic different aspects that remain constant, intersectionality views identities as shaping and evolving as a result of phenomena and other social circumstances. Collins and Chepp's view of intersectionality is at odds with the idea of essentialism, as its practice tends to silence some voices, for example, women and black people, and privileges others, especially those of the dominant white male-gendered group. In this sense, their intersectionality rejects the practice of wilful blindness, which is the political strategy of not recognizing the dignity and rights of the disadvantaged and marginalized in society.

Collins has further focused on the development of intersectionality as critical inquiry (theory) and praxis (application or use). In her recent book, she offers six core ideas that broaden and deepen understanding of the subject (Collins and Bilge, 2020, pp. 31–6):

1. **Social inequality** is not caused by a single factor, such as only race or only class, but through the intersections among various categories of power.

2. **Intersecting power relations** take into account various and intersecting domains of power. These include the interpersonal domain of power, nation state power working within different philosophies of social democracy and neo-liberalism, the power of politics, economic power and the power of money, which makes having capital an intersectional issue.

3. A core theme of intersectional analysis is the importance of examining power relations in a **social context**, whether that is a global social context or a cultural social context. Social contexts are very much shaped by the zeitgeist.

4. **Relationality** is a component of intersectionality that embraces an

analytic framework that shifts the focus from seeing categories as oppositional to examining their interconnections. Relationality is found in terms such as coalition, dialogue, conversation, interaction and solidarity. Relationality connects and provides opportunities for new possibilities for intersectional enquiry and action.

5. **Social justice** is the work at the heart of intersectionality. What makes intersectionality critical is that it is a tool very much connected to a social justice ethos. As a tool of critical enquiry into the workings of social justice, it can illuminate how justice can be elusive in unequal societies. For example, everyone has the right not to be abused, but what upholds black (British) footballers' right not to be repeatedly racially abused is proved ineffectual, as decades of cheap talk and intent are the only feeble actions sanctioned by the governing bodies concerned.

6. Intersectionality is multifaceted and aims to analyse and make sense of the **complexities** in our world. It therefore engages in critical enquiry, as is the case with the tool of psychoanalysis, and aims to study and uncover what is going on within the nature of social phenomena.

Racialized trauma

Racialized trauma can be described as the ongoing impact of racism that affects every layer of the self and leaves in its wake a weight and a burden that create hauntings for black lives. Related to this is intersectional damage, which can be summed up as the loss of dignity and rights, psychological pain and damage, including the reactivation of racial hauntings. Any or all of this may lead to a diminished quality of life.

Understanding intersectionality: case examples

The following three case examples illustrate the use of the intersectionality analytic tool to help widen and deepen awareness of the impact of racialized trauma. In these examples, I identify the areas where racialized trauma can be missed, marginalized and completely forgotten; this may well be in plain sight, especially in the consulting room, and in the process of dealing with unconscious bias complaints in the workplace.

Case example 1: Bhumi

Bhumi is a 26-year-old single black woman who hails from the Ivory Coast, also known as Côte d'Ivoire, Africa. She has been in the UK for four years, where she feels freer to live her life as a member of the LGBTQ+ community.[3] Bhumi identifies as queer, an identity she wears with pride to express her sexuality and gender, which is complicated, ever-changing and doesn't fit neatly into a category. She enjoyed a rich education in her country of origin and acquired an internationally recognized degree in Business Management. Business was the traditional choice of study, which she followed to please family. Faced with many difficulties in trying to live a more authentic, fluid life beyond the binary of expected heteronormativity, she decided to look outside her African home environment to connect with like-minded people in a more open-umbrella queer community.

In London, she found such a black community that made her feel welcomed and embraced. In this new home, she enjoyed a further sense of progressing with her life by undertaking a Women's Studies course that explored politics, society, media and history from women's and feminist perspectives. In her work as a semi-skilled salesperson in a very large retail company, however, her experiences were very different. Bhumi was one of a handful of ethnic minorities working amongst a predominantly white British workforce. The company had a clear tiered system, wherein the positioning of workers was visible, with white males occupying all managerial and organizational roles at the top. There were white men and fewer white women in the middle tier, taking up positions as supervisors and foremen. In the lowest tier, at the coalface, was the largest group, comprising ethnic minorities; paradoxically they possessed higher education qualifications than their white working-class peers but they were, nevertheless, placed further down the ladder of abilities and responsibilities.

Bhumi's peer, Linda, is a 40-year-old heterosexual white working-class woman. Both Bhumi and Linda are regarded as working class, and, therefore, share certain commonalities within their social grouping: they are both women, engaged in semi-skilled retail work, occupying the same lower position within the hierarchical structure of the company. They are also both on a lower pay structure than their white male counterparts and subjected to experiences of sexism and other forms of gender inequality in the workplace. However, despite these clear similarities, Bhumi's experiences are very different. Apart from the aforementioned gender inequality and sexism, Bhumi has suffered additional layers of discrimination as a direct result of her gendered racial identity, at the intersection of being a woman and black; she has also suffered from racism specifically at the intersection of being a woman and a black African woman – not a mixed-race woman, or a black British woman, but a black African woman. There is a need to recognize that uniformity of blackness limits understanding of the uniqueness in racial diversity and the sensitivities therein for personal preferences with regard to racial, ethnic and national identification. In other words, a mixed-race black British woman born in the UK may experience racism in one way, a naturalized black British woman born in the Caribbean, another way, a black African, a totally different way. All of these nuanced intersections lead to different and very distinct forms of discriminatory experience. Bhumi also finds herself a victim of gendered homophobia in the work culture as a direct result of her sexual identity and membership of the LBGTQ+ community.

In addition, Bhumi is also subject to other forms of oppression, as a result of ageism due to her being seen as too young for the job. This brings judgement on her character and abilities, for no justifiable reason. Bhumi endures a xenophobic work environment, where comments are directed at her immigrant status, which is seen as robbing home-grown whites of a job. Bhumi is particularly hurt by the presence of other forms of prejudice from 'her own people', that is, fellow black workers, who ignore and isolate her for being 'a very different black'. Further humiliation stems from jokes that mimic her pronounced 'African accent', which she feels is pure ignorance, as there is no such thing as an African accent, given that there are countless languages, dialects and accents in the vast continent. What particularly stings is the lowered expectation of intellectual ability that seems to go hand in hand with the accent of someone for whom English is a second, albeit fluently spoken, language. Microaggressions prevail, are accepted as the norm in this toxic working environment and Bhumi suffers from their damaging impact.

Bhumi's various negative experiences overlapped and intersected at the crossroads of her many identities to compound the impact of discrimination in the workplace. Her response to the daily grind and oppressive experiences was to challenge and call out the microaggressions and the negativity. However, in an environment where it felt like the like-minded closed ranks in silent collusion, Bhumi felt unheard, defeated, alone and worn down. She withdrew, became almost mute and suffered in silence. In spite of this enforced positioning, she was singled out as the aggressive, angry, difficult, scary black woman. All of these inaccurate labels belied the unpleasantness and real systemic inequalities in the company's work culture.

Linda, on the other hand, experiences workplace oppression mainly because of gender and class discrimination, but her whiteness differentiates the nature of her experiences, privileging her identity and therefore offering protection and insulation from racism. Bhumi's blackness adds many layers to her experience of intersectional oppression and, as such, it increases the psychological burden.

When Bhumi finally plucked up the courage to complain to her white female manager about her experiences, she was told 'It is just banter', 'You can't be so sensitive to survive here' and 'It's natural for people to pick on strange people'.

Comment

The implementation of an effective intersectional approach to supporting Bhumi in therapy would allow for the unpacking of the multiple social and racialized identities that are contributing to her experience in the workplace. Effective use of this tool will help widen and deepen the practitioner's understanding and, therefore, facilitation of the various levels of distress in the client's experience. Intersectionality as an analytical tool could offer insight into how the interlocking nature of Bhumi's racial oppression affects her multiple identities, including the black-on-black issues of colourism/shadism and race prejudice.

A culturally sensitive approach to Bhumi's workplace difficulties will allow the necessary space for her to be seen in her full hybrid self. Part of this work would include recognition of how workplace rejection may activate wider issues of rejection, such as the rejection of the LGBTQ+ community in her country of origin and aspects of her authentic self. An intersectional approach in therapy will also enable the practitioner to ground their intercultural psychotherapeutic praxis in meaningful approaches for the client's holding, support, healing and empowerment. Ultimately, support should enable Bhumi to actualize her employment rights for dignity and safety in the workplace. Case examples like Bhumi's also raise implications for intersectional pedagogy in counselling, psychotherapy and other psychological and 'diversity' trainings.

The following case example questions are offered to facilitate tutors and students, wider thinking about intersectional themes when dealing with racialized trauma.

Questions to facilitate intercultural psychotherapeutic praxis

- What is stirred up for you by this case example and what are you doing with your responses?
- How might you begin to explore Bhumi's self-identity and perceptions of her experiences as a black woman in a predominantly white working environment?
- How many intersectional identities can you identify in this case study? How does the racialized element influence the impact of trauma?
- What conceptual handles help guide you in your understanding of Bhumi's experiences?
- What might you take to supervision to help review your handling of this case?

Case example 2: a hostile encounter

The following example is from personal experience and identifies where intersectional identities meet. The situation highlights a hostile encounter and presents a case example worthy of intersectional scrutiny.

I am staying for two nights at a luxurious city hotel, provided by the organization who have requested my diversity consultancy services. It's a bonus I am grateful for, although I would be equally happy with a functional travel-chain hotel option. I am charged with facilitating two days' training to managers and staff, with a specific anti-racism focus. The first day has been a great success, and I am pleased to return the next day.

I head down to breakfast, dressed in my smart consultancy trouser suit. As I contemplate the wide array of delicious hot English breakfast choices, I hear an unusual sound, *pssst*, coming in my direction. I ignore it, but, upon hearing it again, I turn around. One of three men seated at a table looks directly at me and impatiently beckons me with a flicking motion of his index finger. The three white males appear to be professional city gents, in smart and crisp business suits, with brief cases and iPads beside them.

I immediately assessed the subtext of this seemingly innocuous incident, and did not feel concussed by this 'race-accident' (that is, naive perception of it as an unintentional incident of mistaken identity). This assessment of what is really at play is something that I and black people are familiar with when we happen to be a minority in a majority setting. Fact: I was the only black person in this predominantly white male-dominated swanky environment. Fact: there were white hotel staff (predominantly of the hidden minority groups of European migrant staff who also suffer frequent discrimination), who were diligently carrying out hospitality services all around us. I immediately knew that I was being cast into the stereotypical role of kitchen staff, waitress or black cleaner. In the comfort of this knowledge, I purposefully decided to enter into the eye of the storm, anticipating the race-infused dynamics that would unfold.

In response to the white forefinger beckoning gesture, which meant *YOU, over here*, I mimicked the most stereotypical servile slave posture possible and genuflected my way over to the white guests. The exchange unfolded thus:

Me: Did you call, SIR (parodying servitude)?
White male: Yes, could you get us some warm plates?
Me: Come again, SIR?
White male: [annoyance clear in his voice/expression] Don't you understand English? I said, could you get us some warm plates!

At this point, I bring my role-playing to a halt, pull myself up to full height and, in the most self-assured fashion, facilitate an equal engagement.

Me: You've made an assumption of my role here. Haven't you?
White male: What are you on about?
Me: I said [pause], you have made an assumption about my role in this establishment. Haven't you? [pause] A role that you feel is only meant to serve people like you [pause] Yes? [eye wide; brows arched]

The other two white males rise with impatience and head to a new table, leaving their colleague to deal with the confrontation.

> **White male:** What's your case?
> **Me:** [calm and modulated] I'll tell you what's 'my case'. You have made an assumption that the only black woman present here today can have no other role or position but to serve white folk. Being black is not my raison d'être. And, while serving is an honourable job, that ain't my role today – sir! I am a fee-paying guest just like you, so I suggest that you get off your bony ass and get your warm plates yourself. Goodbye!

The following questions are offered as guides to facilitate tutors' and students' wider thinking about intersectional themes when dealing with racialized trauma.

Questions to facilitate intercultural psychotherapeutic praxis

- What is stirred up for you by this case example? Where do your feelings take you?
- How many intersectional identities are impacted in this hostile encounter?
- Identify and unpack each intersectional experience with a focus on working therapeutically with the impact of identity wounding.
- What conceptual handles might be helpful in this work?
- What difficulties might you encounter in helping the client in their recovery from this experience?
- What might you take to supervision to review your handling of this case?

This case example highlights wide-ranging intersectional themes in the midst of individual and collective racialized trauma.

Case example 3: Windrush

The treatment of the Windrush generation is a scandal-soaked story of discrimination and betrayal that played out at a national level in Britain just a few years ago. The legal outcome of this shameful case was greatly influenced by the intersectional lens used to scrutinize the multi-layered and overlapping aspects of discrimination and oppression of a generation of black people. This lens exposed shameful breaches of Britain's human rights laws, through the neglectful treatment and deliberate creation of a hostile environment for an ethnic minority group. The scandal was summed up in the national papers as a deliberately rigged system that targeted a black ethnic minority group; it exposed systemic and structural failings in the Home Office, leading to senior politicians losing their jobs.

The story of the Windrush generation is a quintessential example that highlights intersectionality in motion at a nation-state level. In many, and scarily familiar, ways, the analysis has bearings on another national scandal, the Grenfell Tower tragedy.[4]

Over 70 years ago, thousands of Commonwealth citizens left the Caribbean for the UK, at the invitation of the British Government, for labour replacement purposes after the Second World War. The ship HMT *Empire Windrush* set sail from Jamaica to London in 1948 carrying 1027 passengers from various parts of the Caribbean. The 'empire' part of the name was commonly given to merchant ships controlled by the British in the colonial era; the 'Windrush' part became synonymous with that generation who came to fill the labour shortages.

Until 1972, the British Nationality Act 1948 gave citizenship to all people living in the Commonwealth territories. This 'right' enabled members of the Windrush generation and their children to live as British citizens and to work in institutions such as the NHS and the National Rail Service (which remain two key areas still dutifully served by the descendants of this generation). This generation contributed to the development of post-war Britain, and includes many who were ex-service personnel who had already served Britain during the war. They settled here, had families and became part of the fabric of society.

In 2017, citizens of the Windrush generation were told that they would have to prove they had the right to remain in the UK or face deportation. People who had not formalized their status in the UK found themselves subject to the government's Hostile Environment – a package of measures intended to make living in the UK difficult for them, thereby encouraging them to leave.

Many were unable to prove their citizenship, because either they had arrived in the UK on their parents' passport, or landing cards and other records proving their arrival had been destroyed by the Home Office.

Many found themselves no longer able to access healthcare, social care, benefits and housing, as to do so required proof of their British citizenship. Many people suffered despite the fact that they had lived here for decades, working and paying taxes, and raising their British-born families.

The Windrush scandal exclusively affected older people at the crucial time in their lives when they were in need of care and support from their family, friends and the state (in the form of healthcare, social care, benefits and housing). The hostile environment created by the government also resulted in many having their legal aid cut, making it impossible to get legal advice to fight their cases.

The scandal mirrored many dynamics that were seen in that of Grenfell Tower. In both cases it was, in the main, black and other minority ethnic people who were affected, making them clear examples of intersectional racialized trauma. As a result of structural and systemic racism, many faced additional difficulties on top of the initial trauma, such as illness, mental health difficulties and the longstanding psychological impact of racial inequality and death.

In the horrific case of the Grenfell tragedy, the spectre of hauntings remains an enveloping mournful shroud for minorities, not unlike the thick white plastic sheeting that covers the charred skeletal effigy, where 72 spirits roam their burial site. Hauntings will forever remain the unwanted visitor to all those left behind. At the time of writing, *no one* in either the Grenfell tragedy or the Windrush generation case has been prosecuted. The burden of racialized trauma remains a heavy weight to carry, leaving racial hauntings to pay their frequent visits and terrorize the lives of broken souls.

Intercultural psychotherapeutic praxis

The three cases illustrate the intersectional nature of racialized trauma, where dormant historical pain is likely to be activated for the person(s) involved. The unpacking of intersectional wounding is not a perfunctory exercise of seeing how many social identities one can detect in a scenario. It is more about, to use the analogy of going regularly to the gym to build muscle strength, having the stamina and resilience to stay with the client's immediate pain from the present trauma, as well as being alert to the intergenerational-activated pain that stems from family issues and upbringing, as well as ancestral transgenerational pain. It also pays to have the mental endurance necessary for daring to enter psychic spaces that are not always familiar, and to engage in the facilitation process of fielding, holding and containing fragmentation both in the moment and from the past.

Working therapeutically with such clients may also trigger vicarious traumatization for practitioners – both black and white – and so supervision will be vital, and possibly personal therapy too.

The analysis of racialized trauma via the intersectional lens enables us to understand the interlocking elements of discrimination and damage that can befall people on the basis of aspects of their identity. It offers a wider perspective for understanding inequality by providing the practitioner with tools for deepening their way of thinking, frame, categorize, conceptualize and process dynamics of power and privilege. It also enables a more authentic engagement with the corollaries of inequality oppression and their trauma impact on marginalized lives. An intersectional approach in psychotherapy ultimately contributes to dignifying black lives.

The third element

I often conceptualize black racialized trauma in psychotherapeutic work from the perspective of there being a third element in the consulting room, besides myself and the client. The third element is often representative of the external (social, political, or racial) oppressor. History may also be seen as the relational third, creating generational trauma; this affects our ontological security and how we go about living our lives in society. Other times, the third element joins the therapist and client as the client's own internal oppressor, who presents as an enemy-like voice. Working with any aspect of race trauma creates a triad, a tripartite relationship: the three elements are in full engagement.

When the therapist is white, the challenges for both therapist and black client are greater. The intersectional transference and counter-transference dynamics will invariably have very layered dynamics. These might relate to what is going on in the present moment, what has happened to the client in probably a predominantly white working environment and what might be re-enacted in the consulting room. There may be other dynamics relating to what is triggered or retriggered transgenerationally or from the historical element, including what lurks in the shadows of reactivated hauntings. The therapist who struggles to field, hold and contain such complex and powerful dynamics will symbolically leave doors carelessly wide open, leaving the client to feel unsafe and unsupported.

Vicarious racialized traumatization

There is another factor which needs to be acknowledged which relates to cases with a strong media presence that bring the public's attention to global racial injustice. The brutal killings of George Floyd and Steven Lawrence, the gross mistreatment of the Windrush generation, and the years of wilful neglect of minority ethnic residents' housing complaints that led to the Grenfell Tower inferno fall into this category. These traumatic events create visceral vicarious traumatization at a granular (up close) and shared level. These phenomena cause black people (and others who are marginalized) to endure vicarious traumatization, which behaves like an emotional pendulum that swings their moods between the individual and the collective, and between the present day and the past. In these cases, the spectre of racial hauntings lingers, as if being concussed from a major accident. On top of this, there is the reaction of white people who may feel the need to express their own feelings about these events, seeking out black people in order to do so.

Practitioners must recognize these factors when they are dealing with such complex and compounded racialized trauma, and be aware of how they can maintain good mental hygiene in order to facilitate best practice; this includes not resorting or regressing to states of racial guilt and shame.

CHAPTER 9

Working therapeutically with generational trauma

Intercultural practice is like driving an unacquainted car on the opposite side of the road in another country. You are not entirely without skills, but must observe new scenery, note different signs, adjust your orientation and navigate the unusual. The challenge met will cause discomfort, but must be normalized to safely negotiate the unknown and unfamiliar.

Introduction

Although the emphasis of the book is on black lives, it will have relevant application to other racial minorities, and my hope is that it will deepen the knowledge of a reader of any ethnic background and identity persuasion. The tools and concepts in this chapter are offered to practitioners coming from a variety of theoretical modalities and therapeutic backgrounds, and can be made applicable in any setting; it is relevant to one-to-one client work, couple and group settings, and can be utilized in psychodrama, art therapy, milieu therapy and clinical supervision.

Key therapeutic concepts and tools

Working with generational trauma

How it presents
When activated in **crisis situations** look out for:
- hyperarousal of emotions, that is hypervigilance and hypersensitivity

- fight/flight responses
- pressure of speech and thought
- upset and hurt
- anger and rage
- pre-occupation with the trauma event
- adaptation to the majority group by toning down, editing and filtering out one's authenticity
- fawning by adopting a co-opted (false) persona
- feeling a victim
- isolation and victimization
- feelings of inadequacy
- shame and identity wounding
- excessive ego-justification
- strategizing and choreographing one's behaviour in white presence.

In **chronic situations** look out for:
- defeatist thinking
- defunct and outmoded life scripts
- chronic and archaic shame manifesting in negative and defeatist personal scripts
- ever-present low-level depression
- the constant negative presence of the internal oppressor
- feeling stuck and unproductive
- resignation to life
- hardening of character from repeated violence to the soul
- loss of self-esteem and self-confidence
- loss of belief in self
- psychosomatic symptoms, for example hair loss, loss of weight, weight gain, poor sleep, high blood pressure, loss of libido, impotence.

How to address it

Phase 1: working with the manifest content

Facilitate safety through offering the generosity of space for the client to be heard. When generational trauma is triggered by present-day racism, something terribly disruptive occurs intrapsychically and causes a dislocation – a psychic fracture. This is a destabilizing time for the black person, so a careful space must be created for the granular effects of this kind of mental disturbance to be held without too much therapeutic interruption. The client needs to let out and exhaust their distress (the pain-wound) and consequent hauntings that trouble the soul as occurs in the aftershock of an impact.

In the initial stages of this kind of trauma work, the client tends to talk at you, instead of engaging with you. This is an important stage of the process, enabling the reporting of what has happened to the client to be heard. This stage of the process works best if the practitioner can be an attentive listener and safe container for the distress. A genuinely engaged and curious therapist is one who is interested in hearing the minutiae of the trauma, in the knowledge that this is the *rinsing* of the trauma wound. The reporting stage of the trauma work is crucial to helping the person regain a sense of stabilization after the disruptive nature of the traumatic experience. Placing the trauma in a safe pair of hands is critical when working with racialized pain that has also activated historical trauma wounds.

Phase 2: trauma processing
Enable the client to name the dread. Naming what has actually happened enables the client to stabilize the mind and get hold of what needs to be addressed and healed. Identifying, for example, that what the client is experiencing is a clear case of 'workplace harassment' or 'racial profiling' can provide a steadying therapeutic banister rail for negotiating the trauma experience. Reflecting to the client that it appears that they have become tired of being stuck in the circular pattern of a dirty wash cycle could act as a wakeup call and provide reality orientation. Such an intervention can be centring and grounding for the client, meaning that the earlier phase 1 mode of incessant reporting of events starts to be regulated.

In the naming of the dread process, it may be necessary to offer some psychoeducation, an intervention that presents reality and enlightenment via education. For example, it may be helpful to distinguish how microaggressions in society or microinequities in the workplace can lead to a semi-permanent state of feeling 'haunted' by these *soul-injuries*. Self-regulation as the next step in the process is critical in enabling the client to start to take charge of their emotions and begin to see the reasons for them and the need to reclaim control.

If safety, insight, new awareness and self-regulation are all reasonably established at this stage, ego strength continues to build. The ongoing work may highlight other possible themes such as identity shame, identity wounding and forms of historical enmeshment that could also be part of the trauma dynamic.

Phase 3: working with latent content

At this stage of the trauma work, when ego strength is more fully regained, it may feel safer to address the triggering of past trauma, as it is often the case that present-day trauma activates trans- and intergenerational trauma. The aim of latent content work is to look deeper for a broader understanding of the trauma experience. This will help you develop a greater critical consciousness of how to manage inevitable racialized trauma.

This work involves exploring and asking questions such as *What else has been opened up for you as a result of your experience? You have hinted that your current situation has opened up your parents' suffering of overt racism when they came to this country ... can we talk about that?* The aim of holding and fielding carefully what is triggered and activated from the past is important in interrupting the concertina effect, that is, where the emotional impact from old trauma collapses into and on to the present trauma in an uncontrollable way.

If manifest and latent content are fielded well, the client's ego strength can develop. If stability continues, the client may feel reassured enough to bear working through old pain differently and can return to the present challenges with renewed insight and emotional strength. They may even be able to see their contribution or part played in the current trauma situation. For example, they may come to recognize that they have never made their voice heard for fear of reprisal, or they may have tolerated forms of emotional abuse without creating boundaries, or might have kept their head down for a long time so as not to cause a stir; in doing any or all of this, they may see that they have lost sight of a better reality that was there to be enjoyed. Self-ownership, as opposed to externalizing and projecting, is a major step towards healing and reclaiming control. From this point, trauma processing and resource building will hopefully enable a healthier return to mental and emotional wellbeing.

Phase 4: integration and sublimation

This is the last and most dynamic stage of generational trauma work. In this phase, the practitioner facilitates the process of integration of the disrupted selves by creating an encouraging and proactive environment for effective restoration, leading to hope and empowerment. The client will be stronger for having straighter lines of narrative about their experiences, instead of split, disjointed and untreated areas where pain resided. It is important to include reminders of the strengths resulting from overcoming trauma. Strength can be experienced from and within vulnerability. Actively encourage the client's sublimation through their engagement in their choice of activities. Sublimation in this context means utilizing the energies that stemmed from the trauma and redirecting them towards some form of creative pursuit or intellectual endeavour, for example writing, poetry, singing, retraining, meaningful activism.

Working with the internal oppressor (Alleyne, 2006)

Help your client to understand the concept of the internal enemy, which they have created consciously and unconsciously within; they can then develop inner resources to reframe and change its inhibiting impact. The internal oppressor must be distinguished from internalized oppression: it is part of the self, a part of the ego-structure that functions as an inhibitor and interferes with the moving on process in black lives. This is necessary psychoeducative work in generational trauma work.

Start this process by helping the client to identify their internalized scripts and how they were created. Some psychoeducation about what scripts are might be helpful. They can be described as the meaning we give to events that happen to us, a process that usually starts in childhood. Understanding generational and personal scripts that are influenced by what we have internalized from our parents, and those that have been shaped by our societal and cultural experiences, will offer insight and awareness. They may help the client see what might be influencing their thoughts and the patterns in their lives that prevent them from moving on and the actualization process. Deepening an understanding of the internal oppressor can help to reframe, with more positive thoughts and actions, leading to the achievement of full potential and heightened critical consciousness of racialized lived experiences.

Recognizing pitfalls of cultural relativism for cross-cultural competence

Cultural relativism is the idea that a person's belief and practices should be understood based on that person's own culture, and that the norms and values of one culture should not be evaluated against the norms and values of another. For this important reason, it is essential to recognize what are the potential hidden, unsuspected traps, and troublesome areas of difficulty that you might encounter.

Becoming aware of such pitfalls in therapy practice requires an awareness of the rules of cross-cultural engagement. For example, Eurocentric counselling and psychotherapy theories have a goal-orientated focus on (a) independence, (b) self-actualization and (c) personal individuation, and there is a tendency to explain behaviour and psychic phenomena mainly as a function of intrapsychic challenges. The danger of this individual and internal-based focus is that it can exclude and neglect an equally important emphasis on external factors and the collective. For ethnic minorities, what happens to the racial self in the outside world is the reality of their lived experiences. These deserve inclusion – their rightful place in the therapy space. Racism is a real part of clients' lives. Intercultural competency challenges us to create a synthesis between the external and internal, the individual and collective, and to honour the healthy tension between different races and cultures.

Reframing Eurocentrism in therapy practice

It is important to understand Eurocentrism, which is generally defined as a cultural phenomenon that views the cultures and histories of non-Western cultures and societies from a European or western perspective. 'western' and 'non-western' are broad terms used in the context of describing common social norms, belief systems, traditions and so forth, in Europe and the UK and in Africa, Asia and indigenous peoples respectively. Some examples where Eurocentric bias can occur are listed below.

Table 9.1 Eurocentric bias

Western values	Non-western values
Eurocentric values tend to give primacy to individuals, individualism, uniqueness and autonomy	Non-Western values tend to give primacy to the collective, orthodoxy and levels of compliance
In the west, the emphasis is on 'me' and 'my' (the goal of individuation)	Non-western emphasis is more on 'us' and 'our' (collective individuation goals)
There is a striving for self-actualization	Emphasis is on collective actualisation
Eurocentric values place emphasis on the nuclear family structure	Non-western values place emphasis on the extended family culture
Eurocentric values place emphasis on non-conformity	Non-western values place emphasis on conformity
In the west, the emphasis is on freedom	Non-western emphasis is placed more on security
In the west, the emphasis is on youth	Non-western emphasis is placed more on maturity
In the west, there is more openness to expressing views and feelings	In non-western cultures, there is a holding in of views and feelings as a show of respect
In western cultures, there is more of a focus on ideas of creativity	In non-western cultures, education appears to be more about learning by rote and submitting to teachers, tutors and educators
In western cultures, sarcasm (saying the opposite to what you mean), satire (using biting humour to criticize, ridicule and expose), innuendo (often disparaging, sexually suggestive or toilet humour), banter (jokey conversation) and the understatement (deliberately making something less significant than it is), are staples that particularly define British humour	In non-western cultures, humour seems less aggressive, less at the expense of others, less self-enhancing or deprecating, less self-defeating. Humour is relatively benign and observational, with a tendency to highlight and enhance relationships, as well as lift spirits through adversity

Western cultures tend to be more liberal about sex and sexuality	Non-western cultures tend to be more conservative; liberal views and behaviour regarding diversity in sexuality are still taboo
In western cultures, elders are frequently being seen as the dying breed	In non-western cultural, elders still seem to command a particular position and role of influence
In the west, communication is more open, direct and nuanced	In non-western cultures, communication can be more closed and concrete
In the west, shame seems to be managed by verbal dexterity and clever positioning	In non-western cultures, shame is 'loss of face' and damage to the personal integrity needed to function as part of the social order

Understanding cultural myopia

Cultural myopia is a form of near-sightedness, grounded in the belief that one's own culture is appropriate and applicable in all situations to all people. This is a narrow and cockeyed view of seeing all of humanity as the same. Cultural myopia can present as arrogance, ignorance and fear. All of this can lead people to say things like 'I don't see your colour, I see you as a human being'. The question is: why not see colour? We notice that someone is a woman, tall, has brown eyes and wears glasses. What is so wrong in seeing that they are black with dark skin? Seeing the world solely through a limited Eurocentric worldview, and nothing existing outside these comfortable parameters, misses the rest of humanity in a clear view perspective. It is therefore important to notice all of what is different in cross-cultural engagement, including whether someone is black. Noticing difference is not a problem nor is it a race offence. Rather, it normalizes race dynamics so that the black person feels seen, acknowledged and embraced.

Engaging curiosity – an essential tool for working with difference and diversity

Albert Einstein (Quoteslyfe.com) is quoted as saying 'Curiosity is more important than knowledge'. Curiosity leads us to enquire, ask questions, create hunger to explore and delight in new discovery. Curiosity is the very basis of education – and therefore an analytical tool. It is daring to engage with intrigue and suggests a sense of security in one's self to live outside prescribed boxes, take risks, and, above all, challenge oneself to investigate the way the world is and the way we live. Curiosity lets us really listen to other people because we are interested or, quite simply, just want to know who they are. Reciprocally, we open ourselves to receiving, sharing and exchanging. Curiosity makes us interested in a broad range of information about the world around us. It guards against indifference, which is one of the hallmarks of racism.

To be curious about what is different racially and culturally is to feel the challenge of approaching the world with a healthy narcissistic vulnerability that is able to deal with the potential threat of fragmentation. Rather than pursue an agenda or be always knowing for the sake of being in control, curiosity challenges us to follow where our questions lead us. Curiosity is about occupying the space of uncertainty, the unknown and the unfamiliar. We do not naturally like being in this space, as it takes us right back to the nakedness of our shame, and the anxiety of our greatest vulnerability, that is our primordial (primitive and unsophisticated) self.

Fighting against the vulnerability of shame is to minimize, and even get rid of, the healthy disturbance that arises in meeting the unknown and unfamiliar. At worst, it is therapeutic incompetence, for the fact that we cannot achieve cross-cultural competence by avoiding discomfort. The well-known idiom, or commonly used phrase, curiosity killed the cat suggests that being curious gets you into trouble. Curiosity effectively applied in this context will only reward the practitioner nine lives for developing stamina and authentic competence in the work.

Facilitating forgiveness and a state of grace

Facilitating movement towards a state of grace, is permitting the deity(ies) within us. Striving for a state of grace involves, first and foremost, the work of tuning out archaic rage and pain and beginning to settle at the casual core of who one is as a human being. Because the greatest challenge to life exists within us and not outside, these six elements serve as a useful reminder of the work to be done in actualizing the presence of grace:

1. Forgiveness, often seen as the forerunner to grace, means releasing the tyranny of the past that robs the present.

2. Acceptance of all of oneself.
3. Permission for your presence to shine in all its luminescence.
4. Actualization of the rightful entitlement to partake at humanity's feeding table.
5. Freedom to enjoy and just be.
6. Transformation leading to fulfilment.

Like grace, which is often biblically aligned, forgiveness may be construed as the biblical process of pardoning or releasing someone from the sins of their bad behaviour or wrongdoing – but therapeutic forgiveness is quite the opposite. It is not about pardoning, absolving or exonerating the other from their behaviour. Forgiveness, in the context of psychotherapy, enables the client or patient to see and understand that they are no longer participating in the wrongdoing of another person. This awareness enables the process of separating from enmeshed and codependent situations. Forgiveness can therefore be used as a tool for change, reframing, letting go or bringing about closure. When our clients arrive at a place of forgiveness, this can heal their psychic wounds, thereby releasing them from the tyranny or chokehold of the past.

Principles for building real race conversations

- Attunement: this is reactiveness to and full engagement with people generally. In the context of intercultural work, it demands that we shift from our comfort zones to meet the unknown and unfamiliar. Authentic engagement as part of attunement allows the other to have a real sense of being seen and felt.
- Develop the art of being reflective, which is the skill of being able to stand back and examine your own feelings, reactions and motives and how these influence what you do or think in a situation. Reflectivity counters biases, identifies your blind spots and, for those struggling against oppression, strengthens self-awareness, leading to a liberation from the 'burdens' of heritage. Developing reflectivity can be a person's agency for actualizing their full potential.
- Put aside your preconceptions.
- Examine your motivations.
- Embrace the discomfort of not knowing.

- Research and relearn; find out what you don't know. Use Johari's Window as a tool (Luft and Ingham, 1955).
- Acknowledge the advantages of your white privilege.
- Get comfortable with your story. Remember: your story = your background + your life experiences.
- Embrace shame as the source of creativity and learning, for the simple fact that one of the biggest roadblocks to creativity is a feeling of being right. When we think we are absolutely right we stop seeking further information. Being certain puts a halt to curiosity. Healthy shame never allows us to think we know it all and therefore maintains openness to others, the world and all things different.
- Read Eugene Ellis's *The Race Conversation: An essential guide to creating life-changing dialogue* (2021).

Flashforwarding: confronting catastrophic thinking

The flashforward procedure is a specific technique borrowed from EMDR (eye movement desensitization reprocessing (Shapiro, 2001), which I have adapted for basic but effective use in talk therapies. It is a tool that helps walk the client along the corridor of fear when their catastrophic scripts and internal oppressor hold them back from actualizing their full agency and potential. The skill is particularly useful when working with clients who tend to procrastinate and frequently find negative reasons for not moving forward or taking risks. An example of using this skill is taken from my clinical practice with a black female client addressing her imposter syndrome fear.

Therapist: 'What do you believe is stopping you from breaking away and setting up your own company?'
Client: 'I don't know if I can take the risk.'
Therapist: 'What's the fear in taking this risk?'
Client: 'I don't know if I believe enough in me.'
Therapist: 'What would be your worst-case scenario if you took the risk?'
Client: 'Well, failing of course.'
Therapist: 'Where would failing leave you – and what would that look like?'

> **Client:** ... very long pause ... 'Spooky! I can hear the female ancestors saying, you are capable girl.'
> **Therapist:** 'So you are being lifted by the voices of those strong women?'
> **Client:** 'Yes, I know I am capable – very capable – and I can't afford to let me – and them down.'
> **Therapist:** ... using humour ... 'Say that again Michelle! I missed it the first time! And a little louder please.'
> **Client:** ' ... I can do it ... It's what I have been doing FOR white companies for over a decade without recognition. It's time to rise like the phoenix and do it FOR myself ... phew!'

In this illustration, the active and current fear is being processed very closely to address the blocks, reluctance and other catastrophic thoughts. By asking additional questions that focus on the client's fear, the worst-case scenario is 'rinsed' to get the client to her optimal strengths. In this example, I am particularly struck by help coming from the client's ancestry, and it feels important to acknowledge them in the consulting room. The basic tenets of the flash forward procedure in this chosen extract from therapy had paradoxically moved back into the past to help a client move forward with her agency to address and meet her future.

Recognize pitfalls and omissions in your practice

- To strive only to have a theoretical knowledge about how to DO race, difference and cultural diversity work is to strive to be so well educated and equipped to know the right things to say that it may inadvertently educate you away from the immersion and embodiment of fragmentation and rawness of context.
- Those who are particularly engaged in bodywork will be entering the domain where the messiness of the self gets dumped in the therapeutic space. As Van Der Kolk (2015) reminds us, the body keeps the score, so bodywork on its own, or combined with talk therapies, will have the potential for cathecting complex trauma. Be mindful of there being adequate containment and holding for dealing with the charge of complex pain and mental distress.

- Be aware of the aesthetic appeal to de-emphasize the intersectional nature of diversity in intercultural work, where euphemisms are used as sanitized shortcuts to downplay, fuse and avoid what is difficult to name or address. This tempering, and homogenizing effect, perhaps disparagingly referred to as **gentrification** in some quarters, avoids the rawness of context and importance of difference. Here are a few examples of these occurrences that seem to be gaining traction as norms within the field of therapy and organizational diversity work:

Diversity work used instead of the specific issue of **race, black people, race conflict** and the **damage of racism**.
Unconscious bias used as a comfortable blanket term for talking about **racism**.
Brown people used as a lazy catchall instead of specifying, for example, **south Asian, east Indian, Pakistani, Bangladeshi, Malaysian, Mauritian, Arabs, people of mixed heritage**.
Inequality used instead of **racial discrimination**.
Racial prejudice used instead of **racism**.

All of the above examples run the risk of downplaying the specificity and nature of intercultural or cross-cultural work and the following suggestions are aids to these challenges.

- Use your clinical supervision as a place to address challenges of racism and oppression in your therapeutic practice. Refer to McKenzie-Mavinga (2016) to deepen your understanding in this area through fuller engagement with oppression and meeting similar challenges in clinical supervision. Supervision with a culturally competent supervisor enables a more inclusive quality check on what is omitted and what needs to be embraced with regard to best practice in the areas of race and cultural issues.
- Familiarize yourself with different cultural concepts regarding the make-up of family constellations. Know the complex attachment and relationship patterns in your clients' references to those who may not be blood relatives, but attachment figures who either may have provided a corrective emotional experience or were the replacement figures in a black client's life.
- Recognize that, for many black men, there is a continuous

struggle with managing the ever-changing challenges for black masculinity and identity in the absence of the foundation provided by a positive, emotionally available and nurturing black father. If you are a white male or black male therapist, be alert to the fact that, in the transference, you may come to mean much more than what is fostered and introjected in the work.

- Pay attention to archaic personal scripts that see blackness as a 'mark of oppression' and, therefore, a pathology. Such notions will go along with a racist ideology that sees black people as psychologically damaged. The 'damaged black' label has the propensity to engender pity from a white therapist who may, in the therapeutic process, see the malady that is white racism, something to place inside the black person to address therapeutically, as opposed to including and addressing external challenges of societal racism, inequality of opportunity, racial discrimination.

- There is no monolithic black in blackness. This true statement should alert white therapists to the fact that black is on a continuum of identity differences. It is important to allow black clients to describe their own identity and own their own experiences of what black identity means to them.

- Don't expect people of colour, LGBTQIA+, differently abled, women and all others on the diversity dimension spectrum to be your tour guides through the worlds of the underrepresented. Do the homework under your own steam and internalize the pursuit as personal investment for deepening inter- or cross-cultural professional competence.

For black therapists: boundary issues in black-on-black dynamics

Be aware of boundary issues, which include:
- over-sharing
- being overfriendly and overfamiliar in the proper development of the therapeutic relationship
- assuming cultural knowledge and taking things at face value or for granted because of the black-on-black racial proximity
- failing to explore, expand, and allow space for the client's individual voice and racial/cultural experience to be fully explored

- assumptions that both client and counsellor know what is being referred to
- 'like me' biases can lead to collusive therapeutic bonds being fostered. In these overly close and familiar working relationships, favouritism can prevent important challenges being made, 'friendships' (instead of professional relationships) being maintained, and a sense of 'stuckness' not being named
- making the white other the measure of attainment and/or the critical and punitive overseeing, super-ego self
- shifting and slackening of professional and ethical boundaries.

For white therapists: understanding white fragility

Start the process of understanding your white fragility (DiAngelo, 2018) in the context of day-to-day race conversations and working therapeutically with black clients by exploring the following key questions:

- What is your STORY? Remember your story = your background + your life experiences.
- Who taught you that STORY? What values and belief systems were imparted to you about your race, your culture, the black race and black culture.
- Which cultural scripts from your STORY do you hold dear and how have they shaped your racial identity? Focus on your values and beliefs systems.
- How does your STORY influence your thinking and behaviour today?
- What are three things that you do consciously and unconsciously to protect your white comfort when meeting challenges of race and racism?

CHAPTER 10

Healing from the burden of our heritage

'The paradox of trauma is that it has both the power to destroy and the power to transform and resurrect.'

Peter A. Levine (2010, p. 37)

Introduction

The principles of healing offered in this chapter will be of use to both practitioners and general readers.

I have come to the conclusion that, if you have never had the privilege of ownership, your sense of self value changes. The dictionary describes ownership as the state of mind or the fact of being an owner. In the context of healing, this begs the question – owner of what? Of one's rights, of control, of having power over one's life, freedom?

Healing, in the context of this book, is about moving beyond all the hallmarks of oppression and holding on to a hopeful vision that offers movement forward, towards change and individuation. There are two key processes that enable a sense of freedom: transcendence and transformation.

Freedom: a precursor or end-goal of healing?

An observation I have made during the writing of this book is that psychoanalysis seems not to have an entry for 'freedom' in its dictionaries. Counselling and psychology, on the other hand, appear to address it not as a standalone word, but rather to talk about it in terms of, for example, free will, freedom to make choices about one's life, freedom to access one's emotions, and so on, as people in charge of our own destiny. This would be all well and good if equal opportunities, privileges and liberties, which actualize personal goals for freedom, were offered to all. The reality is that existing and new encumbrances and obstacles are heaped in the paths of marginalized groups.

Interpretations of freedom

At its most basic level, freedom is the power or right to act, speak or think as one wants. It's the state of not being imprisoned or enslaved – it is independence. Freedom is not necessarily synonymous with happiness. In my view, these are two distinct concepts, but interlinked.

At a more layered level, freedom is commonly known as the quality or state of being free from governmental oppression. Political freedom, in this sense, is the absence of interference of an individual by the use of coercion or aggression. What coincides with these two definitions is the notion that liberty and freedom create power and resources to fulfil one's own potential. Determinists argue that all human actions are predetermined and thus freedom is an illusion. This opens up a whole debate on the concept of free will. Plato talked about freedom from tyranny of the soul. He described being free from the dominion of the six tyrants: anger, jealousy, fear, desire, pleasure and pain – not only for the individual, but also for society. Other philosophers (Chakrabarti, 2017; Wenzel and Marchal, 2017) describe freedom as non-attachment to the senses and the physical world, thoughts, feelings and emotions.

What strikes me about the concept of freedom in the world of counselling and psychotherapy is that it is still not very clear what it is, ultimately, for racially marginalized people – and what psychological yardsticks are used to measure this transformative process for them. It feels important to include the concept of freedom as a standalone goal which assesses personal responsibility, free will, personal choice, entitlement to equal opportunity and self-value. Facilitative questions that might help black and brown focus more deeply are:

- What does personal freedom mean to you?
- What would it look like?
- How will it impact your life?
- How will you want to use it for yourself and others?

- What could be the obstacles to your freedom?
- How would you negotiate these obstacles and blocks?
- How can we use this therapy space to work towards achieving it?

Transcendence and transformation

Both transcendence and transformation are means towards psychic healing, but I see them as different and complementary to each other. In the context of healing from the burden of heritage, transcendence is the pursuit of a higher state of being. This may be achieved through a lifetime dedicated to meditation, spiritual practice, faith healing and a whole host of complementary and alternative therapies. A multitude of paths may be chosen and followed to ultimately move beyond the four basic freedoms: freedom of speech; freedom of worship; freedom from want; freedom from fear. However, we immediately come up against unfairness in this human quest, as marginalized groups struggle to lay claim to the basic civil liberties and rights that democratic societies are meant to afford to all citizens equally. At the starting line, minorities are often positioned unfairly, as if paying some penalty about which they know nothing. First place is always occupied by the privileged majority, who get off to a head start. So the vertical challenge of moving beyond 'the burden' and seeking a higher and stiller state of being is always fraught with difficulties and greater challenges.

In psychotherapy, transformation is often seen as a series of corrective experiences facilitated by a skilled therapist, and a breakthrough in the client's effort to engage in new behaviour, adopt healthier ways of relating to others and gain a more positive view of self. As such, corrective experiences play a central role in the transformation process. Yet, as an active process, there seems to be scant attention devoted to the nature of transformation: what it is, how it is achieved, what mechanisms trigger its evolution and the consequences for positive outcome. The existential approach does address transformation, for example van Deurzen (2009), but, in the intercultural context of black generational trauma, there is a paucity of information.

In our current zeitgeist, which I have already described in Chapter 4, black clients seem to be asking and wanting something bigger, deeper changes that lead towards wholeness and more authentic connection

– both within the self and in their external reality. The following composite quote expresses this, along with the impediments that stall individuals in repetitive behaviours and thought patterns, way beyond their sell-by date:

> *I feel I am doing all the right things ... eating right, sleeping tight, really into meditating, karma cleansing, yogic practice, breath work ... I love my chanting and drumming, do black women's studies, shelves full of black books for enlightenment of the soul ... I am doing all of this stuff, but I don't feel filled up ... why am I holding myself back? ... Why am I still hiding? ... Why do I still feel empty? ... Why can't I trust myself more to believe in me? ... What am I afraid of? ... Am I terrified I might be found out to be a fraud? ... I feel I am frightened of my own shadow ... I end up doing, doing, doing with very little being ...*

In order to address this in therapy, a more active transformational process is required, demanding that the therapist embrace the impact of racialized trauma on black life. Steven Frosh (2013) adopts a vertical and horizontal perspective in his analytic examination of hauntings and ghostly transmissions in psychoanalysis. I find this axial compass helpful in thinking about healing in the black context, which I see as stepping proudly and fully into life with all of our identities.

Vertical analysis

In a nutshell (or jam jar, as will be revealed in the poignant example below), a vertical analysis facilitates a top-down focus on the transmission trajectory of the client's generational history, and can create a therapeutic opening to look at latent historical content in the clinical presentation. A vertical analysis enables identification of what is transmitted from one generation to the other, and gets repeated and subsequently internalized. Alongside this, it helps identify the relational and not yet fully understood epigenetic transmissions which hamper the natural propensity towards growth and actualization. The benefit of this approach for the client enables a fuller insight into the generational repetition that they are trying to repair.

A vertical exploration helps to name familiar racialized pain by moving across the client's generational scripts. Identification of these historical patterns allows for straighter lines of narratives to be created and, thus, clearer connections between past and present. Only when clarity of the generational burden being carried is gained and its resultant personal discomfort identified does the work of negotiating change become urgent. If the discomfort can be tolerated, despite its negative or damaging impact, change is stymied. This phenomenon has led to a familiar refrain that I share with my clients: 'We do not shift until we feel sufficiently uncomfortable with the status quo'. Therefore, if we coast in the midst of the trauma transmissions, transformation will seem out of reach and clients become resigned to how things are for their ethnic and racial group.

Horizontal analysis

A horizontal approach moves across the client's daily life, with its focus very much on the present, dealing with situations that penetrate black people's personal psychic boundaries, thereby impacting their present functioning. The careful therapeutic attendance to these trauma experiences leads to a better understanding of the correlation between situation and psychological impact and the elevation from the pain. Horizontal analysis embraces the current intersectional impact of racialized trauma and creates the right space to deal with consequent hauntings. Working horizontally with the manifest content of the client's day-to-day struggle patterns enables better accounting of their agency, both individually, within the black collective, and how they negotiate the white world.

A horizontal analysis of racialized trauma can become a more potent tool when used in conjunction with the vertical. Combining the tools can initially focus the client on a single incident of racialized trauma; once this manifest content is fully exhausted in therapy through a horizontal analysis, the vertical analysis can facilitate exploration of the latent content for a deeper understanding. A combined approach interrupts the cycle of the dreaded events and subsequent hauntings, eventually lightening the burden that is part of black heritage.

Self-actualization

> 'The organism has one basic tendency and striving – to actualize, maintain, and enhance the experiencing organism.'
>
> (Rogers, 1951, p. 487)

A vivid childhood experience came to mind, which beautifully encapsulates the challenge for the process of transformation. Its simplicity is a poignant reminder of what Carl Rogers (1959) honours as the uniqueness of one of nature's most instinctual human drives: self-actualization.

Rogers believed that humans have one core motive in life – to reach self-actualization, which means to fulfil one's potential. For a person to grow, Rogers believed that they need an environment characterized by genuineness (openness and self-disclosure), acceptance (being seen with unconditional positive regard), and empathy (being listened to and understood).

This is the transformation process – without these, personalities will not develop as they should, much as a tree will not grow without sunlight and water.

A child's fortuitous experience

'We delight in the beauty of the butterfly, but rarely admit the changes it has gone through to achieve that beauty.'

Maya Angelou

As a 10 year old living in the Caribbean, my curiosity led to the accidental hobby of collecting the most unusual and colourful caterpillars I could find near our home in the remote area of Mara, a sugar plantation in Berbice (one of the three counties of Guyana). Caterpillars, butterflies and other exotic insects were plentiful in the rich flora of the lush and unpolluted tropics. With no prompts or directions from adults, I saved up twenty empty jam jars, into which I individually placed a different species of caterpillar, with leaves from the corresponding plants and bushes where I had found them.

Twenty jam jars with their residents were lined up on a long veranda ledge and I delighted in looking after my new pets. Little did I know that I had created the ideal conditions for the wondrous process of transformation. I watched the veritable eating machines grow plumper and longer as they stuffed themselves with the leaves that I fed them daily. After a few weeks, when they seemed to reach a critical size, they stopped eating; I was puzzled and became confused as to what to do. I noticed strange things happening to their skin, as a silky skein formed around their bodies.

Soon they became encapsulated in a dull-looking protective casing and it appeared that nothing was happening. Thinking they were all dead, my naive 10-year-old self became quite impatient. I poked at one caterpillar with a twig, trying to will it into life, only to realize with horror that I had disturbed the magical living process that would promptly kill the larva. I remember walking around in a state of upset and resignation for another week, until my hopes were lifted by the sight of activity taking place inside the remaining nineteen cocoons. The signs of life taught me to be patient and I quickly learnt to just watch, be still and wait for nature to do its thing. Around the twenty-eighth day of this bizarrely exciting and disturbing new learning experience, nineteen one-and-a-half-inch brown capsules metamorphosed into beautiful airborne fairies. Some emerged slowly, lingering on the rim of the jar to sun their wings before flying off. Others simply took their first flying leap into the air and floated off into the wide green tropical surroundings. I was profoundly affected and, fifty-plus years on, still clearly remember this personal character-forming experience.

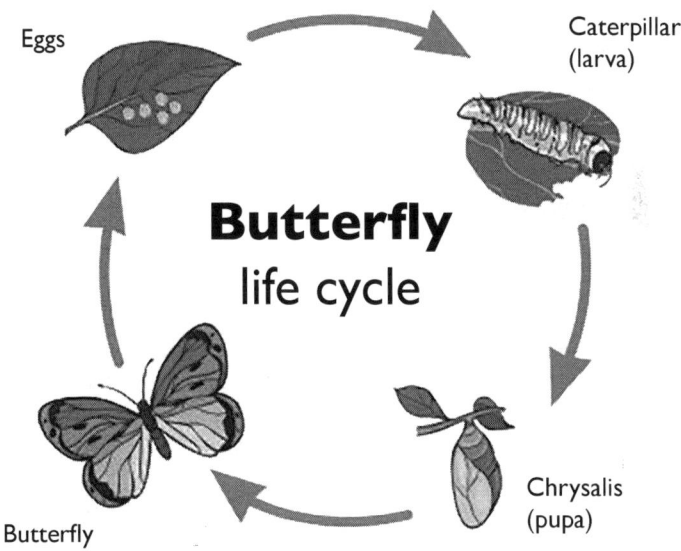

Figure 10.1 *The Butterfly life cycle. Source: Getty Images*

The child bearing witness to this enchanted experience seems to me a perfect and powerful metaphor for transformation – a slow and meticulous process of negotiating a rite of passage that involves the shedding of skin (the weight of old burdens attached to the old self) and release from trappings that no longer serve the new existence. This long held magical introjection has become deeply embedded in my psyche, shaping the trajectory of my career and fundamental belief that we all have the (natural) potential to change our circumstances if we work hard to create the conditions for transformation – even when societal blocks threaten and deny the actualization process.

Transformation: an active, moving process

Transformation is about having the right conditions within the self for the creation of our fullest aliveness to be experienced. For those whose generational histories have been perpetually marred by white oppression, this active process requires us to:

- create straighter lines in our trauma narratives, in order to have a more joined-up understanding of their relationship with the past, present and future
- re-white (rewrite) our whitewashed internalized identity scripts, for example, *Whites are more intelligent; I will never fit in. They will always be on top*
- shed archaic and outmoded values and belief systems
- readjust old character traits
- conduct regular mental hygiene checks for stronger ontological security (balance in life)
- let go of the psychological burdens of heritage and leave behind old fears and anxieties that are not fit for present purpose
- turn down the volume of all negative voices of the internal oppressor (Alleyne, 2006), which is the internal enemy – for those voices no longer speak a truth that helps our agency
- separate from habits that keep us stuck in old and familiar comfort zones
- practise reliable self-regulation skills in preparation for new experiences and unknown and unfamiliar challenges
- capitalize on every opportunity to step fully into the power of our hybrid selves.

In my thirty-plus years of clinical practice, I was not always aware of how client difficulties, distress, and 'dis-ease' were influenced by or enmeshed with relational aspects of historical trauma. It was not always clear how the transmissions of the past were interlocked with the black client's material in the present. From my observations of particular patterns emerging over time, however, I soon recognized that the fact of these occurrences in several black clients' lives was not a coincidence. Familiar patterns of behaviour in attempting to manage racialized trauma and the particular ways people became stuck with their psychological blocks, as if investing in the very thing that was not working, could not be accidental. I came to the conclusion that what had ceased to be coincidence in these repetitive observations, was indeed a phenomenon of intergenerational trauma.

The drive to understand these observable occurrences heavily influenced the focus and thrust of all my subsequent academic and research studies. The end results identified relational aspects of the past being very much alive in the present, with the intersectional components of race, ancestry and history intertwined. The phenomenon leaves me to conceptualize transformation through two succinct sayings:

> Transformation is the journey you are on. You are exploring the wisdom of your soul. You are shedding old ways and beliefs that no longer fit who you are becoming. Be brave ... you are becoming your authentic self.

And in the specific context generational trauma:

> Maybe the journey isn't so much about becoming anything. Maybe it's about un-becoming everything that isn't really you, so you can be who you were meant to be in the first place.

The identification of the transformation phenomenon made something real, which I was able to name, anchor and use as a conceptual handle to steady myself in my therapeutic work with black clients. The phenomenon is real and ever present, and it impacts black lives.

Interruptions to the black transformation process behave like a pendulum. The trauma 'alarm' is set in motion when white racism is experienced. The trauma response punctures and permeates the ego (and semiotic) coverings, triggering the pendulum to swing into the wake of the past, where dormant ancestral trauma sediments become reactivated. As we must live life in the present and not the past, the pendulum is inevitably pushed back into the present, but now it is more heavily burdened by the compound trauma effect. It finally comes to a standstill in the wake of the aftershock and hauntings.

Transformation is a state of being and therefore inextricably linked to our healing process. How we, as black people, understand and manage these trauma effects is crucial to maintaining ontological security. My observations suggest that how effectively we heal from the burden of our heritage is very much dependent on our early childhood experiences and how our transgenerational, intergenerational and immediate family attachment styles and patterns have been formed. The more secure and healthy our early family attachments are, the stronger our ability and capacity for resilience, transformation and healing. The weaker these foundations, the greater the challenges will be for recovery from the reverberations of racialized trauma. It is said that, when we experience a traumatic event, it has a ricocheting effect of opening all other doors where trauma reside. Often we have little control over this intrapsychic activity, and therefore an aspect of transformation and healing is knowing how to manage these ripple effects.

Celebration of black resilience

One way I have chosen to highlight the uniqueness of black resilience is to measure it against the power and ability to recover and remain mentally robust in the midst of the following daunting odds: the type and nature of human trauma; the degree to which the trauma perforates the essence of identity; the size of the group affected (wherever in the world); the time, length and range of the trauma event; and the granular level at which objectification occurs from the outside world. I use the word granular, in this sense, to mean seemingly small and insignificant racialized incidents which have the profound opposite effect of penetrating deeply in harmful ways. This is the anatomy of racial hauntings that is often invisible and therefore hiding in plain sight.

I would argue that those who are accustomed to social privilege and racial dominance (acknowledged or unacknowledged) would find it impossible to tolerate (and survive) the same degree of historical and ongoing oppression. My own observations bear this out; for example white attendees on my unconscious bias training often comment on how *wiped out*, *discombobulated* and *disorientated* they feel after a six-hour training session – even set against a genuine will to engage with the subject, one day of engagement is enough. In another example, I observe extreme anxiety and discomfort in a white person after a mere one-hour pre-consultancy discussion about conflict resolution in a racially mixed team. In another similar meeting, a white male director said to me, banter-style, 'I need to lie on the ground for a week after this'. Such casual humour speaks loudly of a weight that feels too heavy to hold, and this is before the training has begun.

The more racially privileged may also find their capacity challenged in race conversations, where they become anxious, defensive, apologetic, or dogmatic; many get up and leave the room, because they have had enough. Some choose to leave mentally, shutting down while present. Either way, these actions indicate intolerance and unbearable discomfort aroused by race challenges.

Other indicators of little to zero capacity to contain racial discomfort by dominant others can be seen in the hasty and premature resignation of senior staff when the spotlight is shone on their racial transgressions; these public 'outings' shame the intact self, and the slipping of their semiotic cover becomes a terror that must be avoided at all costs. There is also the nimble mechanism of impenetrable powerful ranks being closed to protect the guilty in similar incidents, as in the decades of widely documented well-known cases of institutional racism within Metropolitan Police office culture and practice. A more recent phenomenon can be observed whereby parties guilty of serious race demeanour use the shield of their mental health to plead diminished responsibility and/or loss of mental capacity when faced with punishment for their racial crime. In all of the aforementioned examples, there is a silent terror and inability to stay with and hold responsibility relating to racial discomfort. The avoidance response is to retreat, freeze, close ranks or 'pull up the drawbridge' in order to protect the self – and, in some cases, their race.

Peoples of the black diaspora are recognized the world over for their innate ability to be resourceful and resilient, even in the direst of circumstances. We have only to think of parts of war-torn Africa, where conflict-ravaged people manage to eke out a meagre existence after repeated natural and man-made disasters. Many have mastered the amazing art of being resilient. Although battle-weary by life's circumstances, black people are still able to work well, play well, love well and expect well. Many have moved from the position of mere surviving to thriving. Countless others are aware of the fact that hurt people who hurt others must seek opportunities to move away from the position of victim to that of victor. These may sound like trendy sound bites, but they are celebrated aspects of black life that can sometimes be easily forgotten in discourses and texts focused on trauma.

Guiding principles for healing from generational trauma

The following principles are a practical guide to various audiences for the work of transcending generational trauma. Central to the guide is the knowledge that positive change can arise from the place of trauma:

- **Compassion** Being a regular visitor to the pain of racialized trauma can equip you with a better understanding of the struggles of other racial and cultural minorities. Your increased compassion can enable easier access to others' suffering and pain, particularly in the mental and psychological health professions.
- **Heightened instincts** Heightened instincts can be a useful psychological tool that helps you detect pathological narcissism in others. This is the narcissism that can be found in racial superiority and other circumstances where you become the perceived target or convenient container into which others project their unwanted feelings. Be mindful, however, to learn the art of self-regulation in the use of this psychological tool, so as not to let it take over and push you into states of hypervigilance, hypersensitivity, paranoia and general mistrust of all people.
- **Heightened morals** Some people develop a clarity of what is right and wrong and strongly follow this moral stance. Morals might be compounded by faith and religious beliefs, which serve as guiding principles for life. But be mindful that, in our rapidly changing climate, rigidity in morals can leave you behind others who lead more fluid lives (with less conservatism and cultural orthodoxies, that is, belief and value systems).

- **Resilience** There is general acknowledgment and recognition of black people's abilities to be emotionally resilient and strong in the face of adversity. Many of us have grown up with family stories, folklore and sayings that attest to these strengths.
- **Sublimation** Following on from this, strength from intact emotional abilities can be sublimated into many forms, for example, creative and artistic expression, as acknowledged in previous chapters.
- **Personal boundaries and our relationship with time** It is important to recognize that maintaining boundaries is not entrapment or being anal (rigid). It is also not the case that respecting time boundaries means being 'too white' or following 'the white man's rules'. Creating good and effective boundaries is a marker of self-discipline, self-care and self-respect, as well as respect for other people. This single achievement can be a positive factor in becoming more competent and productive in what we do. Healthy boundaries make life less stressful and cluttered and enable a sense of calm and spaciousness.
- **Belief in oneself** This is about increased self-esteem and self-worth that allows for the pursuit of dreams and hopes, key tenets of transformation. Healing from the burden of heritage, by whatever means, is to individuate and actualize one's fullest potential. Healing that leads to transformation allows for a completely different view of life and the world, where one can achieve a profound sense of strength and personal permission.
- **Recognition of the importance of self-worth and self-care** For those who carry the compound weight of being carers to their families, other people's families, the sick, disabled and needy, and to the masses within the areas of hospitality and the lower echelons of the retail and ancillary industries, the alert is move the value of self-care and self-compassion to the top of the list. To those in jobs in the care sector, often populated by black women who look after others physically, psychologically, socially, medically and spiritually, the message is crucial. For those who fetch, carry, clean, hold, contain and tend to the needs of needy and privileged others, often without adequate recognition or financial reward, the principle of self-care is urgent. These complex demands take their toll. I suggest

personal mottos relating to 'Care for the Caretaker' be scripted in as the number one priority to protect personal boundaries and preserve self-respect. Although caring is a strength, the overwhelming desire to help others may unwittingly leave us entangled in unhealthy spaces where abuse and enmeshment patterns are re-enacted. Recognize outmoded personal and inherited scripts that have passed their sell-by-date and reframe these defunct ways of conducting one's life.

No one, in my view, speaks more powerfully to boundaries and self-care than Audre Lorde (1988, pp. 64–5), who reminds us: 'Caring for myself is not self-indulgence, it is self-preservation, and that is an act of political warfare.' Lorde recognized that freedom was meaningless if she didn't have the courage to deliver it to her own self. 'If we don't care for ourselves and each other, who gets to enjoy the fruits of our labour? Are we again positioning ourselves to be the world's mules? All work and no reward? You are living your ancestors' wildest dream and your oppressors' worst nightmare every time you rest.' (ibid.)

Recognize your personal triggers on meeting the white world

- Differentiate between what is imagined and presumed, and what is real and factual. This will lessen confusion, misjudgement and projection.
- Assess what is your stuff and what belongs to the other. There is less of a tendency to project personal disgruntlements if we own our baggage. This distinction assists cross-cultural interactions and relationships.
- Reflect critically on your attitudinal disposition and default position in mixed interactions. Be aware of tendencies to be hypercritical, hypersensitive and overcautious. These may inadvertently limit your expansion and enjoyment from wider social interactions.
- Be mindful of how hauntings cause obsessive worry and preoccupation long after racially motivated incidents and

situations have occurred. Notice how you deal with ruminations; how much time you pick over things, spend surfing social media platforms, obsess about others and struggle with shutting off these activities. Such repetitive behaviour only serves to intensify emotional defeat and triggers mental health disturbance.

- Be aware of the downsides to your coping strategies, such as routinely wearing a metaphoric bullet-proof vest that acts as psychological armoury for meeting the menace of racism. These forms of self-protection may give off the wrong message that keep people at arm's length. An example is the adopted mannerism, colloquially referred to as, wearing the 'resting-bitch face' (RBF). Unfortunate misreading of 'RBF' may inadvertently add to the stereotype of black women being aggressive, angry, difficult and a problem. Psychological armours may provide protection, but they also weigh us down.

- Notice your responses to being made to feel invisible, indifferent or objectified by the absence of recognition or gaze of the dominant other. Do you hold on to a quiet sense of rejection, harbour resentment and shame? Or do you react in the heat of the moment, or simply surrender to the status quo? Remember control is lost when we allow the outside world to dictate how we feel about ourselves. Granted, we are influenced by our surroundings, but acting from a place of autonomy and strength is a key principle to negotiating the work of generational healing.

Recognize your historical trauma triggers

Get to know and differentiate your trauma triggers so as not to become entangled and become a hostage to your past. If archaic pain material leaks too heavily into current difficulties and struggles, it is very likely to contribute to your losing the plot. What this means is that there will be no clear overview or focus and productive energy to engage in the right fight. Some fights are worth it; others steal our energies. It is therefore necessary to uncouple from archaic trauma triggers with therapeutic support that enables healing and closure of untreated trauma. Working through old wounds, where pain continues to be easily triggered, requires work that changes the old wash cycle from churning around the familiar heavy load in exhaustive and futile ways.

Deal effectively with historical trauma triggers that lead to a new approach to healing. The process offers a clearer overview of what one is entangled in, what needs to be separated and let go of, and what can be reframed and rebuilt. This is needed for better self-regulation, assured ego strengthening and contentment, which has aptly been described as natural spiritual wealth that is not dependent upon the balance in one's checking account. Ego strengthening allows for gratification to be experienced by healthier internalizations that fulfil areas of loss and need. In these corrective modes of operating, movement towards authentic goals can be achieved. Missing or delaying support that can actualize these skills may unwittingly keep a person stuck in the destructive cycle that is the burden of heritage.

The following questionnaires will help you to identify and recognize your trauma triggers and know it is time to engage in appropriate healing work that suits your needs.

As a black person, have you found yourself:

- preoccupied with experiences of racial discrimination to the extent that the disturbance has manifested in recurring or disturbing dreams?

- avoiding the place where the racialized trauma occurred?

- hating all white people and all things white?

- carrying feelings of victimhood because of your racial identity?

- questioning your worth and entitlement in life?

- suffering social anxiety because you don't trust interactions with others different from your racial group?

- feeling paranoid about what people might think of or say to you?

- mistrustful and hopeless for the future?

- becoming overly dependent on one person for all of your support?

- avoiding risk-taking and sticking to what is safe and familiar?

Add your own observations to this list.

As a black person, do you:

- hold yourself back by creating prohibitions (no-go areas in your life, for example, 'this is not for me', 'that wouldn't work', 'I am happy with my lot', 'I don't trust mixing with white people')?

- gauge yourself against what white people feel and think about you?

- daydream or romanticize frequently that, one day, it will all come good for you?

- give up ALL of your agency to a God, because only 'he can make things happen' for you?

- seek to prove to others at all costs that you are somebody?

- judge yourself according to your family, church, cultural group and societal expectations?

- feel happy for other black people's achievements or burned by the light of their success or brilliance?

- doubt or question your abilities and end up feeling a fraud, not worthy, not entitled?

- continually return to the past to explain your present-day struggles and challenges?

- carry a guilt or burden complex about delighting in your earned successes because you deem it not right, unfair or selfish to celebrate openly when other black people are not as lucky?

Add your own observations to this list.

As a mixed-race/ mixed-heritage person, do you:

- negate any part of your racial heritage because of shame, blame, betrayal, hurt or hate?
- split the parts of your racial identity by idolizing the perceived dominant part and denigrate the other/others?
- secretly wish you were white, so you wouldn't have to deal with the social pressures and difficulties of straddling both black and white worlds?
- feel angry with or envious of other black people because you perceive their experience of racism as being more straightforward and yours complicated, and therefore worse, because you have to deal with both black and white prejudice and negativity?
- struggle with feelings of belonging to a racial home as a direct consequence of your dual (or other) heritage?
- secretly feel ashamed of the minority ethnic parent and align yourself with the parent from the dominant majority ethnic group?

Add your own observations to this list.

Recognize and reframe historical enmeshment scripts

Scripts are usually derived from what we internalize from family scenarios and interactions, and particularly formative experiences and events. They are held internally, like commandments that become guiding principles for life, for example, 'As a black person, I must work twice as hard to ever be noticed and valued.' Scripts act as codes for our conduct, for example, 'Never show vulnerability, as that will be taken as weakness.' Our connection to scripts shapes not only our behaviour but also our personality traits, attachment patterns and attachment styles. There are family scripts and these are represented in every personal script.

Transactional analysis talks about life scripts, which encompass an individual's whole life span, for example, 'I will never leave myself wanting and reliant on anyone', but also many scripts that may be enacted in the moment 'I won't employ that black firm to work for me because they will ultimately let me down'. There are family scripts that span and connect generations, for example, 'Every first-born in my father's lineage developed mental health problems; we may have to take action if our first born is male'. Scripts get passed on and blended into our own lives and continue to overlap through the generations.

Re-white dysfunctional 'me-now' scripts

- Create clear narratives about your trauma, which means joining up the dots and straightening out confused and entangled areas of your life, so that you have a clearer picture of your life history. It is most helpful if you can do this with a non-judgemental witness, such as a counsellor or a psychotherapist.
- Have the boldness of heart to embrace your own unorthodoxy, which means giving yourself permission to be different and not have to conform to what is expected or laid down by culture, tradition or generational norms.
- Review your relationship with time. This, in my view, is the single most important boundary issue that impacts black life. Are you unconsciously rebelling against time? 'I will get there in my own sweet time, thank you very much.' Do you delay time? 'It will have to be enough if I just show my face at the end of the

meeting or event.' Are you expecting concessions with regard to time? 'Isn't it good enough for you that I tried to get within the vicinity of the expected time?' Are you fed up with deadlines? 'Don't rush me.' Are you tired of the demands of time? 'Don't touch me.' Are you angry with time? 'Leave me alone.' Are you mourning the loss of time? 'Why am I still hiding?' Any fight with time *takes* time. Disregard for time fosters negativity that moves you away from being close to your purpose and focus, preventing you from actualizing needs and achieving goals.

Scripts can be helpful or unhelpful. Eric Berne (1972, p. 136) offers seven elements of the types of scripts to illustrate how they function in different ways. Starting off are scripts that are **payoffs or a curse**; these are messages from our parents or parental figures on how we will end up. Then there are the **injunctions or stoppers**, which act as negative commands or prohibitions from the parent – these negate what we really want to do. There are the **counter scripts**, which, according to Berne, occur later in life and shape life plans based on parental principles or rules. **Model and copy behaviour** scripts begin to form from what we see and hear around us at a very early age. Then there is the **provocation** script, which encourages and confirms our script beliefs as coming automatically from the instinctive part of our make-up, which allows us to play and indulge. The **demon** script is always seen as coming from the unpredictable, impulsive rebellious voice that gives in to basic urges, needs and desires. And, finally, there is the **anti-script, the spell breaker**, which is a self-releasing freeing script, which saves a person from self-destruction.

You may find it helpful to know your own scripts. Make a list of the following types of script and take the time to explore and reflect on them on your own or in your counselling or therapy sessions.

The following suggestions are a guide to knowing your scripts, how they function and influence your behaviour, and for what purposes and gains you may hold on to them or consider it is time to reframe them.

Knowing your scripts

- Make a list of your generational and family scripts (include who or what influenced your internalizations).

- Make a list of general internalized personal scripts (which ones have you retained, and which have you ditched?).

- Make a list of your 'me-now' scripts (current scripts, both positive and negative).

- Reimagine or reframe your shame scripts as part of your personal therapy.

- If risk is the price of progress, then start to action your personal scripts.

- *Re-white* your historical enmeshment scripts. Identify what does not fit or serve you any longer and cease investment in these defunct scripts.

- Who taught you to be a man/woman? What were their scripts? In what ways did these influence and shape?

Review every six months for maintenance of good mental hygiene

Fight imposter syndrome

Impostor syndrome can stifle our potential for growth and meaning, by preventing us from pursuing new opportunities for growth at work, in relationships or in our hobbies and social pursuits. Confronting impostor syndrome can therefore help us continue to grow and thrive.

The following dos and don'ts are a guide to knowing your imposter syndrome scripts and get a handle on rescripting them for more effective agency.

Some dos and don'ts for overcoming imposter syndrome

- Don't let the saboteur in.

- Know your MO (modus operandi) and where you position yourself in meeting the white world.

- Don't repeat defeat.

- Know when you are fighting against the very things you want to correct.

- Get to know your hauntings (discerning who or what has just evacuated their mess on to you), so that you avoid becoming too contaminated.

- Know your *internal oppressor* so that you can take full responsibility for its preoccupations.

- Don't allow the *internal oppressor* to win.

- Be aware of your disavowals, that is, knowing what you give over, what you give away and what you give into that reduces your power to shine.

- Deal with shame-defeating scripts by reframing old values and belief systems.

- Be alert to when you might be playing up to stereotypes.

- Don't dumb down your authenticity or creativity.

- Engage in less guilt tripping of yourself when you have needs and wants.

- Know when it is time to stop remembering the past and let new energy in.

- Don't shut the door on opportunities to grow the shoots of your creativity.

- Don't wait for others to acknowledge your worth. Start the process yourself by celebrating yourself.

Add your own observations to this list.

Know your internal oppressor

The internal oppressor (Alleyne, 2004) is distinct from internalized oppression. It is a part of the self and ego structure that functions as an inhibitor, leading to problems with moving on. It inhibits movement towards negotiating the transformation process. As an internal inhibitor, it holds us back and can be viewed as the internal adversary or the enemy within. Be especially mindful of how your internal enemy works to make you question yourself, your worth, your abilities and actions. Get to know it as a saboteur. This is the part of you that doesn't believe in you and questions your every move because of low self-confidence and self-esteem. Get to know this familiar voice that becomes the loudest sound you hear, testing you and holding you back. Spend less energy catastrophizing because of the negative messages from the inner enemy voice. Give less time to thinking of the worst-case scenarios and worry less about what other people will say. Test out your desires, drives and wishes. Take calculated risks to remove yourself from your comfort zone and get used to *not* staying in your lane as dictated and expected by others. Give yourself permission to be, and do not expect to always get it right first time. Unfriend contacts who do not enrich your life, but who just take from your life and mentally expunge all defunct scripts that have become set codes for living your life. By deactivating your attachment to these unhealthy attachments, you will create room for new scripts and energies for self-advancement and self-respect.

The most powerful and proactive way to deal with the internal oppressor is to educate the mind for critical consciousness and exercise control over your life. Critical consciousness is an essential process for people of colour to engage in. It is the individual (and collective) work of coming into one's own being and knowing oneself. It is the vital tool needed to disrupt default patterns that are oppressive to us. Critical consciousness stimulates action that is the precursor to psychological individuation and collective activism for a more just and equal world.

Embrace the therapeutic notion of forgiveness

Forgiveness in the context of therapeutic healing bears little resemblance to the biblical definitions of forgiveness. Scripturally, this act of mercy is privileged as being the process of forgiving someone or being forgiven. Forgiveness itself is defined as the letting go of sin, which is an act of obedience and gratefulness to God, and it focuses more on making reparations and reconciliation with the perpetrator.

In the context of psychotherapy and counselling I see forgiveness as being compassionate to oneself. In this therapeutic context, therefore, it is the process of healing through releasing or relinquishing the tyranny of the past. Tyranny can be the internal oppressor that holds us back. It can also be the arrested state of being emotionally ravaged by racial hauntings that cause a particular ants-in-your pants type of mental dis-ease or restlessness. Forgiveness is the active and mental process of letting go and soothing the soul. Forgiveness can free up mental space for new experiences to be owned and enjoyed. Forgiveness also frees up relationship dynamics that have been stuck for a long time. Forgiveness allows us to have the opportunity to work at improving generational family conflict, and thus change attachment patterns for more productive and meaningful bonds.

It is important to note that the unconscious process of hanging on to pain, shame and trauma might give a false sense of having something to do and may, thus, keep hope alive. But like any letting-go process that has passed its sell-by date, we run the risk of not serving ourselves well, and may end up investing in non-profitable attachments that lead nowhere.

Understand notions of freedom

The following list is both a catalyst and an invitation to explore what freedom means to you and its role in how you shape your life.

Freedom is ...

- Freedom is the art of knowing why you are picking up and carrying the weight others have refused to hold themselves and dumped on you, and when to put it down or give it back.

- Freedom is deciding when to lend precious time to deal with other people's projections and when to call them out and disengage.

- Freedom is knowing when to see (observe) and when to oversee (be proactive).

- Freedom is knowing when to look and when to overlook.

- Freedom is deciding when to care and not to care too much.

- Freedom is the art of remembering and forgetting.

- Freedom is releasing or relinquishing oneself from the tyranny of the past.

- Freedom is not being hostage to the *internal oppressor*.

- Freedom is having a reliable and sustained routine for your mental hygiene.

Add your own thoughts, notions and sense of meaning of this concept for your life.

Know when to step out of other people's dreams and into your own

Don't waste your time by making a bigger space for other people, while keeping yourself small. Collectivism and community building are integral to being an interactive and full social being, but be mindful that you may be hiding behind assumed scripts, such as 'I am a team player' or 'Going solo is not for me'. Find the necessary courage and self-worth to negotiate your own journey, which sees you graduate with the fulfilment of achieving your dreams and wishes. Inhabit the home of your own authenticity and award yourself all opportunities to actualize your giftedness. Make no excuses for negotiating this journey with style and grace.

Limit reliance on favours and waivers

Favours and waivers are unconsciously employed to deal with the unmet needs of not being seen, unwittingly assuming the victim position and dealing with loss of expectations from a significant other, for example, a parent, partner or society. They are formed from trauma scripts that shout, 'You owe me one', 'It is my right', 'I deserve this', 'Can't you see ...?'.

The receiver of such a request might be faced with two forms of communication: the favour or waiver being asked, and an overt or covert attitudinal defiance that the request cannot be refused on any terms. Often the person requesting frequent favours and waivers comes across as asking for special treatment because of what they feel are their particular or unique circumstances. Dependency on favours and waivers is often requested with explanations such as, 'You know my circumstances, so getting here half an hour late, as opposed to my usual hour lateness, is good enough', or 'I deserve help because no one was there for me'. Often, and unintentionally, the person asking may not be aware that their request is really about being rescued or demanding to be made to feel special. A reliance on favours and waivers not only creates unhealthy dependence on other people, it also diminishes agency in the person requesting, preventing them from achieving autonomy and independence.

Be aware of black-on-black bias

Black-on-black bias may include feelings such as envy and jealousy, as we experience ourselves in competition with other black people. It manifests mainly as not being able to delight in our own people's light as, instead, we feel burnt in its presence. This indicates that there are also challenges to be found in some black-on-black dynamics.

An example of this can be found in **misogynoir**, a term first coined in 2008, by queer black feminist scholar, Moya Bailey. It is a combination of the English 'misogyny' (hatred of women) and French 'noir' (black) and highlights the hatred that black women face in the public realm. It includes the contempt or internalized prejudice men generally may hold, but also black men specifically, against black women. Black women in the pop industry and in politics, for example, where they publicly voice their opposition, can be met with hatred of their race and gender.

Recognize and understand your investment in co-opted personas from the majority society

Co-opted personas from the majority society are the assimilated traits that members of racial minorities may adopt in order to gain entry into the established privileged group. It involves neutralizing or dumbing down aspects of identity that are deemed by the majority to cause offence or amplifying perceived favoured aspects of one's identity to gain acceptance. In the psychology of Jung, a persona is the mask or façade presented to satisfy external demands; it doesn't represent the inner personality of the individual. Because the co-opted persona can reap rewards of acceptance and inclusion, one can think oneself into believing that it is the true self.

Check your stockpile of co-opted personas and get to know how you were seized by them and what price you are paying for personal convenience and gains:

- Explore the identities and roles you have adopted to be accepted in society.
- Assess levels of authenticity in these selves through getting to know yourself.
- How do these personas work for you?

Shame affirmations

Use the affirmations below to embrace loving thoughts toward yourself:

- I am worthy of love and healing.
- I release the chokehold of my past; it has no power over me.
- I choose to practise self-compassion.
- I deserve good things.
- I recognize that I am a courageous survivor.
- I let go of the anger and hurt I've been carrying.
- I treat myself with kindness and love.
- I am intentionally creating the life I want.
- I embrace the gifts and talents I have.
- I release all self-judgement and embrace self-forgiveness.
- I am on a journey towards healing.
- I accept myself fully and completely.
- I refuse to live in the past, for it robs me of my glorious present.
- I create beauty and joy wherever I go.
- I believe my future is bright and filled with good things.
- I am an integrated hybrid being.

Be a self-starter

A self-starter is usually described as an ambitious person who eagerly goes after what is desired. Such a person has initiative, drive and belief in themselves. A self-starter is proactive, has a go-getter attitude and likes things to be done. They tend not to procrastinate and, therefore, have a healthy relationship with time, as they see taking action as better than stalling progress. A self-starter believes in making progress and figuring things out as they go along. Such an attitude utilizes energy rather than remaining stuck in the romanticized notion that 'It will happen one day'; 'My day will come'; 'Walk in Jah light and Jah provide the bread'; 'One day!'

Guidance for black men

There is much that can be accessed about black men's health in the form of, for example, self-help books, black men's groups, tailored services that focus on mental health, systemic discrimination, the impact of negative racial stigmatization and the nurturing of black boys, and so on. The plethora of information available suggests the need for such support services.

In keeping with this chapter's theme on healing from the burden of heritage, I wish to highlight a particular phenomenon that has emerged over the years from my clinical work. It is the profound psychological impact on black males who have missed out on the active and sustained presence of a loving father, particularly in the crucial developmental stages of early life. Struggles with achieving a well-balanced manhood and male identity, relating to other men, actualizing fullest potential and managing issues of intimacy and trust in close affectional bonds are key themes for black men in therapy.

In the very focused work with black men, I have found the following facilitative questions useful for enabling black men to explore their male identity and sexualities, and discover where trauma wounds may lie for the work in therapy:

- What kind of a man are you?
- Who taught you to be a man?
- What is your relationship with women like, for example, with your mother or sister(s)?

- How have family dynamics impacted your moving-on process?
- What is your most profound positive experience of being shown love by a close male family figure?
- What is the most damaging experience at the hand of a significant male?
- What does your friendship network offers you?
- In the absence of your own father, what will help you to be a proactive ever-present father?

Guidance for black mothers

As with the above, the plethora of information available on black women's health suggests a real need for support services that address the impact of racial stigmatization that impedes the nurture of black girls and women.

I wish to highlight one key phenomenon emerging from my clinical work, which relates to the relational aspects of black mother/son relationships in the absence of the steady presence of a positive male father figure. What I have observed as a recurring theme, and therefore a phenomenon, is the profound psychological impact of a mother/son relationship enmeshment, which impacts in the following ways:

- Mothers become overly protective of their sons or exceptionally hostile if the son becomes a constant reminder of her emotional hurt from the abandoning partner.
- Mothers invest emotionally in their son's happiness, to the point where it is often difficult to know where mother's needs end and her son's begin. They are enmeshed and the son's maturation process into full adulthood either stalls or is completely stymied.
- In these enmeshments, sons become deeply entangled with their mother, and struggle to separate and form a healthy intimate relationship with an equal other, as they choose partners who mirror the only intimate attachment they know, which is unhealthy, dependent and enmeshed.
- Enmeshment issues cause black males to be perpetually torn between two loyalties: to their mother and to a desired partner. Being torn leads to being stuck and ambivalent, unable to be separately independent of the parent and commit fully to their partners in a healthy and productive way.

- Being torn between two loyalties leads to many black males feeling stuck and unable to grow away from mother. They may view and experience commitment in intimate outside relationships as entrapment and this may lead to missing out on the opportunity to evolve into free individuals. When it comes to engaging in the process of creating a couple relationship, this might feel like a return to the mother/son entrapment. Such men may inadvertently earn the label of player, lone wolf or sigma male.

Finally, single black mothers are advised to pay closer attention to how they choose a partner after relationship breakdown. Choosing someone based solely on how they may get on with their children might be great in the short term but could create problems in the longer term. In such partnership bonds, women may overlook and lose out on getting their personal needs met.

Guidance for black trainers

From my experience as a consultant trainer and facilitator in a wide area of addressing diversity challenges, there is clear evidence that the catchall term 'diversity' is often used euphemistically to address thornier issues of 'race' and (white) racism that underlie it. In the broadest context, diversity applies to traits, qualities, characteristics, beliefs, values and mannerisms, in self and others. It is displayed through predetermined factors such as race, ethnicity, gender, age, disability (visible and non-visible), national origin, sexual orientation and other changeable features, such as citizenship, world views, language, schooling, religious beliefs, marital status, parental status, socioeconomic status, regional and work experiences. It calls into question many other factors such as identity, cultural inclusiveness and exclusion, and racism as a lived experience for racial minorities. The pedagogical dimensions of diversity are expansive, yet, in my experience as a consultant, diversity has become the more palatable, go-to word for organizations, rather than naming the specific challenges of race dynamics, unconscious race bias and systemic/structural racism in their workplaces.

This is true of my experience for the majority of 'diversity' training requests in the fields of education, Social Services, the NHS and many areas of the private, public and charitable organizational sectors. This regular occurrence is not mere coincidence, but a phenomenon of our times, observed as a trainer in the field. It is as if the hidden message is: *Yes, we have dealt with gender, age and disability, and we feel we understand the temperament and disposition of Asians ... but the damn spiky issue is how to manage race* and this, in turn, is a euphemism for *How do we deal with black people?* It can often feel this is the bald nature of what is unsaid.

Diversity training takes place on many levels and its demand has increased exponentially since 25 May 2020, following the murder of George Floyd and subsequent reverberation of the BLM movement. The training involves an experienced trainer, usually black or Asian, being called in by an organization to work with predominantly white teams who have marginal diversity membership, who want to engage more proactively in Equality, Diversity and Inclusion (EDI) challenges in the workplace. Often, a request will hide the fact that the real, but hidden, work is about conflict resolution between predominant white staff membership and minority black and brown team members. Other times, it might be about the 'new guard's' disgruntlements with the 'old guard', who, with their archaic principles and old-fashioned policies, drag their feet resentfully to keep up with the changing pace.

Diversity consultancy therefore addresses a myriad of individual and organizational diversity challenges; these may relate to policies, systems, procedures, workplace culture, ethics, identity, equality and dignity in the workplace. The trainer's initial assessment of what is really being requested is therefore key, so that they can delineate what is needed, how, and when. Such consultancy work places unusually high demands upon the trainer compared with those conducting other trainings. Added to this challenge, the current BBCCT[1] zeitgeist has generated very difficult and contentious discourses, all of which have compounded high levels of anxiety, which has become the main precursor to the demands for such trainings.

Consequently, I (and many other black and brown trainers), find myself in the position of having to carve out time not only to craft such training programmes, but also for thinking about how to field the anxiety projected in the request. 'Fielding' is my term for holding all the balls that come from unusual and different directions; it is a special skill of delivering complex diversity material sensitively, inclusively and mindfully, while holding the sensitivities of people who feel naked, exposed, deskilled and anxious. In many ways, these are trauma signs and part of what a diversity consultant is confronted with and needs to field and hold well, while imparting knowledge, guidance and tools for change.

In such programmes, what is not known and heeded is the fact that diversity consultants are now having to bear the additional invisible weight of addressing themes of trauma, shame, pain, resistance, projections, and aggression, to name just some. These elements predictably and inevitably emerge from all diversity – but very specifically race – work. The aggression met, albeit often in a linguistically subtle and behaviourally covert manner, requires skilful handling and containment by the trainer. The extraordinary task is to be both a facilitator within the arena of trauma and people dynamics and an educator in the learning space where your group is vulnerable. This is exceptional work. The emotional drain from such careful fielding can and does take its toll on the trainer – a unique hidden cost of pedagogical diversity training. It is therefore difficult to escape the unavoidable vicarious traumatization in the process, yet as black trainers we seldomly speak openly about this emotional cost. My years of training experience have enabled me to manage these teaching challenges reasonably well, often supplemented by paid supervision support and debriefing via my known and tested ways of unwinding (a long walk by the sea and sweating it out at the gym). Nevertheless, the nature of teaching 'diversity' awareness is demanding on multiple levels. I am therefore very clear about how I honour my own professional worth and contributions to this field.

I call upon other trainers to do the same and to bear in mind the following care-taking tips:

- Keep an eye on how much you extend your work and mental health bandwidth.
- Ensure that there is adequate care for the caretaker.
- Be mindful of the insidious effect of vicarious traumatization, which is the fallout from holding other people's stress.
- Be bold in asking for what you want and need, without being held back by the inhibiting voice of the internal oppressor or imposter syndrome.
- Accept when you have graduated into professional prominence and present this self without apology, but as a self that has been earned.
- Seek out like-minded peers to share and get support.

- Know when to say NO. Be mindful of overextending yourself. You are not omnipotent or indispensable.

Holding the tension for building resilience

I am aware that this book's title may leave the reader with a view that the black existence is one long, hard slog, the word burden implying something immoveable and a permanent weight. Granted, burden in the context of black life does imply hardship, overload, rupture and more. *But this is not all of black life.* Such a belief would, at best, be a cock-eyed view of black life; at worst, it is absurd racist thinking that homogenizes a whole race. I am not going to neglect to create a proud and celebratory space for the multitude of virtues that black people possess and delight in, while, at the same time, addressing the burden. This is the tension in being black – and the challenge in a racially divided world.

The burden is created by whatever the majority in society finds difficult and intolerable within itself – this is evacuated into and on to black people, as if blackness is the default repository for humanity's aggregate mess. But, in spite of these real and ever-present burdensome experiences, what black people have suffered historically – and continue to suffer – marks the toughness of a people, made durable by the wonder of their resilience and aliveness of spirit. The trajectory is sobering. This diasporic group of people has gone through, among other realities: slavery, colonization, segregation, legal barriers to voting and education, police brutality, bomb attacks, the assassination of black leaders, daily discriminations, systemic and personal racism, right-wing extremist hatred, refusal of housing, public services, unemployment – all of this on the grounds of race and yet we rise. This is quintessentially the personification of resilience and, although the past is never dead, and the hauntings continue against our will ... I leave it to Maya Angelou as she says it best in her poem that speaks to the concept of transformation.

And Still I Rise

You may write me down in history.
With your bitter, twisted lies,
You may trod me in the very dirt
But still, like dust, I'll rise.

Does my sassiness upset you?
Why are you beset with gloom?
'Cause I walk like I've got oil wells
Pumping in my living room.
Just like moon and like suns,
With certainty of tides,
Just like hopes springing high,
Still I'll rise.

Did you want to see me broken?
Bowed head and lowered eyes?
Shoulders falling like teardrops,
Weakened by my soulful cries?

Does my haughtiness offend you?
Don't you take it awful hard
'Cause I laugh like I've got gold mines
Digging in my own backyard.

You may shoot me with your words,
You may cut me with your eyes.
You may kill me with your hatefulness,
But still, like air, I'll rise.

Does my sexiness upset you?
Does it come as a surprise?
That I dance like I've got diamonds at the meeting of my thighs?

Out of the huts of history's shame.
I rise
Up from a past that's rooted in pain.
I rise
I am a black ocean, leaping and wide,
Welling and swelling I bear in the tide
Leaving behind nights of terror and fear
I rise
Into a daybreak that's wondrously clear
I rise

Bringing the gifts that my ancestors gave,
I am the dream and the hope of the slave.
I rise
I rise
I rise.

'Still I Rise' from *And Still I Rise: A Book of Poems* by Maya Angelou

Epilogue

As I journeyed through the writing of this book – a period just shy of two years – it was an experience of joy, pain and release. The physical pain from sitting for long hours at the computer, and the vicarious nature of writing about generational trauma that took its toll and settled excruciatingly in my sacroiliac area (lower back and hips). The last four chapters of the book were written via the support of strong painkillers, regular deep tissue massages and Stairmaster gym workouts. My reliance on these supporting banister rails was the only way to ease the somatization of the activated trauma within my body. Mental release from the agony was guaranteed by bearing the untold story inside me.

Contrastingly, the joy from the project was experienced through getting my words out because I have something to say and share. I thoroughly enjoyed the crafting of my sense-making of the race trauma phenomenon in my own inimitable style. Surprisingly and unexpectedly, something else evolved in the many joyful spaces halfway through and then towards the end of this journey. An unfamiliar organic and separate process evolved in the form of poetry. It's an art form I had never paid much attention to before, except for when listening to it performed on stage or read to an audience in some other capacity. You see, I live by the sea, which is a most contemplative place to be, and, in two sittings, the quality of the reverie gifted by these calm surroundings spurred me to write free-flowing pourings from my thoughts in a new and unaccustomed way.

The following poems are the by-products of this creative writing process. In many ways, it is a brand-new manifestation of my sublimation and healing process. Remarkably, as I completed the epilogue, this last part of the book, my lower back pain dramatically eased, as if to mark the act of letting go as I reached the end.

Humanity Matters

Brutalizing an African in 2020
Killing sacred animals, leaving
scarcely any
Seems to be their MO to cause
mass destruction to many.

From past to present
Loud silence gave rights to decades of consent
But in 2020 the world experienced a collective haunting,
That triggered dissent and many to repent
About a horror that caused untold grief and rage to vent
For an unforgettable tragedy that reversed and changed time to a large
extent
Transgenerational wounds amassed and passed from historical times
Leave painful memories and legacies from these awful crimes

NO MORE is the NOW message that reverberates loudly as it chimes
Only positives must be built from the devastation of those times.
Whatever the transitional objects, be it therapy, an inner goddess
or some alternative buttress
Whether Buddha, Jehovah, Allah, Inshallah إِنْ شَاءَ اللّٰه
Or burying defunct scripts to move on to new endeavours
The journey begins in earnest
For a better forever.

The Generational Wake

Referred to as the 'visitation' and 'viewing'
The Caribbean Wake is a celebration of life
Paying homage to the journey of the human spirit into the afterlife.
In Jamaica it's nine nights; in Guyana, a mere one night
But for five generations of black peoples, it's a different kind of occurrence
That triggers internal disquiet, mental fight or flight;

Wakes occur to bring comfort to families
And uplift loved ones in times of sorrow
But the echoes from slavery create and leave a hollow
Where hauntings wallow, disturbed by external provocations
That occupy our todays and tomorrows.

It is as if the reverberations of the past cannot be stilled or come to rest
Not unlike the analogous situation I see daily living by the sea
Where I watch large merchant ships leave foamy trails long after their passing.
And I think of the generational wake with its own transmissions
Just like the huge, majestic vessel gliding through the waves
Creating its own drag from the path of its vibrations
That generates a charge and life of its own.

It's remarkable how such lofty structures
Create invisible currents beneath the innocuous white foam
That ripple outwards with quiet impact,
And disturb every moored and stable craft
That gets caught up in the aftermath.

The generational wake provokes racial hauntings to come alive in its path
And not unlike the analogous situation I witness by the sea
They remain present and disturb mental moorings in our reverie
Making black life perpetually burdensome to be toll-free and just be able to be.

This poem gives a nod to Christina Sharpe's (2016) seminal work 'In the Wake: On Blackness and Being'. Duke University Press.

The Ubiquity of the Knee

Taking the knee is a sign of respect
Tapping on the knee is a way to detect
Using the knee is a potential offence
And to bow the knee is showing deference
Dropping to the knee is a sign of reverence
And a drop knee might be considered a manoeuvre of defence.

Bringing someone to their knee indicates submission
Kissing the knee is a mark of adoration
Sinking to one's knee can signify appreciation
And to rest the old knees is a sign of relaxation.

Crouching on the knee signals preparedness for action
Like pregnant women, knees akimbo
After choosing natural birth over C-section.

Hiding a face betwixt the knee says get ready for an emergency,
Nursing a knee injury might lead to surgery to restore productivity,
To drop someone on the knee is agony and a wrestling violation,
Elevating the knee is universal,
It aids circulation and promotes the healing action,
Showing the knee says to heck with all decency,
And being bent over one's knee could be a pleasurable activity,
But enforced, could lead to a stiff penalty,
Historically, to cross the knee was a sign of modesty.
Selling girls the trope that was the way to maintain dignity.

BUT...

Enough of the above fun and games playing with the knee
And let's be serious for 7 minutes and 46 seconds, just you and me
A knee on the neck is enforced brutality
The universality of this symbol profoundly shames human morality
'Cause on 25 May 2020, the world witnessed a brutal fatality
By a law enforcer who stared blankly, arm akimbo
To steady a deadly knee to inflict his righteous finality

Impound all literal (and symbolic) knee obstructions for nature's
sanity
And reclaim the ubiquity of its use for liberation and restoration
To end all repeats of horrors reminiscent of colonial plantations
We must protect future generations from this indignity
And give civilization a better chance to restore its humanity in
perpetuity.

The treatment of generational trauma in this book has focused on the
burden and its impact, of which hauntings are a key feature, and the
healing necessary for black lives. The book's focus on black lives is hugely
significant, as only we (black folk) can heal our own wounds. However,
as with the universal experience of trauma, there exists the relational
dynamic of the wounded and the violator (my preferred choice of terms).
Experiences of this profound nature and level of psychological injury
(level 3 and level 4 trauma) require repair involving both sides – the
sufferer and the contributor. Black people's trauma has its genesis in
white colonial historical oppression. Healing is therefore not a one-sided
task for black people alone to do, but a process involving a formal act
of reckoning of the impact of the wrongdoings by the oppressor. This is
necessary atonement work, which is as much for the dominant collective
to manage its own generational guilt and shame, which lies supressed and
repressed within white collective unconscious, as it is about black people
needing a profound public gesture of recognition of their historical
trauma.

The art of forgetting and remembering

Someone once said history is the art of forgetting and remembering.
What a stunning truth! There is a tyranny for both black identity shame
and white identity shame, as a direct result of this fact. Each group's
relatedness to its history continues to impact race relations and lived
experiences for both sides. It is therefore a crying shame when it appears
that any move towards equality for all is experienced as oppression for
and by the privileged.

For a people who have been, and still are, negatively affected by colonial legacies, the challenge in relationship to history lies in remembering the past, but not remaining stuck and hostage to it. The mental and psychological challenge for black people, therefore, is to master the art of both forgetting and remembering, while not allowing present-day trauma triggers to intrude and take over. Slavery is conspicuously absent from European writers' consciousness and, similarly, from this nation's efforts to demonstrate proper healing of its historical colonial conscience. It is in the omission of the moral imperative to manage colonial legacies that the hidden white identity shame lies – and the burden of heritage for black lives. Dominant powers have a duty to history not to ignore and not to fail in remembering their past. Seeking public clemency is one national act that can serve the collective purpose of healing white historical and archaic shame. Such a rite of passage could truly assuage a collective national guilt regarding the evils of a dreadful colonial past; it could also restore humility, which will be the antidote to white shame. It feels important to qualify that the atonement that I speak about is not financial largesse (that is, money gifted as compensation), as is often disparagingly posited as what black people are asking of white governments. A true atonement would be properly acknowledging the collective trauma of a shameful past, which should no longer be left out of conscious recognition and conveniently carried by others.

Lest we forget

I would posit that, if humility as the antidote to historical shame could be realized, what a watershed healing moment it could be for the colonizer and the colonized. To this end, I would suggest a remembrance day dedicated to the recognition of historical black lives suffered and lost, lest we forget. A national day of commemoration would be most fitting a gesture of atonement for Britain's significant and atrocious 400-year past. For when the concept of shame being both gatekeeper and conscience is applied to the inhumanities of slavery, the important act of atonement becomes more pertinent in dealing with the tyranny of the burden on both sides: the burden of pain for blacks and the burden of shame for whites. *Lest we forget the burdens still borne* would be my contribution to a fitting motto that could be adopted by Britain (and other European colonizers).

The first three words borrowed from Rudyard Kipling form part of my chosen epithet for such a redemptive act. When Kipling's famous phrase, from his Recessional poem, was first published in *The Times* on 17 July 1987, it was not intended for the remembrance of fallen soldiers. Written at the height of the colonial period, Kipling warned of the dangers of imperialism, and intended to remind us of the impermanent nature of British Imperial power.

How healing would it be, then, for all sides, if these three little universal words, *Lest we forget*, were accorded to the black souls that suffered during one of the longest periods – 400 years – of man's inhumanity to man. The gesture has been employed in the form of Holocaust Memorial Day, 27 January, and Remembrance Day, commemorated every second Sunday in November. The latter marks the symbolic moment when hostilities ended, following the heroic efforts, achievements and sacrifices in past wars. These days are proudly kept alive in order to honour the healing function they provide. Memorials are also erected for a host of reasons, not least for lives that mattered. However, the lives lost during one of the darkest points in English history are still not counted – and still await remembrance.

My contribution to the crafting of the key text for such a memorial:

Lest We Forget

Lest we forget traumatic imprints of history

Lest we forget haunted memories from wounds endured

To benefactors from history whose choice was to ignore

Lest we forget immoral gains of loot

And transmogrifications of history that distorted truth

Lest we forget ... damaged souls and pay tribute

And lift mental burdens to meet a new dawn to salute

We Repair

Appendix I

Glossary of terms

Baby mothers and baby fathers terms that refer to a parent of the infant who is not married to or in an exclusive relationship with the infant's other parent.

'BBCCT' Zeitgeist (Brexit, Black Lives Matter Movement, Covid-19, Climate Change, Trumpism) is the term coined by the author to identify key significant phenomenon shaping our current times in the UK. #Me-Too Movement is a key aspect of the Zeitgeist, but has been evolving over a much longer period of time.

BIPOC is an acronym meaning, black, indigenous, and people of colour and is used to refer to members of non-white communities. Many BIPOC are also recent immigrants or asylum seekers.

Black is a racialized classification of people that includes people with known African heritage, who can be discriminated against because of the colour of their skin. The term black is also used as a prideful political term, rooted in racial oppression that pervaded directly from the trans-Atlantic slave trade, giving birth to the civil rights movement and all subsequent human justice campaigns for social and political change. Black as a political term is often viewed negatively and perceived by some white people as derogatory, despite black people owning the signifier and their black identity with pride and dignity. Black is sometimes used as an overarching term to include Asian minorities, but this is increasingly resisted with preference for the aggregate expression 'black and brown (Asian) minority groups' or 'people of colour'. People of mixed black and white racial heritage may also choose the category 'people of colour'. Others may opt to see themselves politically as black, as in the most well-known example of President Obama, America's first-ever black president, a mixed-race man with a black father and white mother.

Black identity trauma is a term used to describe the negative and harmful effects caused by racism and other forms of racial oppression which can have damaging effects on one's sense of self and security in being in the world.

Black internalized oppression means believing the stereotypes and misinformation about one's own group are true and acting from this premise in self-defeating and damaging ways, which hinder self-development.

Black-on-black discrimination is a term used to describe the ways in which we [black people] act out, among ourselves, internalized negative views and beliefs about our race in such ways as to hinder and prejudice collective and interpersonal relationships.

Black/white relations will refer to problematic, 'dependent' and historically entwined dynamics embedded in the dyadic relationship between black and white people, contributing to difficulties relating to power and powerlessness and the dominant and dominated.

Black ontology Ontology is the branch of western philosophy that studies concepts such as existence, being, becoming and reality. Ontology is contentious as it has not created an inclusive space for understanding black people's lived experience as integral to their existence, being and becoming. Black ontology permits the different realities of black lives to be taken into account for a more comprehensive understanding of black people's stability, security and sense of self in an unequal and divided world.

Brown has gradually entered the lexicon of race language and is now used as a term of racial identification and differentiation from black. It is a widely misused and misunderstood term, even among so-called 'brown minorities'. It makes sense to use 'brown', as an aggregate term to denote affiliation and membership, for example, 'This service is for black and brown minorities'. The aggregation refers to commonality within a collective experience, while recognizing differences in racial classification minority group experiences. South Asians, Pakistanis, Malaysians, Mauritians, Arabs, Samoans, may all, for example, refer to being from the brown ethnic minority group. However, the term 'brown' used as an identity descriptor, for example, 'I am a brown woman', is meaningless and lacks substance. This particular shorthand term seems to hide true ethnic identities, begging the question what is difficult and/ or problematic in honouring one's ethnic origin, for example, 'I am British, of Bangladeshi heritage', or 'I am British Mauritian'. 'Brown' as a standalone ethnic signifier seems, at worst, vacuous.

The inclusive term '**people of colour**' embraces a wide range of people who are not white or of full European heritage, that is, racial groups whose geographical origins are from south Asia, or the Indian subcontinent including China, Japan, Malaysia, Pakistan, to name a few. Mixed-race or mixed-heritage people are included in this category, and the term is also used interchangeably in instances where black people choose to aggregate with the experiences of ethnic minorities.

Codependency is defined as being psychologically influenced by another person to the degree that personal needs are supressed and ignored. This is a state of being held back in personal development; autonomy and independence are severely impeded and can sometimes be lost in the process of being reliant upon, controlled by, and needing the other to fulfil one's own needs or to complete oneself.

Co-opted self refers to the way in which black and brown ethnic minorities assimilate in order to find a safe space in the white majority group. Lennox Thomas's *proxy-self* concept (1995) refers to the same phenomenon, with reference to Donald Winnicott's false self (1960). Thomas studied children in therapy who, in order to feel accepted by their therapist and in a white world, developed a proxy-self as a coping mechanism which enabled them to fit in without fear of racism or psychological trauma. The negative side of this co-opted self was that it affected their ability to express their true or authentic self.

Critical praxis in its simplest form means theory plus action. It indicates life practice formed from both reflection and action. It is a threefold process that includes self-reflection, reflective action and collaborative reflective practice. For people from marginalized groups and those fighting oppression, critical praxis is a challenge to be inventive in ways that encourage free creative reflection and thoughtful action in order to effect change while being transformed in the process.

Culture consists of the values, beliefs, systems, language, communication and practices that are learned, shared, inherited and passed on from generation to generation. In this sense, culture is like collective programming of the mind and living patterns, and these distinguish one group of people from another. Although culture is forever changing, the values, symbols, interpretations and perspectives society places on culture still serve as identification markers for our sense of belonging to a particular group. Culture continually informs social structure and economic aspects of society

Cultural myopia is a form of near-sightedness, grounded in the belief that one's own culture is appropriate and applicable in all situations to all people. It is a narrow and cock-eyed view of seeing all of humanity as the same, and can manifest as arrogance, ignorance and fear in someone's world view.

Cultural relativism is a concept that establishes that cultures are essentially different from each other, and that our understanding is based on its standings and not judging it with one's own culture. In this context, cultural relativism is fundamentally a moral theory, aiming to show that no culture is superior. Cultural relativism aims to assist people in relating to different cultures that are not their own and to develop appreciation of other people's way of life around the world.

Differentiation is an important aspect of self-development and a process of separating out from the things that bind you. Differentiating of *self* is a psychological state of being in which someone is able to maintain their sense of identity, sense of self, thoughts and emotions, in their attachments, and particularly with intense or intimate relationships. Differentiation in family dynamics is the process of freeing yourself from family process in order to define yourself. This means being able to have different opinions and values than your family members, but still be able to stay emotionally connected to them. Social differentiation involves a similar process of knowing thyself, but with the added challenge of understanding the role of social divisions and the implications for selfhood within the hierarchical ranking of social strata.

Enmeshment is a merging of identity so that neither person functions like a whole independent person. In merging with the other, the two identities become one or pathologically dependent on each other for survival. More simply put, enmeshment is present when our sense of wholeness comes from another person. It is, in short, engulfment.

Ethnicity (broad term) is based on cultural expression and place of origin. It recognizes differences between people mostly on the basis of language and shared culture. Ethnicity is typically acquired, or self-ascribed, based on factors such as where we live or the culture we share with others.

Homogenization and specifically as it relates to cultural homogenization is the process by which dominant entities, for example, white western cultures, impose their culture on to others in ways that erode the uniqueness of cultural diversity and transform groups in ways to be changed or assimilated into the dominant culture. Cultural homogenization impacts racial and national identity and can be seen as a form of cultural imperialism.

Epigenetics is the study of how behaviours and environment can cause changes that affect the way our genes work. Epigenetics, as it relates to trauma, reveals how the impact of trauma transmissions passed down as generational trauma can become imprinted in genes. Historic and ongoing systemic racism may impact the genes of affected people potentially into future generations.

False self is an analytic concept introduced by Donald Winnicott (1960) to describe a defensive structure, which develops during infancy if the environment does not provide a nurturing and facilitative condition for the development of the *true self*. The true self, according to Winnicott, is one that has achieved optimal adaptation and development through the nurturing of a good-enough mother.

Horizontal dimension of hauntings identifies the phenomenon of black life that is often interrupted by the impact of racism. The resulting racialized trauma trigger, the charge that is still present in the unresolved pain of the past. The horizontal dimension distinguishes racialized hauntings as lived experiences for black people that powerfully open up the wounds of the past. (See also Vertical dimension.)

Hybrid, with specific reference to hybrid selves and cultural hybridity, is a concept that has gained prominence since the 1980s. In cultural studies, the term is used as a way of conceptualizing difference that aims to avoid ideas of closed identities and monolithic selves. Hybrid and cultural hybridity, as descriptors, avoid the process of making things uniform or similar, which haunts theories of multiculturalism.

Identity politics aims to secure the political freedom for people from a particular constituency, such as identities from gender, religion, race, social background, social class or other identifying factor groups. Identity politics emerged out of the 1960s' Black Civil Rights Movement, second wave feminism and gay and lesbian liberation, and it influenced political agendas that were based on these identities. It is a way of governing that takes into consideration the experiences of injustice of the collective groups.

Identity shame results from the struggle and difficulty in accepting one's racial and ethnic identity. The contributing factors are not feeling a prideful sense of belonging and acceptance to an ethnic, social or nation group and internalizing and responding to the negative stereotypes about one's racial group. Identity shame creates real problems for building self-worth, self-esteem and healthy interpersonal relationships.

Identity wounding is a term used to describe the deep hurt and offence caused to one's sense of self by the experience of being targeted or singled out for negative, discriminatory or unfavourable treatment.

Individuation is a term used by Jung (1917) to describe the process of psychological development over a lifetime in which a person discovers the self they desire to be that is quite distinct from all others. Individuation involves the achievement of selfhood, self-realization and emotional maturity, brought about by the gradual fulfilment of the person's fullest potential and functions.

Intercultural psychotherapeutic praxis is not just the process of linking cultural theories, which is knowledge, and practice, which is the act of doing therapy, but combing the work with a disposition to act with genuine concern for understanding other people and meeting challenges of race and cultural diversity. The skill demands a continual engagement in the interplay between working with the unknown and known.

Intergenerational trauma is concerned with the transmission of historical trauma within families. It is about what is psychologically – and epigenetically – inherited, internalized and passed on in ways that influence family life, dynamics, behaviours and so on, within people's experiences in the wider world. A generation is approximately 25–30 years (an average interval of time between the birth of parents and the birth of their offspring), which sociologists refer to as a 'familial generation'.

Intersectionality describes and investigates the ways in which systems of inequality, based on race, class, gender identity, ethnicity, sexual orientation, disability, class, religion and other forms of discrimination, overlap and intersect to contribute to the specific type of discrimination and systemic oppression experienced by an individual or group.

Institutional racism is a term used to define the collective failure of an organization to provide an appropriate and professional service to people because of their colour, culture or ethnic origin. This may be seen or detected in processes, attitudes and behaviour which amount to discrimination through unwitting prejudice, ignorance, thoughtlessness and racist stereotyping that disadvantage minority ethnic people.

Interpsychic refers to dynamics involving, relating to or arising from the interaction between the psyches of two or more people. Interpsychic problems are those we have because others frustrate or trigger us, especially in conflicts relating to race, cultural diversity and racialized trauma.

Intrapsychic is a psychological term referring to internal psychological processes occurring within the mind, psyche or personality of the individual. A negative intrapsychic might be stress arising from racism or experiencing crisis of identity. The process can also be positive or neutral.

Levelling is a microaggression that sends the message that you should 'stay in your lane'. This form of racial prejudice occurs when white people employ conscious, unconscious and subtle actions, (for example, off-the-cuff remarks, gestures, silence) to belittle/disparage/demean and question the justifiable positions black people attain in society, because they are perceived as threats to the traditional status quo.

Macroaggressions are similar to microaggressions in every respect but differ in that they are directed at the wider racial group and/or community as a whole.

Microaggression is a term used by Russell (1998) to describe covert racial assaults. Such snubs, slights, insults and casual remarks often stem from subtle, automatic, non-verbal and verbal communication by whites that put down black and brown people. Their capacity to 'stun' the receiver invariably results in upset, shame and hurt. They are largely experienced as hostile, marginalizing and erasing.

Minority or **minority group** is used in the sense as defined by Wirth (1945, p. 347): 'a group of people who, because of physical and cultural characteristics, are singled out from others in society in which they live for differential and unequal treatment, and who therefore regard themselves as objects of collective discrimination ... Minority status carries with it the exclusion from full participation in the life of the society.' The term includes hidden white minorities, such as Travellers, Gypsies, Irish and Jewish, the last whose group is often mistakenly categorized as a cultural or religious minority only.

Ontology is the branch of philosophy that studies concepts such as existence, being, becoming and reality.

Parental introjects are formed through the process of taking in negative and positive aspect derived from parents' attitudes, values and beliefs and absorbing these into one's system. Parental introjects influence the shaping and formation of the self and therefore are a central developmental influence in the creation of identity and personality. Positive introjects help with coping with life. Negative introjects create problems in managing the challenges of life.

Race (narrow term) is understood to be a mixture of physical, behavioural and cultural attributes. This definition carries the perception that race is something that is inherent in our biology and, therefore, inherited across generations. Race also covers nationality, national origin, skin colour and ethnicity or ethnic origin. Essential to this definition is the fact that the word is also a social construct, used as a political concept and pawn by the power-dominant group in maintaining the oppression of minority groups. Social construction has no objective reality, but rather, becomes set by what and how people think of it and decide it should be.

Racism is any behaviour or pattern of behaviour tending to systematically deny access to opportunities or privileges to members of one racial group, while perpetuating access to opportunities and privileges to members of another racial group. Bowser (2017) specifies three levels of racism:

(a) Racism at the *cultural level* provides a way of accounting for the intergenerational continuity of racial enmity, despite efforts to eliminate it. At this level, racism is subtle and pervasive and, therefore, an empirical fact based on distinct norms, attitudes, beliefs and values that constitute a particular worldview.

(b) Racism at the *institutional level* pervades the system and includes the intentional or unintentional manipulation or toleration of institutional policies that unfairly treat and restrict opportunities for minority ethnic or targeted groups.

(c) Racism at the *individual level* includes the individual expressions (conscious or unconscious) of the superiority of one race's cultural heritage and concomitant value system over that of other races.

Racial oppression is the experience of collective and/or varied forms of racism, for example, individual, institutional and cultural, together with other occurrences of related harassment, for example, bullying, scapegoating, sexual and racial aggravation. The term highlights issues of power and powerlessness and dynamics involving the dominant and dominated.

Sublimation is the process of dealing with the energies that stem from a place of trauma and redirecting them towards some form of intellectual pursuit or creative endeavour. Sublimation, therefore, is a form of healthy displacement whereby the ego is provided a healthy channel for these drives, whether, traumatic, aggressive, depressive or sexual.

Splitting describes a division into two within the psyche. The term is used in three main ways. First, to indicate the division between the conscious, the preconscious and the unconscious levels within the psyche. Second, the splitting of the ego, which refers to divisions within the self as a response to conflict, where only one side is enjoyed and the other denied. Third, the splitting of objects into good and bad, and black or white, as a defence against the anxiety of having to deal with contradictions from holding differing views and perspectives.

Stigmatic stress refers to the kind of stress that arises from the act of 'being marked' (that is, singled out for unfavourable and discriminatory treatment) and then pushed into a state of hypervigilance and over-sensitivity.

Transcendence is the pursuit of a higher state of being.

Transformation – in psychotherapy, this process is often seen as a series of corrective experiences facilitated by a skilled therapist, and a breakthrough in the client's effort to engage in new behaviour, adopt healthier ways of relating to others and gain a more positive view of self.

Transgenerational trauma refers to the negative and damaging impact of an oppressive history on a people, society, group or collective. It is about history and how what happened in one generation can affect future generations, even a few hundred years later. In this book's context, black historical trauma is 400 years old (from 1619 to the present day).

Vertical dimension of hauntings directs understanding of generational trauma as a burden still carried. The top-down vertical axis highlights how internalization of historical trauma is embodied as a continued heaviness representative of the psychological pain still borne from a past. (See also Horizontal dimension.)

Vicarious traumatization, which is also referred to as emotional fatigue, is the impact of second-hand experiences or indirect exposure to traumatic events. It can derive from the cost of caring for others, witnessing, hearing or reading about trauma events and feeling or empathizing with the pain of others who are experiencing the trauma. Vicarious traumatization can affect the carer's own mental capacities, leading to burn out.

White is a racialized classification generally used for Caucasian people, for example, of European origin defined by their light (or white) skin, among other racial characteristics. The term 'white race' and 'white people' was first used in the context of the Atlantic slave trade. The modern concept tends to focus on white as a privileged group at the top of a racial hierarchical system. This social default makes whiteness a construct directly connected to the correlating construct of non-white people as 'other' in society.

White fright–guilt complex is repressed historical guilt that manifests as hyperalertness to any perceived danger from the black presence or witnessing black equality and independence as an existential threat.

White ontology is identified in this text to address semantic components within the broader and more generalized definition of ontology. Race as one key factor, highlights the important elements of existence, being and becoming for white people, as having prescribed advantage and privilege for living and evolving. This default status, which is key to self and collective actualization, positions white people at an established vantage point. The process of 'being through others' is comparatively different when compared with the black people ontological process which will be interrupted by social obstacles that impinge progress towards being.

White-Passing is a term used for a very light skinned Person of Colour, usually of black or brown and white parents, who is recognized as only being white. This labeling occurs when mixed identities are perceived in stereotypes.

Zeitgeist refers to the mood or spirit of a period of history that is defined by the ideas and beliefs of the times. My 'BBCCT' zeitgeist (Brexit, Black Lives Matter Movement, Covid-19, Climate Change, Trumpism), as described in Chapter 5, are key significant elements shaping our current times. #Me-Too Movement is a key aspect of the zeitgeist, but has been evolving over a much longer period of time.

Appendix II

Recognizing my own ancestral burden

I am here because YOU were there …

Introduction to my genealogical search

The research undertaken up to the time of writing has involved an uncompleted genealogy exploration. First, I wanted to discover the make-up of my ethnic origin. Secondly, I wanted to uncover the ancestral origins of my white English-language surname, Alleyne – where did it originate and who are the people behind my genetic makeup? I wanted to uncover this by following all links leading back to the very first genetically related Alleyne in my father's bloodline. The genealogical research is not complete, and may never be possible to complete, but I will share my discoveries to date and how they have brought meaning to my sense of self and identity. The hope was to find the related DNA root connections and, although this who-do-you-think-you-are[1] exercise is unfinished, the journey thus far has added pieces to my identity jigsaw puzzle. I am a little clearer about the trauma trails that link my root connections with slavery and the slave trade. Although I am aware that, throughout the sixteenth, seventeenth and eighteenth centuries, European empire builders all gained strength, wealth and power from raping the resources of indigenous people – that is, the people who inhabited the land first – the strongest colonial connection and 'mother country' attachment for me, as a Caribbean native, has been with Britain, not with the rest of Europe.

I know I am Guyanese, born of African ancestry, Caribbean background, naturalized black British and a British citizen for 47 years, living in England. However, I wanted to know more about my ethnic origin, the ethnic makeup of my identity and heritage. I wanted to gain a more intimate understanding of the complex hybrid self I have constructed to negotiate my complicated existence in a predominantly white society. I had also hoped to be able to understand more fully the content of self and character that has learnt to thrive, in spite of being on the receiving end of racial and cultural microaggressions. The personal journey I have been on in crafting the book, searching for who am I, reclaiming my kin and offering all of this up for scrutiny has been exposing and healing at the same time. The writing process has been a deeply triggering experience, filled with a mixture of frustration with being stuck, despondency, upset, pain, mourning, feeling burdened and anger. But the work has also activated a sense of deeper 'knowing' of memory that was lost, leading to healing and empowerment, and a true sense of being a little bit more liberated.

My ancestral search fulfils (in part) the adage, best expressed by the Maya Angelou quote (accessed 2021): 'if you don't know where you've come from, you don't know where you're going. I have respect for the past, but I am a person of the moment. I'm here, and I do my best to be completely centred at the place I'm at, then I go forward to the next place' (Maya Angelou, 2011, *The Arizona Republic* interview).

The story of Guyana

My own country of origin, now the modern Co-operative Republic of Guyana, and simply know as Guyana, is on the northern mainland of South America. Guyana originated about 35,000 years ago with the first nomadic people crossing over from Asia. The original settler people were, however, native American peoples who were from the Arawak and Carib tribes. Christopher Columbus, in his four transatlantic voyages in the fourteenth and fifteenth centuries, is known for opening the way for European exploration, exploitation and colonization of the Americas. 'The Guianas' was one such territory. Previously Dutch colonies between 1580 and 1796, and again between 1802 and 1803, Demerara, Essequibo and Berbice were reinstated under British rule in 1814. The colony of British Guiana was created in 1831, when the administration of the three territories was centralized in Georgetown. British Guiana remained under colonial role until 25 May 1966, when the country became independent under the name Guyana.

The French were awarded part of The Guianas in 1667, for trading purposes, and only took full occupation in 1852, using the territory as a penal colony for deporting 70,000 of its French convicts. French Guiana remains the only territory of The Guianas still under colonial role. The lesser chunk of The Guianas was awarded to the Dutch, and it remained under their rule until its independence in 1975. Dutch Guiana is now named Suriname.

The term 'West Indies' distinguished the territories (sub-regions of North America) encountered by Columbus from discovery claims by other powers. Nowadays, the term 'West Indies' is used interchangeably with 'Caribbean'. Europeans supplanted 'Caribbean' and used the term 'West Indies' to describe their own acquired territories, and also to distinguish the region from the 'Indies' (India) and the East Indies of south Asia and southeast Asia.

For me and other Guyanese people, our historical, cultural and emotional attachments remain strong with the mother country, Britain. The impact of history has created a colonial bond, which is ambivalent and conflictual. Historically, and even after Guyana's political independence in 1966, the trans- and intergenerational trauma impact for healing remains a sore wound for the Guyanese and the rest of the people of the Caribbean/West Indies. The Caribbean was occupied by indigenous people whose population was decimated by brutal labour practices, enslavement and disease when the Europeans arrived.

Understanding and dealing with the burden of one's heritage is a liberation best put by Bach, '... the inner Enemy is like a throwback, a vestigial tail we no longer need now that we have conquered the elements and are in fact no longer at the mercy of fire, thunder and wild animals' (Bach, 1985, p. 47). Bach's 'inner enemy' can be regarded in tandem with my concept of 'the internal oppressor' (Alleyne, 2004).

Conducting a genealogical search

The process of discovering one's ethnic identity is extremely complex, but mine was initially helped by the guides to using Ancestry.com (Hendrickson, 2018). This process of discovering roots is even more difficult for black and brown people worldwide, who are underrepresented groups when it comes to our life experiences being recorded accurately, documented fully, logged properly and stored judiciously for posterity.

My attempt at my own genealogical search was assisted by a genealogist with knowledge of European settlers in the Caribbean colony of Barbados. The who-do-you-think-you-are exercise is complex, complicated, confusing, time-consuming, frustrating and expensive.

The results can both elate and deflate. The actual task of finding out my ethnic background and ethnicity makeup was, however, relatively easily achieved by doing a simple DNA test. It has surprisingly and joyfully brought me quickly in contact with several unknown Alleyne cousins, some as far back as eighth and ninth bloodline relations. Knowing that I am black Caribbean (and naturalized British for more than half of my life) is one sure thing about my ethnicity, but having a bit more knowledge of the specific ethnic make-up of my black identity has proved informative, empowering and stabilizing. The process affirmed the saying that knowledge is power. This journey to discover the origins of my ethnicity also highlighted the painful transgenerational affiliations and ambivalent attachments black and brown Caribbean peoples still have with Britain.

My DNA test summary and ethnicity estimate

The following is a breakdown of what informs my racial identity and can be seen as just one example of how Britain and other European colonial powers have played a part in keeping the black diaspora under subjugation. Although it consists of an estimation of make-up, the ethnic breakdown also gives a clear indication of a rich and, in some cases, prosperous and powerful existence once experienced by black people prior to slavery. The hereditary search confirmed for me that black people were part of, and enjoyed, a civilization before slavery, and that my (our) existence as black people did not start with slavery.

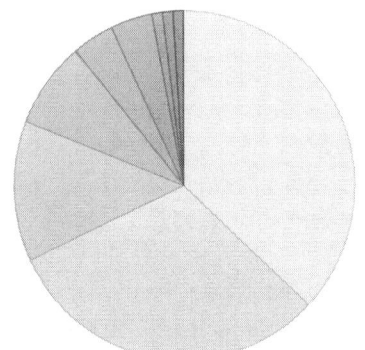

Nigeria - 37%
Cameroon, Congo and Western Bantu
          Peoples - 31%
Benin and Togo - 13%
Ivory Coast & Ghana - 8%
Mali - 4%
England and North-western Europe - 4%
Southern Italy - 1%
Wales - 1%
Scotland - 1%

Figure A2.1 *An ethnicity estimate from 9 regions*

Figure A2.1 is a pictorial representation of my DNA story, emerging from my submission of DNA material for research. The approximations highlight the specific elements of my black ethnic makeup, which have no doubt influenced my spiritual and metaphysical character. I was excited to be in possession of this information, as it enlightened me to the places, histories and cultures that have genetically shaped who I am today through who and what I am connected to. This important discovery has fostered a deep curiosity and determination to delve even deeper to discover who am I.

Making sense of ethnic identity

Jean Phinney (1989) suggests that, like ego identity, the process of ethnic identity can be conceptualized in terms of stages, with an individual moving from the unexamined attitudes of childhood, through a period of examination and exploration, to a more secure place of achieved ethnic identity. The four stages of the process were identified as:

(a) ethnic self-identification
(b) sense of belonging
(c) positive and negative attitudes towards one ethnic group
(d) involvement in cultural events.

She was clear in distinguishing between the development of ethnic identity, which is the 'process' of discovering, and understanding ethnic identity, which is the 'content'.

Process: discovering your racial ethnic group membership and its importance, which includes history, origin and knowing thyself.

Content: understanding values, beliefs, attitudes and behaviours that are inherited and are thereby internalized. This background endorses one's engagement with the world and becomes what we are in our identity.

Both are important for racial or ethnic identity development but, sadly, they have become personal work relegated to minorities because they are the ones who are seen as having a deficit. Finney's conceptual model was not intended to replace or usurp Erikson's (1968) developmental model of identity development and, in my view, it adds to it in a fundamental way and is applicable to all ethnic majority and minority groups, not just people with known African or Indian heritage.

Uncovering the origins of my surname

One thing I have discovered, with great frustration, is the complexity of discovering the origins of what I have concluded is my English slave-related surname, Alleyne. I do know that 'Alleyne' originates in Brittany, France, and came to England during the battle of Hastings; the first Alleyne came to England with William the Conqueror.

Notable writers and genealogists, such as Robyn N. Smith (website last accessed 5 June 2022) and Guy Grannum (2012), suggest that a novice researcher who walks into a library or archive and asks to see the slave records for a specific community will likely leave the archivist confused. They note that most of the records used to study enslaved persons are not called that; rather, the information sought is to be found in the official and administrative documentation of life: probate records, land records, court records, church records, vital records. I have learnt that black ancestral research cannot be done entirely from online digitized records, as important sources will be missed from your family history. These may include, as in my case, an interest in what psychological traits I may have inherited from the various tribal ethnic groups that may have shaped my blend of ethnic identity. Black professional genealogists suggest the following:

- Do not start your genealogical research in the blind.
- Take classes at the National Archives.
- Buy and read new genealogy books as they are published.
- Understand the concept of identity.
- Read case studies in genealogy journals.
- Read about the history of slavery and the transatlantic slave trade, and its specific impact on the region of your birth.
- Read about colonialism and European settlers in the colonies – and for those reclaiming kin from the Caribbean, read about British imperialism.
- Take the time to establish a way to organize the process of your research. Digitize documents and information discovered. Organize genealogy physical files and digitize files by surname and region.

In addition to the above preparation for the onerous task of tracing ancestry, there are reasons why trying to discover how former slaves typically acquired a surname is very difficult. Grannum (2012) points out that although it was assumed that most freed slaves adopted or were given the surname of their owner, research shows there were other options available to freed slave men and women. A few options included: adopting the surname of their mother; using their last forename, as additional names were often given to slaves to differentiate them; using a chosen surname; using a surname given to them by the church or state for official purposes.

Grannum explains that, while freed slaves could choose their surnames on emancipation, the majority chose surnames already existing in the local population. Individuals could, and did, change surnames, and so the same individual might be recorded using a different surname on different documents. This complex system of name identity for the black freed slave makes the whole process of finding ancestral connections particularly difficult.

In my case, the key reasons for coming to a halt in my search are that records are not easily available to be studied. They are sparse, particularly in certain places such as the Caribbean, Barbados and Guyana to be specific. Only some historical information is digitized and, often, handwritten documents are extremely hard to come by, as these were either damaged in floods or through poor storage methods. In addition to these difficulties, British records reveal that slaves were not humanized with full name recognition and records. In one publication, the first mention of a 'negro' was in a family will:

> ... To daughters Benjamina Woodbridge Alleyne ... half of furniture and chinaware and Negro girl Patience, and the right to live in house while she is unmarried .... Patience, a negro Infant daughter of June servant to Miss Benjamina, Woodbridge Alleyne of Braintree, was baptized privately at the House of Madam Alleyne Sunday evening November 7, 1778. (Brandow, 2001)

In another entry, Bristol, a negro child of Philip, servant to Mrs Mary Alleyne, was baptised privately on 2 July 1765. In both of these entries, the negro is given neither a surname nor an age. They are just a first name with no title. There was no clear tendency for slaves to bear their own native surnames or the surnames of their owners or slave masters. They were just a first name and, in some cases of freed slaves who assumed a surname in one of the aforementioned ways, a former slave owner might use the strange phrase 'he calls himself', as if having a given name and a surname was absurd and laughable.

The compulsive interest to trace my name origin and learn about my ancestors took me to *Barbados and the Genealogies of Barbadian Families* (Brandow, 2001) which is an A–Z history of names in Barbados. I summarize from Brandow what I have gathered to date:

- The Alleyne family probably originated in Staffordshire (1375), but, as yet, no definite proof of connection between the Alleyne family of the UK and the Barbados (Caribbean) branch of the Alleyne family has been found.
- Reynold Alleyne (1609–1651), the progenitor of the Barbados family, who arrived within three years of the first British settlement of the island, was the son of Reverend Richard Alleyne, (1572–1651), the rector of Stowting in the County of Kent.
- In June 1630, Reynold Alleyne is first mentioned in the records of Barbados as one of the counsellors in the government under Captain Henry Hawley, who went to Barbados as governor. Reynold Alleyne is nearly 21 years old.
- In 1938, his name appears as Reynold Allen on a list of owners of land and property in Barbados. He trades in cotton and tobacco and is an agent for a London merchant.
- In October 1651, Colonel Reynold Alleyne is employed by the British navy to protect their conquest, Barbados. History tells us that colonial rule over the Caribbean islands created conflict among European colonists. Reynold developed considerable interest in and ownership of the island, having led his soldiers to gain it outright.
- Reynold Alleyne became the owner of a plantation for growing cotton and tobacco, and house servants/slaves are mentioned as being owned by his progeny (consisting of his wife, three sons and a daughter) after his death in 1651.

Although my genealogical search has frustratingly come to a halt at this juncture of completing the book, I can only surmise that it could have been quite possible that my ancestral links may be connected to any one of millions of slaves wrenched from their African homelands during the slave trade between 1500 and 1900. West African slaves specifically were bought to work the plantations, or service the slave master's plantation homes, in the Caribbean and the United States of America. The search for my origins remains a compelling itch that I must continue to scratch, until soothed.

Recognizing and understanding of my own ancestral burden

The trauma borne by a single person, family or community invariably and inevitably finds its way into wider society. Trauma legacies weave and wire their roots deeply in the psyche. In turn, this weaving profoundly informs how we see and live in our worlds and relate to and understand one another. This understanding has lent itself to my ambivalent relationship with white Britain and my choice to make it my home. On a slightly facetious level, when I am asked why I have chosen to live here, my immediate response is to reply *I am here because you were there.*

Part of my ambivalence was created by my parents, who pushed for my further education in Britain, the mother country. Clearly, the notion that the mother will look after and nurture is deeply embedded. These internalizations were quickly dashed from lived experiences in the UK, adding reality to my internalized parental romanticisation of Britain. Part of 'burden' is living with the ambivalence in the healthiest way possible. It is my contention that in order to do this successfully, one has to know thyself.

My research to date has been about the specific nature of my ethnic make-up, which has enabled me to gain a fuller understanding of what the word 'burden' entails. Burden is what I carry silently and seems to be in a constant flux of healing and being opened up again by racial hauntings. It can often feel unresolved and sometimes resolved, but in the current climate of what I have personally termed our 'BBCCT' (Brexit, Black Lives Matter Movement, Covid-19, Climate Change and Trumpism) zeitgeist, there is a collective trauma burden with its accompanying collective racial hauntings that has impacted my own personal unresolved burdens. Many other wounds have been activated as I feel caught in the intersection of various traumatic events.

Burden is what I carry for parents and wider family who were not always aware of the enmeshment with our Caribbean colonial past and the importance of unyoking from this unhealthy attachment. Burden is what I, and we, seem to carry as members of the black race; burden is what I hold for others, which they themselves do not want to hold under any circumstance; burden is both mine and other people's disavowed, displaced and repressed lived experiences. To put it this way makes the meaning of burden, in the context of race, the conflation of carrying a personal weight while lumbered by an outside imposition. Burden then becomes both a responsibility to resolve and an encumbrance to release and return to its sender. This definition makes perfect sense when it is viewed in the context of Sampson's description of the context of power:

> The other is a figure constructed to be serviceable to the historically dominant white male group. In order to provide the service, the other cannot be permitted to have a voice, a position, a being of its own, but must remain mute or speak only in the ways permitted by the dominant other ... The other is an essential presence without whom the dominant protagonists could not be who they claim to be ... The other must remain part of, and party to the self-celebratory monologues of the dominant group ... no real dialogue can be permitted to intervene, lest in permitting others actually to speak in their own terms, expressing their own point of view, the entire Western scheme of Western civilization would collapse. (Sampson, 1993, p. 13).

The burden is explicit in Sampson's description, which highlights the roles of the dominant and dominated. The serviceable other is like a mule, subjugated to the predestined role of carrying the heavy load of/for the dominant other, while also needing the mental and physical strength to haul its own heavy load.

Understanding the nuanced nature of historical burden has helped me discern where I position myself in the midst of all of this in the society I have chosen to live in. There are also additional challenges for me and my multidimensional hybrid self in being black, an older woman, educated, assertive and who uses the voice I have developed and own outright without indebtedness to anyone. Knowing where to position myself in this predominantly white UK society first means doing the homework of untying myself from the burdens of the past. This meant to reject being defined only by my minority status, to disallow the label of wearing a badge of suffering and oppression and therefore only capable of anger and rage. Knowing where to position myself is to allow myself a rainbow of emotions, which include joy, delight, pleasure, thrill and bliss from life experiences. I have dared to step out of a traditional box that I had once upon a time created for myself, by fulfilling previously envious wishes to own my own motorbike and ride regularly with a Harley Davidson posse in the countryside, learn the physical and mental skills of modern fencing and experience one of Britain's longest ziplines. These pursuits conquered, and thoroughly enjoyed, were internalized as not for black people, and certainly not a black woman.

I have also had to challenge the unintentional infantilization, the 'fixing' and 'levelling'[2] that are among the myriad ways in which white people find to belittle or question black and brown people who are in positions of power and influence. This includes those who are simply in control of their lives and work hard to stand near the taller poppies in the field. An example of this occurred in a visit to a local pharmacy to collect my repeat prescription for high blood pressure, a hereditary condition. After handing over the prescription, the white female at the counter looked at it, then quizzingly at me, then back to the prescription and asked, 'Is this for *you*?' My reply was yes, to which she asked, 'Are you a real doctor?' The irony of being there to collect medication for hypertension was not lost on me, and I immediately and deliberately settled myself internally so that my blood pressure would not be activated by this microaggression. However, the trigger of such blatant, yet paradoxically covert, racism was set off, and I replied, 'If I were white and male, would you see it fit to ask that question?', to which her embarrassment was palpable and visibly denuding. Knowing, based on experience, that what would follow would be a defensive covering up of personal shame, I cut short her explanations, by quietly but firmly directing her to discuss the incident with her colleagues at lunch and, between them, analyse the many aspects of the encounter. I promptly left with my medication and my blood pressure intact. In my experience, I have found that on several occasions, when injurious experiences are retold in white presence, what is received feels perceptibly like performative empathy or flabby dramatic outrage. Such responses only add insult to injury.

Knowing where to position myself means never lapsing into the victim position of needing to be rescued because Britain owes me and black people. Yes, there is a definite role for national atonement and reparation, but this is not confined to monetary handouts or largesse.

Unburdening the past therefore means, in essence, finding a way to keep the memory and knowledge of the past properly processed and filed away, so that your trauma is not easily and readily activated (or, if it is, knowing how to respond to it in a way that does not leave you destabilized, as demonstrated by my example above). To be inflicted with the suffering of constantly being triggered is to allow the other to continue to exert a level of control over our lives. As I have come to understand and conclude, to heal from all forms of trauma, one has to learn the art of knowing when to stop remembering – this goal is not about forgetting, but realizing that separation is necessary before healing from generational trauma can begin to take place.

How to master the art of living with the tension of generational trauma

The mental work of not allowing the past to continually reactivate is a big ask of the historically subjugated. This invisible task of trying to achieve effective self-regulation and healthy ontology is a major drain on our psychological resources. I am now more aware of the phenomenon of the silent killer of so many black people, namely the higher prevalence of high blood pressure. To date, researchers do not have a definite answer to the question as to why high blood pressure is so common in black people but, apart from the more recognized factors of dietary habits, hereditary factors and excessive weight, the environmental factors unique to the black experience – economic inequality, discrimination and racism – are now being recognized as risk factors for high blood pressure (Fuchs, 2011). The intersection at which racial oppression is felt has an impact on mental and psychological health over time. There is a long list of triggers that impede my ongoing healing process, from microaggressions that attack my black identity, forms of oppression that can be seen, for example, in a denial of equal service when I am going about my everyday life, to news items of racial assault or the murder of a black person. All of these take place against the backdrop of those in power turning a blind eye to overt systematic and structural racism. It is as if the chronic wound is constantly being reopened, thus rendering it difficult to heal properly.

I have developed the following techniques, based on my own experience and the work that I have done with my clients, which have helped me to ground myself when the wound is reopened:

- Remember that when we are triggered and experience our personal history being involuntary activated, this is a trauma response. It does not matter if it is a small T, middle T or big T trauma; trauma at the end of the day is about rupture and psychological injury. A trigger, like the example from the pharmacy, can spark an immediate ripple effect that reopens the doors of old personal and historical trauma wounds.

- Learn to identify and know when you are being triggered, or your archaic material activated. Watch out for the 4 F responses: flight, fight, freeze, and fawn (that is, compliant and sucking up to) reactions and behaviours. Although these are natural responses to trauma, they are also trauma reactions that may result in defensive, hypervigilant and unhelpful barriers to regaining and feeling in control.

- Name the trigger. Anchor it concretely by identifying in words what has caused the activation. Follow this up by removing it from within you and putting it on the ground, so to speak. The way to do this work is to get in touch with and recognize which of the five senses – sight, smell, touch, taste, hearing – is signalling distress or pain.

- Detect where the activated presence of racial hauntings is somatized in the body. If it helps, write down what your brain and body signals are conveying to you. Use conscious breathing as soon as the stress hits.

- Engage in positive self-talk, telling yourself you are larger than your fear and you are not a slave to the situation. Apply mantras such as *I am more than a colour* to engage the mental hygiene process. Be compassionate to yourself by remembering that you are worthy.

- Separate what is the manifest content (in the moment) and what is the latent content (past historical material) of your experience. This is the art of separating what belongs to you and what is rightfully the burden of the other. Clarity in recognizing what is yours and what is the other person's stuff will allow for rationality and a return to a more secure ontological base.

- De-escalate the trauma arousal by practising all of the above and regulating the impact of the old wounds that have been vicariously triggered. Focus more on processing the manifest issues for a here-and-now resolution. The inability to maintain this clarity will inevitably leave the sufferer fused and confused, with the potential to prolong their experience and the risk of further harm and hurt.

It is only when these elements are successfully employed that self-regulation is experienced, control is reclaimed and the trigger can be properly examined and regulated. You can learn from every situation how best and effectively you handled your trauma reactions. From there, you can get better and quicker at anticipating the pitfalls and traps that trigger you. Learn to develop a sense of preparedness without ending up hypervigilant, obsessively tracking the moves of the other in every encounter.

The process of trying to heal from generational trauma amidst the constant activation of old wounds, by living in a divided world, is, in and of itself, a burden. We know that racism will never be wiped completely from our human world and nations may forever struggle to brave those important roundtable and kitchen table conversations that kickstart the process of facing up to the past. There will remain obstacles in the path of being entirely free from the burden carried and activations of racial hauntings of black heritage. Knowing this fact, it behoves me to build the right emotional muscles, as I do at the gym for regular routine workouts, in order to gain the strength to have a quality of life, without overtaxing or damaging myself. Therefore, to do one's healing is to learn and master the art of living with the tension of always having to mediate between the inside and outside, and private and public aspects of self and identity. Mastering this task is to build immunity – with regular boosters – to the world's race disease.

Appendix III

Values and principles underpinning good practice in working with issues of difference and diversity

The list below is an encapsulated guide to good practice in working with difference and diversity in therapy practice. The information can also be used as a training handout for tutors and trainers on counselling and psychotherapy trainings.

Guide to good practice

Working with lesbian, gay, bisexual, transgendered, intersex, queer/questioning and pansexual clients

(1) Acknowledge the existence of, and work through, external and internalized homophobia, heterosexist messages, and rigid ways of viewing sexuality and gender identities.

(2) Maintain empathy by learning about and understanding LGBT+ identities, culture and needs.

(3) Affirm LGBT+ lifestyles as viable and legitimate life choices (that is, that they can exist healthily and enjoy legal and social recognition).

(4) Validate LBGT+ rights by challenging clients, peers, colleagues and organizations for change.

(5) Recognize the diversity within LBGT+ communities. Understand social and political issues that lead to feelings of powerlessness, systematic exclusion and marginalization for

LGBT+ people who are from black and other ethnic minority groups, and those with disabilities.

Working with refugees

(1) Acknowledge the fact that English may be the second language for refugee clients and that effective work with such individuals may require allocation of extra time and the assistance of interpreters/translators.

(2) Recognize the social, political and emotional problems for refugees. Endeavour to seek specialist knowledge in order to work with issues of cultural displacement, homesickness, political torture, effects of war on the human psyche, culture shock, family disruption, isolation, housing and immigration problems.

(3) Work with the effects of post-traumatic experiences that manifest mainly as loss, bereavement and mental distress – trauma.

(4) Act appropriately as an advocate when dealing with the system, without taking away the client's agency and dignity.

Working with people with disabilities

(1) Avoid the tendency to make decisions on behalf of the disabled person which denies them control over their own lives.

(2) Be careful not to reinforce 'medical' definitions of disability that focus on 'impairment' and 'special needs', which direct attention and approaches to these aspects of disability.

(3) Acknowledge and address ways in which society and its institutions are organized to exclude people with disabilities from mainstream provision and employment.

(4) Recognize that the 'problem' for people with disabilities lies not within individual bodies but within the way in which society fails to organize its resources to include people with disabilities.

Working with Black and Asian clients

(1) Acknowledge and actively deal with racism operating at these levels: individual, institutional, intentional, unintentional and intersectional.

(2) Take account of support structures within different communities, for example, the church, the role of religion, religious practices and rituals, the extended family and other non-traditional and traditional family support structures.

(3) Respect the need to include helping agencies relevant to the different communities, for example, spiritual healers, the imam, the priest, elders and other specialist agencies.

(4) Recognize the influence of the community and primacy of the collective.

(5) Redefine and work appropriately with Eurocentric concepts of mental health.

(6) Reappraise what psychological yardsticks are culturally relevant in determining what is psychic equilibrium and progress in the counselling/therapy process.

Working with women

(1) Be aware of the biological, psychological, cultural and social issues that have an impact on women in general and on particular groups of women in society.

(2) Recognize and be aware of all forms of oppression and how these interact and intersect with sexism, classism, racism and sexuality.

(3) Increase your ability to utilize skills that are particularly facilitative to women in general and to particular racial and cultural groups of women.

(4) Be aware of sexist language that may be unintentionally used in counselling, supervision, teaching, daily interactions and journal publications.

(5) Understand the effects of sex-role socialization on women's development and functioning.

Working with racism and the racist

(1) Remember those who remain silent to racist behaviour stand to benefit from its effects; therefore, maintain a positive stance by challenging offensive, oppressive and all other forms of behaviour that excludes black people, Asians, Jews, Irish people and those members who represent 'the hidden white minority', for example, Polish, Romanian, Bulgarian, Croatian people.

(2) Failure to combat racism in any form is not just a simple act of racism; it is a *perpetuation* of racism. If you are not part of the solution, you are part of the problem.

(3) Comment clearly on offending behaviour (for example, I did not find it funny when you mimicked the black cleaner's accent). Spell out the consequence of the behaviour, for example, racial mimicry is always negative because its intention is to highlight an aspect of the person's identity for ridicule).

(4) Spell out the positive consequences of the behaviour you are requesting change in; people need to know the positive effects of the change before shifting from their old position.

(5) Use forms of communication that are appropriate for the individual and take account of the need for privacy and respect. Remember feedback should always give value to the receiver – not release for the giver.

(6) Support others actively to complain about discrimination. Deal with covert problems, which undermine and affect personal morale, by making them overt in individual supervision, staff meetings and special training, and CPD (continuing professional development) sessions. Consider group external training consultancy if circumstances permit.

Working with yourself

(1) Re-examine your own values and beliefs and how they were influenced. What has changed with experience, new knowledge and changing sensitivities?

(2) Be willing to learn new patterns of thinking, perceiving and behaving.

(3) Be open to meeting the unknown and unfamiliar.

(4) Be prepared to admit to your own shortcomings; there is strength in owning one's ignorance and naivety about other cultures and being willing to embrace new knowledge.

(5) Stay with the natural and sometimes inevitable discomforts that will be stirred up by difference and allow yourself to become familiar with the new effects.

(6) Do your own homework about difference and diversity. Do not expect the client to feed you continuously in your learning process. This is an imposition and tantamount to abuse.

(7) Consciousness-raising on its own is not enough in working with cultural and racial diversity. Action must follow intent.

(8) The priority should be to identify and change personal behaviour that limits full engagement with others. Remember, cross-cultural competence is essentially a relational skill, mandatory for all work with clients, colleagues – and for one's self in the world.

(9) Do not engage in sexual activity (includes social media, sexting and texting, and so on) with any client under any circumstances. Be aware of the continuum of psychological covert to overt abuse, which includes professional voyeurism, sexual gazes (covert) to sexual remarks, unacceptable touching and more overt sexual contact.

Endnotes

Chapter 1

1. An image of the memorial statue can be seen via: www.theguardian.com/commentisfree/2019/oct/23/memorial-2007-enslaved-africans-black-history-britain. The disavowal is plain to see in the differing treatments directed at the reparative acts for Holocaust descendants and descendants of slavery: www.bbc.co.uk/news/uk-england-london-50287345.

Chapter 2

1. In 2018 Michelle Obama described her feeling of imposter syndrome: www.theguardian.com/us-news/2018/dec/03/michelle-obama-tells-london-school-she-still-has-imposter-syndrome.
2. By 'hybrid capacity' I am referring to a multidimensional and multi-layered self, rather than the superficial and stereotypical way in which black people are often regarded.

Chapter 3

1. Taken from the Care Quality Commission, 'Monitoring the Mental Health Act in 2017/18'. The report was presented to Parliament pursuant to Section 120D (3) of the Mental Health Act 1983. This publication is available at: https://www.cqc.org.uk/sites/default/files/20190320_mhareport1718_report.pdf

Chapter 5

1. At the time, this was one of south London's largest and best-known department stores; it closed in the 1980s.
2. The #MeToo movement could have been added to this acronym, but its powerful impact has been evolving over a much longer period.
3. Formal permission has been given to publicly share this letter.

Chapter 6

1. A British colloquial expression meaning to ostracize someone by ceasing to speak to them.
2. Considered reflections from my white colleague and co-wrangler, Jane Ryan, as borne out of our robust race conversations.

Chapter 7

1. The National Health Service. This is the government-funded health care service that is available to those living in the UK whereby users are not asked to pay the full cost of the service and receive some services free of charge.

Chapter 8

1. Brahmins consisted of mainly priests and intellectuals and were considered to be at the top of the caste system.
2. Identity politics is a political approach, wherein people of a particular gender, religion, race, social background, class – or defined through other aspects of identity – develop political agendas and theoretical systems based on how oppression may affect their lives.
3. LGBTQ+: lesbian, gay, bisexual, transgender, queer (or questioning) and others (including pansexual, intersex, non-binary individuals).
4. Grenfell Tower is the name of a 24-storey block of flats in London that was engulfed in flames in June 2017, resulting in the death of 72 people. An enquiry revealed that the cladding used to coat the block, which enabled the spread of fire, had been selected in order to keep costs down, despite safety concerns having been raised in previous years.

Chapter 10

1. BBCCT: Brexit – Black Lives Matter – Covid-19 – Climate change – Trumpism.

Appendix 2

1. *Who Do You Think You Are?* Is the name of a BBC series in which celebrities trace their family trees with the help of professional genealogists.
2. Levelling is what happens when white people employ conscious, unconscious and subtle actions (for example, off-the-cuff remarks, gestures, silence) to belittle/disparage/demean and question the authentic positions in society of black people, who they perceive as threats to the traditional status quo.

Bibliography

Online resources

Angelou, M. www.goodreads.com, accessed 16 December 2021.

Angelou, M. www.brainyquote.com/quotes/maya_angelou_634505, accessed 28 March 2021.

BBC (2019). 'Time running out' for London slavery memorial. www.bbc.co.uk/news/uk-england-london-50287345, accessed 16 May 2021.

BBC World Service. *The Story of Africa*. www.bbc.co.uk/programmes/p03njn4f, accessed 6 June 2022.

Black History Month (2022). www.blackhistorymonth.org.uk/article/section/history-of-slavery/africa-before-transatlantic-enslavement, accessed 22 January 2022.

Brandow, J. (2001). information on the name Alleyne, www.burrowes.org/ruby/gedrelay.rbx?type=html&target=FB1010, accessed 5 June 2022.

Butterworth, B. (2021). *What does 'woke' mean? Origins of term, and how the meaning has changed*. Available at https://inews.co.uk/news/uk/woke-what-mean-meaning-origins-term-definition-culture-387962, accessed 30 September 2021.

Cameron, David (2013). 'We should be proud of our Empire rule' says Cameron, www.express.co.uk/news/uk/379138/We-should-be-proud-of-our-Empire-rule-says-Cameron, accessed 25 January 2022.

Care Quality Commission (2019). *Monitoring the Mental Health Act in 2017/18* available at www.cqc.org.uk/sites/default/files/20190320_mhareport1718_report.pdf, accessed 25 January 2022.

Cole, Nicki Lisa, PhD. 'Defining Racism Beyond its Dictionary Meaning'. ThoughtCo. www.thoughtco.com/racism-definition-3026511, accessed 5 June 2022.

Dahlgreen, W. (2014). *The British Empire is 'something to be proud of'*. https://yougov.co.uk/topics/politics/articles-reports/2014/07/26/britain-proud-its-empire, accessed 25 January 2022.

DeNoon, D. J. (2005). 'Why 7 deadly diseases strike blacks most', www.webmd.com/hypertension-high-blood-pressure/features/why-7-deadly-diseases-strike-blacks-most, accessed 23 April 2021.

Einstein, A. www.quoteslyfe.com/quote/Imagination-is-more-important-than-knowledge-268931, accessed 21 October 2021.

Fuchs, D. F. (2011). 'Why Do Black Americans Have Higher Prevalence of Hypertension? An Enigma Still Unsolved'. Originally published 7 Feb 2011, https://doi.org/10.1161/HYPERTENSIONAHA.110.163196, accessed 5 June 2022.

Grannum, G. (2011) 'Researching African-Caribbean Family History' www.bbc.co.uk/history/familyhistory/next_steps/genealogy_article_01.shtml, accessed 5 June 2022.

Grant, C. (2020). 'Forced out by Kevin Maxwell review – prejudice between police'. *The Guardian*. www.theguardian.com/books/2020/may/27/forced-out-by-kevin-maxwell-review-prejudice-between-police, accessed 16 October 2021.

Hirsch, A. (2019) 'Britain was built on the backs of slaves. A memorial is the least they deserve'. www.theguardian.com/commentisfree/2019/oct/23/memorial-2007-enslaved-africans-black-history-britain, accessed 23 January 2022.

Hoffman, E.T.A. (1817). Der Sandmann (The Sand-Man). English translation by John Oxenford. https://germanstories.vcu.edu, accessed 06 June 2022.

Isaacson, R. L. (2003). 'Limbic System'. https://doi.org/10.1038/npg.els.0000155, accessed 6 June 2022.

McLeod, S. (2014) Carl Rogers Theory. www.simplypsychology.org/carl-rogers.html, accessed 6 June 2022.

Mohatt, N., Thompson, A., Thai, N. and Tebes, J. et al (2014). 'Historical trauma as public narrative: A conceptual review of how history impacts present-day health'. www.ncbi.nlm.nih.gov/pmc/articles/PMC4001826/, accessed 6 June 2022.

Obama, M. (2018). 'Michelle Obama tells London school she still has impostor syndrome'. *The Guardian*. www.theguardian.com/us-news/2018/dec/03/michelle-obama-tells-london-school-she-still-has-imposter-syndrome, accessed 16 May 2021.

Smith, R. N. Reclaiming Kin website http://reclaimingkin.com, accessed 2 July 2021.

Tim, 'Socrates: Know Yourself, March 24, 2012,' in *Philosophy & Philosophers*, March 24, 2012, https://www.the-philosophy.com/socrates-know-yourself.

Wilson, A. (2021). 'I'm not the defendant': the trials of a black barrister. *The Guardian*. www.theguardian.com/books/2021/apr/17/im-not-the-defendant-the-trials-of-a-black-barrister. accessed 16 October 2021.

Yehuda, R., Schmeidler, J., Wainberg M, Binder-Brynes, K, and Duvdevani, T. (1998).'Vulnerability to Posttraumatic Stress Disorder in Adult Offspring of Holocaust Survivors'. *The American Journal of Psychiatry*. Published Online: 1 September 1998 https://doi.org/10.1176/ajp.155.9.1163, accessed 25 January 2022.

Print resources

Abraham, N. (1994 [1974]). 'Notes on the Phantom: A Complement to Freud's Metapsychology'. In *The Shell and The Kernel* vol. 1, pp. 171–176. Chicago, IL: University Press.

Abraham, N. and Torok, M. (1994 [1972]). 'Mourning or Melancholia: Introjection versus Incorporation'. In *The Shell and The Kernel* vol. 1, pp. 125–138. Chicago, IL: University Press.

Abraham, N. and Torok, M. (1994). 'Secrets and Posterity: The Theory of the Transgenerational Phantom'. In *The Shell and the Kernel*. London: University of Chicago Press.

Akbar, N. (1979). 'African roots of Black personality', in W. Smith, K. Burlew, M. Mosley and W. Whitney (eds) *Reflections on Black Psychology*, pp. 136–144. Washington DC: University Press of America.

Akala. (2019). *Natives: race and class in the ruins of empire*. London: Two Roads.

Akbar, N. (1996). *Breaking the Chains of Psychological Slavery*. Tallahassee, FL: Mind Productions.

Alleyne, A. (1992). *Cycle of Events*. MA dissertation (unpublished), University of Hertfordshire.

Alleyne, A. (2002). 'Spiral of Events'. In G. Tuckwell, *Racial Identity, White Counsellors and Therapists*. Bucks: Open University Press.

Alleyne, A. (2004a). 'Black Identity and workplace oppression'. *Counselling and Psychotherapy Research*, 4(1).

Alleyne, A. (2004b). 'Race-specific workplace stress'. *Counselling and Psychotherapy Journal*, 15(8), 30–33.

Alleyne, A. (2004c). 'The internal oppressor and black identity wounding'. *Counselling and Psychotherapy Journal*, 15(10), 48–50.

Alleyne, A. (2005a). 'Invisible injuries and silent witnesses: The shadow of racial oppression in workplace contexts'. *Psychodynamic Practice: Individuals, Groups and Organisations*, 11(3), 283–299.

Alleyne, A. (2005b). 'The internal oppressor – the veiled companion of external racial oppression'. *The Psychotherapist*, 26, 10–13.

Alleyne. A. (2006) Doctorate in Psychotherapy (DPsych) *A Psychotherapeutic Understanding of Black Identity in Workplace Contexts*. Middlesex University, Metanoia Institute.

Alleyne, A. (2009). *Cycle of Events*. PhD, University of Middlesex.

Alleyne, A. (2011). 'Overcoming Racism, Discrimination and Oppression in Psychotherapy'. In C. Lago (ed.), *The Handbook of Transcultural Counselling & Psychotherapy*. New York: McGraw-Hill.

Alleyne, A. (2022) 'Shame and black identity wounding: the legacy of internalised oppression'. In O. Badouk Epstein (ed.), *Shame Matters: Attachment and Relational Perspectives for Psychotherapists*. Abingdon: Routledge.

Angelou, M. (1978). 'Still I Rise' from *And Still I Rise: A Book of Poems*. New York: Random House.

Angelou, M. (2009). *I Know Why the Caged Bird Sings*. New York: Random House.

Ashcroft, B., Griffiths, G. and Tiffin, H. (2013). *Post-Colonial Studies: The Key Concepts*. Abingdon: Routledge.

Atkinson, J. (2002). *Trauma trails, recreating song lines: The transgenerational effects of trauma in Indigenous Australia*. Melbourne: Spinifex Press.

Bach. G. (1985). *The Inner Enemy: How To Fight Fair With Yourself*. New York: Berkley Publishing Group.

Balibar, E. and Wallerstein, I. M. (1991) *Race, Nation, Class: Ambiguous Identities*. New York: Verso Publishers.

Banks, N. (1992). 'Techniques for direct identity work with black children'. *Adoption and Fostering*, 16(3).

Bar-On D, Eland J, Kleber RJ, Krell R, Moore Y, Sagi A, van Ijzendoorn MH. (1998). 'Multigenerational perspectives on coping with the Holocaust experience: An attachment perspective for understanding the developmental sequelae of trauma across generations'. *International Journal of Behavioral Development*, 22(2), 315–338.

Berkley-Hill, O. (1924). 'The 'colour question' from a psychoanalytic standpoint'. *Psychoanalysis Review*, 11.

Berne, E. (1972). *What Do You Say After You Say Hello?*. New York: Grove Press.

Bhui, K. (Ed.). (2002). *Racism and Mental Health. Prejudice and Suffering*. London: Jessica Kingsley Publishers.

Bowlby, J. (1969). *Attachment and Loss*, Volume 1: *Attachment*. New York: Basic Books.

Bowlby, J. (1973). *Attachment and Loss*, Volume 2: *Separation*. New York: Basic Books.

Bowser, B. (2017). 'Racism: Origin and Theory'. *Journal of Black Studies*, 48(6), 572–590.

Brandow. J. (2001). *Genealogies of Barbados Families: from Caribbeana and the Journal of the Barbados Museum and Historical Society*. Baltimore, MD: Genealogical Publishing Company.

Brooks Higginbotham, E. (1992). 'African-American Women's History and the Metalanguage of Race'. *Signs: Journal of Women in Culture and Society*, 17(2), 251-274.

Burke, A. (1984). 'Racism and psychological disturbance among West Indians in Britain', *International Journal of Social Psychiatry*, 30(3-2), 50–68.

Chakrabarti, A. (2017) 'The Subject Is Freedom'. *Philosophy East and West* 68(1), 277–297.

Chandler, C. (2002). *Semiotics: The Basics*. New York: Routledge.

Chasseguet-Smirgel, J. (1990). 'Reflections of a psychoanalyst upon the Nazi biocracy and genocide'. *International Review of Psychoanalysis* 17(2), 167–176.

Churchill, W. S. (2008). *The Second World War: Alone*. Published by AudioGo.

Clance, P. R. and Imes, S. (1978) 'The Imposter Phenomenon in High Achieving Women: Dynamics and Therapeutic Intervention'. *Psychotherapy Theory, Research and Practice* 15(3), 241–247.

Cobbs, P. and Grier, W. (1968). *Black Rage*. New York: Basic Books.

Collins, P. H. (2002). *Black Feminist Thought: Knowledge, Consciousness, and the Politics of Empowerment*. New York: Routledge.

Collins, P. H. (2019). *Intersectionality as Critical Social Theory*. Durham, NC: Duke University Press.

Collins, P. H. and Bilge. S. (2020). *Intersectionality*. Cambridge: Polity Press.

Collins, P. H. and Chepp. V. (2013). 'Intersectionality'. In G. Waylen, K. Celis, J. Kantola, and S. Laurel Weldon (eds) *Oxford Handbook of Gender and Politics*, pp. 57–58. New York: Oxford University Press.

Crenshaw, K. W. (1989). 'Demarginalizing the Intersection of Race and Sex. A Black Feminist Critique of Anti-Discrimination Doctrine, Feminist Theory, and Anti-Racist Politics'. *University of Chicago Legal Forum* 140, 139–167.

Crenshaw, K. (1996). *Critical Race Theory*. New York: The New Press.

Cross, W. E. (1971). 'The Negro to Black Conversion Experience: Toward a Psychology of Black Liberation'. *Black World*, 20(9), 3–27.

Cross, W.E. (1978). 'The Cross and Thomas Models of Psychological Nigrescence'. *Journal of Black Psychology*, 5(1), 13–19.

Danieli, Y. (1981). 'Differing adaptational styles in families of survivors of the Nazi Holocaust: Some implications for treatment'. *Children Today*, 10, 6–10.

Danieli, Y. (1982). 'Families of survivors of the Nazi Holocaust: Some short- and long-term effects'. In C.D. Spielberger, I.G. Sarason and N. Milgram (eds), *Stress and Anxiety*, vol. 8, pp. 405–421. New York: McGrawHill/Hemisphere.

Danieli, Y. (1984). 'Psychotherapists' participation in the conspiracy of silence about the Holocaust'. *Psychoanalytic Psychology*, 1(1), 23–42.

Danieli, Y. (1985). 'The treatment and prevention of long-term effects and intergenerational transmission of victimization: A lesson from Holocaust survivors and their children'. In C.R. Figley (ed.), *Trauma and its wake: Volume 1. The study and treatment of post-traumatic stress disorder*, pp. 295–313. New York: Brunner/Mazel.

Danieli, Y. (1998) *International Handbook of Multigenerational Legacies of Trauma*. London: Springer.

Danto, B.L. (1968). *Analytical Philosophy of Knowledge*. Cambridge: Cambridge University Press.

Davids, M. F. (2011). *Internal Racism: A Psychoanalytic Approach to Race and Difference*. London: Bloomsbury Publishing PLC.

DeAngelis, T. (2019) *The legacy of trauma*, 50(2). Worcester, MA: American Psychological Association.

DeGruy Leary, J. (2005). *Post Traumatic Slave Syndrome: America's Legacy of Enduring Injury and Healing*. Milwaukie, OR: Uptone Press.

DiAngelo, R. (2011). 'White Fragility' in *International Journal of Critical Pedagogy*, 3(3), 54–70.

DiAngelo, R. (2018). *White Fragility: Why It's So Hard for White People to Talk About Racism*. Boston, MA: Beacon Press.

Dollard, J. (1938). 'Hostility and fear in social life'. *Social Forces*, 17, 15–26.

Du Bois, W. E. B.(1994). *The Souls of Black Folk*. New York: Dover Publications.

Du Bois, W. E. B.(1995). *Black Folk, Then and Now*. Millwood, New York: Kraus-Thomson Organization Limited.

Duran, E.(2006). *Healing the Soul Wound: Counseling with American Indians and Other Native Peoples*. New York: Teachers College Press.

Duran E. and Duran B. 1995. *Native American Postcolonial Psychology*. Albany, New York: State University of New York Press. www.researchgate.net/publication/304781933_ Native_American_Postcolonial_Psychology, accessed 5 June 2022.

Eddo-Lodge. R. (2017). *Why I'm No Longer Talking to White People about Race*. London: Bloomsbury Publishing.

Ellis, E. (2021). *The Race Conversation An Essential Guide to Creating Life-Changing Dialogue*. London: Confer Books.

Erikson, E. H. (1963). *Childhood and Society* 2nd edn. New York: Norton.

Erikson , E. H. (1968). *Identity: Youth and crisis*. New York: Norton.

Erikson K. T. (1976). *Everything in its Path*. New York: Simon and Schuster.

Evaristo, B. (2019). *Girl, Woman, Other*. New York: Black Cat.

Fanon, F. (1961). *Les damnés de la terre*. Paris: François Maspero.

Fanon, F. (1986). *Black Skin, White Masks*. London: Pluto Press.

Fernando, S. (1991). *Mental Health, Race and Culture*. London: Macmillan/MIND Publications.

Fernando, S. (1996). 'Black people working in white institutions: lessons from personal experience'. *The Journal of Systemic Consultation of Management* , 7(2–3), 143–154.

Fleminger, D. (2008). *The Cradle of Humankind*. Havertown, PA: 30° South Publishers.

Fletchman Smith, B. (2011). *Transcending the Legacies of Slavery: A Psychoanalytic View*. London: Routledge.

Fletchman-Smith, B. (2000) *Mental Slavery: Psychoanalytic Studies of Caribbean People*. London: Karnac Books.

Fothergill, A. (2003). 'Civilization, and "Savagery": Marlow Imagining the Other'. In A. Fothergill, *Heart of Darkness*. New Delhi: Viva Books.

Foucault, M. (2003). In 'Society Must Be Defended': Lectures at the Collège de France, 1975–1976. D. Macey translator. M. Bertani and A. Fontana (eds). New York: Picador.

Freire, P. (1970). *Pedagogy of the Oppressed*. New York: Seabury.

Freud, A. (1937). *The Ego and the Mechanisms of Defence*. London: Hogarth Press.

Freud, A. (1992). *The Ego and the Mechanisms of Defence*. London: Routledge.

Freud, S. (1900). *The interpretation of dreams*. SE 4–5, pp. ix–627. London: Hogarth Press.

Freud, S. (1905). *Fragment of an analysis of a case of hysteria*. SE 7, pp. 1–122. London: Hogarth Press.

Freud, S. (1915). *Repression*. SE 14, pp. 141–158. London: Hogarth Press.

Freud, S. (1919). *The Uncanny*. New York: Penguin Classics.

Freud, S. (1920). *Beyond the Pleasure Principle*. Dover Thrift Editions. New York: Dover Publications.

Freud, S. (1997). *The Interpretation of Dreams*. Translated by A. A. Brill. Herts, UK:

Wordsworth Editions.

Frosh, S. (1989). *Psychoanalysis and Psychology: Minding the Gap*. Princeton, NJ: Njc University Press.

Frosh, S. (2012). 'Hauntings: Psychoanalysis and Ghostly Transmission'. *The American Imago*, 69(2), 241–264.

Frosh, S. (2013). *Hauntings: Psychoanalysis and Ghostly Transmissions*. London: Palgrave.

Gabbard, G. O. (1989). 'Two subtypes of narcissistic personality disorder'. *Bulletin of the Menninger Clinic*, 53(6), 527–532.

Gordon, A. (1997). *Ghostly matters: Haunting and the sociological imagination*. Minneapolis, MN: University of Minnesota Press.

Gordon, G. (2004). 'Souls in armour: Thoughts on psychoanalysis and racism'. *British Journal of Psychotherapy*, 21, 277–294.

Grannum, G. (2012). *Tracing Your Caribbean Ancestors: A National Archives Guide*, 3rd revised edn. A&C Black Business Information and Development.

Grier. W. and Cobbs. P. (1969) *Black Rage*. New York: Bantam Books.

Hacker, A. (1992). *Two Nations: Black and White: Separate, hostile, unequal*. New York: Ballantine Books.

Hall, S. (1985). 'Signification, representation, ideology: Althusser and the poststructuralist debates'. *Critical Studies in Media Communication*: 2(2), 91–114.

Hall, S. (1996). *Critical Dialogues in Cultural Studies*. Routledge.

Hancock, A. M. (2016). *Intersectionality: An Intellectual History*. New York: Oxford University Press.

Hendrickson. N. (2018). *Unofficial Guide to Ancestry.com: How to Find Your Family History on #1 Genealogy Website*. Family Tree Books, F+W Media Inc.

Hill, R. A. (ed.) (1992). *Marcus Garvey: Life and Lessons: A Centennial Companion to the Marcus Garvey and Universal Negro Improvement Association Papers*. Oakland, CA: University of California Press.

Hinshelwood, R. D. (1989). 'Social possession of identity'. In B. Richards (ed.), *Crises of the self: Further essays on psychoanalysis and politics*. London: Free Association Books.

hooks, b. (1981). *ain't i a woman: black women and feminism*. Boston, MA: South End.

hooks, b. (1989). *talking back: thinking feminist, thinking black*. Boston, MA: South End Press.

hooks, b. (1996). *killing rage: ending racism*. Harmondsworth: Penguin Books.

Hughes, D. and Dodge, M. (1997). 'African American women in the workplace: Relations between job conditions, racial bias at work, and perceived job quality', *American Journal of Community Psychology*, 25(5), 581–599.

Jacobson, E. (1964). *The Self and the Object World*. New York: International University Press.

Jones, A. and Seagull, A. A. (1977). 'Dimensions of the relationship between the Black client and the White therapist'. *American Psychologist* 32(10), 850–855

Jones, J. M. (1972). *Prejudice and racism*. Reading, Massachusetts: Addison Wesley.

Jung. C. G. (1917). 'The Psychology of the unconscious'. In *Two Essays on Analytical Psychology*. CW7. London: Routledge & Keegan Paul.

Jung, C.G. (1923). *Psychological types: or the psychology of individuation*. New York: Harcourt, Brace.

Jung. C. G. (1964). *Man and His Symbols*. New York: Anchor Doubleday.

Jung. C. G. (1989). *Memories, Dreams, Reflections*. New York: Vintage Books.

Kaufman. G. (1992). *Shame: The Power of Caring*, 3rd edn. Schenkman Books.

Kaufman. G. (2004). *The Psychology of Shame: Theory and Treatment of Shame-Based*

Syndromes, 2nd edn. London: Springer Publishing Company.

Kellerman, N. P. F. (2001). 'Psychopathology in children of Holocaust survivors: A review of the research literature'. *Israel Journal of Psychiatry and Related Sciences*, 38(1), 36–46.

Kohut, H. (1977). *The Restoration of the Self*. New York: International Universities Press.

Kovel, J. (1970). *White Racism – a psychohistory*, New York: Pantheon Books.

Laing. R. D. (1960). *The Divided Self*. London: Penguin Books.

Lederman, N. G. and Lederman J. S. (2015). 'What is a Theoretical Framework? A Practical Answer'. *Journal of Science Teacher Education*, 26, 593–597.

Levine, J. (2001). 'Working with victims of persecution: Lessons from Holocaust survivors'. *Social Work*, 46, 350–360.

Levine, P. A. (2010) *In an Unspoken Voice: How the Body Releases Trauma and Restores Goodness*. Berkeley, CA: North Atlantic Books.

Levine, P.A. and Kline, M. (2007). *Trauma through a child's eyes*. Berkeley, CA: North Atlantic Books.

Lewis, Charlton, T. (1890) *An Elementary Latin Dictionary*. New York, Cincinnati, and Chicago: American Book Company.

Lewis, J. A., Mendenhall, R., Harwood, S. A. and Browne Huntt, M. B. (2013). 'Coping with gendered racial microaggressions among Black women college students' in *Journal of African American Studies* 17(1), 51–73.

Libet, B. (1985). 'Unconscious cerebral initiative and the role of conscious will in voluntary action'. *Behavioral and Brain Sciences*, 8, 529–566.

Lipsky, S. (1987). *Internalised Racism*. Seattle, WA: Rational Island Publishers.

Locke, D. (1992). *Perceived racism in the workplace: consequences for longevity. Increasing multicultural understanding: A comprehensive model*. Newbury Park, CA: Sage.

Lorde, A. (1984). *Sister Outsider: Essays and Speeches*. Berkeley, CA: Crossing Press.

Lorde, A. (1988). *A Burst of Light, Essays*. London: Sheba Feminist Publishers.

Lovejoy, P.E. (1982)'The Volume of the Atlantic slave trade: A Synthesis', *The Journal of African History*, 483–497.

Lowe, F. (2006) 'Racism as a borderline issue: the avoidance and marginalization of race in psychotherapy'. In A. Foster, A. Dickinson, B. Bishop and J. Klein (eds), *Difference: An Avoided Topic in Practise*, pp. 43–60. London: Karnac.

Lowe, F. (2014) *Thinking Space: Promoting Thinking about Race, Culture, and Diversity in Psychotherapy and Beyond*. London: Routledge.

Luft, J. and Ingham, H. (1955). *The Johari Window: a graphic model for interpersonal relations*. University of California Western Training Lab.

Markham, V. (1995). *Managing Stress: the Stress Survival Guide for Today*. London: Element Books.

Maxime, J. E. (1993). 'The importance of racial identity for psychological wellbeing of black children', *Association of Child Psychology and Psychiatry Newsletter*, 15(4), 173–179.

Maxime, J. E. (1994). *Black Like Me: Workbook 1: Black Identity* 3rd edn. Emani Publications.

Mayer, C. (2017). 'Shame – "A Soul Feeding Emotion". Archetypal Work and the Transformation of the Shadow of Shame in a Group Development Process'. In E. Vanderheiden and C. Mayer, *The Value of Shame Exploring a Health Resource in Cultural Contexts*, pp. 277–302. London: Springer.

McIntosh, P. (1989) 'White Privilege: Unpacking the Knapsack of White Privilege', *Peace and Freedom*, July/August, pp. 10–12.

McKenzie-Mavinga, I. (2009). *Black Issues in the Therapeutic Process*. London: Palgrave Macmillan.

McKenzie-Mavinga, I. (2016). *The Challenge of Racism in Therapeutic Practice*. London:

Palgrave Macmillan.

Minuchin, S. (1974). *Families and family therapy*. Cambridge, MA: Harvard University Press.

Mohatt, N. V, Thompson, A. B., Thai, N. D. and Tebes, J. K. (2014) 'Historical trauma as public narrative: A conceptual review of how history impacts present-day health'. *Social Science & Medicine* 106, 128–36.

Money-Kyrle, R. (1960). 'On prejudice: a psychoanalytical approach'. *British Journal of Medical Psychology*, 33, 205–209.

Moosa, F., Straker, G. and Eagle, G. (2004). 'Forgiveness in the Context of Political Trauma'. In S. Ransley and T. Spy (eds), *Forgiveness in a Changing Age*, pp 128–150. New York: Brunner Routledge.

Morgan, H. (2008). 'Issues of 'Race' in Psychoanalytic Psychotherapy: Whose problem Is It Anyway?' *Journal Compilation*. Oxford: BAP and Blackwell Publishing Ltd.

Morrison, T. (1970). *The Bluest Eye*. New York: Washington Square Press.

Morrison, T. (1974). *Sula: Toni Morrison*. New York: Knopf.

Morrison, T. (1987). *Beloved*. New York: Knopf.

Newell, J.M. and MacNeal, G.A. (2010). 'Professional burnout, vicarious trauma, secondary traumatic stress, and compassion fatigue: A review of theoretical terms, risk factors and preventive methods for clinicians and researchers'. *Best Practices in Mental Health*, 6, 56–68.

Norcross, J. C. (2000). 'Psychotherapist self-care: Practitioner-tested, research-informed strategies'. *Professional Psychology*, 31, 710–713.

Norcross, J.C. and Guy, J.D. (2007). *Leaving it at the office: A guide to psychotherapists self-care*. New York: Guilford Press.

Ogden, T. (1994). 'The analytic third: working with intersubjective clinical facts'. In *Subjects of Analysis*. London: Karnac Books.

Olusoga, D. (2016). *Black and British: a forgotten history*. London, Macmillan.

Orwell, G. (1949) *1984*. London: Secker and Warburg Print.

Pearlman, L. A. (1995). 'Self-care for trauma therapists: Ameliorating vicarious traumatization'. In B. H. Stamm (ed.), *Secondary traumatic stress: Self-care for clinicians, researchers and educators*. Lutherville, MD: Sidran Press.

Phinney, J. (1989). 'Stages of ethnic identity in minority group adolescents'. *Journal of Early Adolescence*, 9, 34–49.

Pupavac, V. (2002). 'Pathologizing populations and colonizing minds: International psychosocial programs in Kosovo'. *Alternatives* 27, 489–511.

Rakoff, V., Sigal, J. J. and Epstein, N. B. (1966). 'Children and Families of Concentration Camp Survivors'. *Canada's Mental Health*, 14, 24–26.

Rick, J., Perryman, S., Young, K., Guppy, A. and Hillage, J. (1998). *Workplace Trauma and its Management*. Norwich: Health and Safety Executive.

Ridley, C. (1989). 'Racism in counselling as an adverse behavioural process' in P. B. Pedersen, et al. (eds), *Counselling across cultures*, 3rd edn. Honolulu: University of Hawaii Press.

Rogers, C. (1951). *Client-Centered Therapy: Its Current Practice, Implications and Theory*. London: Constable.

Rogers, C. (1959). 'A theory of therapy, personality and interpersonal relationships as developed in the client-centered framework'. In S. Koch (ed.), *Psychology: A study of a science. Vol. 3: Formulations of the person and the social context*. New York: McGraw Hill.

Russell, K. (1998). *The Colour of Crime, Racial Hoaxes, White Fear, Black Protectionism,*

    Police Harassment and Other Macroaggressions. New York: New York University Press.

Rustin, M. (1991). 'Psychoanalysis, racism and anti-racism'. In *The good society and the inner world: Psychoanalysis, politics and culture.* London: Verso.

Rycroft, C. (1972). *A Critical Dictionary of Psychoanalysis.* Harmondsworth: Penguin.

Saad, L. (2020). *Me and white supremacy: how to recognise your privilege, combat racism and change the world.* London: Quercus.

Sampson. E. (1993). *Celebrating the Other: A Dialogic Account of Human Nature.* London: Harvester Weatsheaf Publishers.

Sartre, J-P. (1943). *Being and Nothingness (Original title: L'Être et le Néant).* London: Routledge (1956).

Sarup, M. (1996). *Identity, Culture and the Postmodern World.* Edinburgh: Edinburgh University Press.

Segal, H. (1982). *Introduction to the work of Melanie Klein.* London: Hogarth Press and the Institute of Psychoanalysis.

Shapiro, F. (2001). *Eye movement desensitization and reprocessing: Basic principles, protocols and procedures,* 2nd edn. New York: Guilford Press.

Solomon E. S. and Heide, K. M. (1999). 'Type III Trauma: Towards a More Effective Conceptualization of Psychological Trauma'. *Journal of Offender Therapy and Comparative Criminology,* 43(2), 202–210.

Sterba, R. (1947). 'Some psychological factors in Negro race hatred and in antiNegro Riots' in G. Roheim (ed.), *Psychoanalysis and the social sciences,* pp. 411–427. Madison, CT: International Universities Press.

Stone, J. B. (2003). *Post-colonial stress disorder and post-traumatic stress disorder: Implications for tribal/native substance abuse, mental health, and dual diagnosis assessment and treatment.* Portland, OR: National Indian Child Welfare Association.

Straker, G. (1999). 'Psychoanalytic Reflections on the South African Truth and Reconciliation Commission'. *Psychoanalytic Dialogues,* 9(2), 245–274.

Straker, G. (2001). 'Child Soldiers in South Africa: Past Present Future'. In C. Stones (ed.), *Socio-Political and Psychological Perspectives on South Africa,* pp. 20–27. New York: Nova Science Publishers.

Straker, G. (2004). 'Integrating the Diverse Languages of Psychotherapy'. *British Journal of Psychotherapy Integration: A process,* 1(1), 4–13.

Sue, D. W. (ed.). (2010). *Microaggressions and marginality: Manifestation, dynamics, and impact.* London: John Wiley & Sons.

Sue, D. W. (2010). *Microaggressions in everyday life: Race, gender, and sexual orientation.* London: John Wiley & Sons.

Sue, D. W. (2014). 'Microaggressions and Marginality: Manifestation, Dynamics and Impact'. Best Practices in Diversity Strategic Planning Workshop, Teacher's College, Columbia University, New York, NY.

Terr, L. C. (1991). 'Childhood traumas: An outline and overview'. *American Journal of Psychiatry,* 148(1), 10–20.

Thomas, L. (1995). 'Psychotherapy in the context of race and culture'. In S. Fernando (ed.), *Mental health in a multi-ethnic society: a multi-disciplinary handbook.* New York: Routledge.

Timimi, S. (1996). 'Race and colour in internal and external reality'. *British Journal of Psychotherapy,* 13, 184–199.

Turner, D. (2021) *Intersections of Privilege and Otherness in Counselling and Psychotherapy.* New York: Routledge.

van Deurzen, E. (2009). *Psychotherapy and the Quest for Happiness*. London: Sage Publications Ltd.

Van Der Kolk, B. (2015). *The Body Keeps The Score: Mind, brain and body in the transformation of trauma*. London: Penguin Random House.

Vannoy-Adams, M. (1996). *The Multicultural Imagination, 'Race', Color and the Unconscious*. London: Routledge.

Vanzant, I. (1996). *Faith in the Valley: Lessons for Women on the Journey to Peace*. New York: Atria Books.

Walker, A. (1983). *The color purple*. London: Women's Press.

Ward, I. (1997). 'Race and racisms: A reply to Sami Timimi'. *British Journal of Psychotherapy*, 14, 92–97.

Wegner, D.M. (2003). 'The mind's best trick: how we experience conscious will'. *Trends in Cognitive Sciences*, 7(2), 65–69.

Wenzel. C.H. and Marchal, K. (2017) 'Chinese Perspectives on Free Will' In K. Timpe, M. Griffith and N. Levy (eds.), *Routledge Companion to Free Will*, pp. 374–388. Routledge.

Whitbeck, L. B., Chen, X., Hoyt, D. R. and Adams, G. W. (2004). 'Discrimination, historical loss and enculturation: Culturally specific risk and resiliency factors for alcohol abuse among American Indians'. *Journal of Studies on Alcohol*, 65(4), 409–418.

White, J. (1989) *Racism and psychosis: Whose madness is it anyway?* Paper presented at 'Psychoanalysis and the Public Sphere' conference, University of East London, September 1989.

Wilson, J. P. and Raphael, B. (eds.) (1993). *International handbook of traumatic stress syndromes*. New York: Plenum Press.

Winnicott, D. W. (1958). 'The Capacity to Be Alone'. In D. W. Winnicott (ed.), *The Maturational Processes and the Facilitating Environment*, pp. 29–36. London: Karnac Books.

Winnicott, D. W. (1960). 'Ego distortions in terms of the true and false self'. In D. W. Winnicott (ed.), *The Maturational Process and the Facilitating Environment*. London: Hogarth Press.

Winnicott, D. W. (1971). *Playing and Reality*. London: Penguin Books.

Winnicott, D. W. (1990) 'Ego distortion in terms of the true and false self'. In D. W. Winnicott (ed.), *The maturational processes and the facilitating environment*. London: Karnac.

Wirth, L. (1945). 'The problem of minority groups'. In R. Linton (ed.) *The Science of Man in World Crisis*. New York: Columbia University Press.

Wurmser, L. (1981). *The Mask of Shame*. London: The John Hopkins University Press.

Yehuda, R. and Lehrner, A. (2018) 'Intergenerational transmission of trauma effects: putative role of epigenetic mechanisms'. *World Psychiatry*, 17(3), 243–257.

Young, R. M. (1987) 'Racist Society, Racist Science'. In D. Gill and L. Levidow (eds), *Anti-Racist Science Teaching*. Free Association Books. Reprinted in D. Gill et al. (eds) (1992) *Racism and Education: Structures and Strategies*. London: Sage.

Young, R. M. (1992). 'Benign and virulent projective identification in group and institutions'. Paper delivered to the First European Conference of the Rowantree Foundation on 'Projective Identification in Institutions', Wierden, The Netherlands.

Index